# The *Twilight* Saga

## *Exploring the Global Phenomenon*

### Edited by Claudia Bucciferro

THE SCARECROW PRESS, INC.
Lanham • Boulder • New York • Toronto • Plymouth, UK
2013

Published by Scarecrow Press, Inc.
A wholly owned subsidiary of Rowman & Littlefield
4501 Forbes Boulevard, Suite 200, Lanham, Maryland 20706
www.rowman.com

10 Thornbury Road, Plymouth PL6 7PP, United Kingdom

British Library Cataloguing in Publication Information Available

**Library of Congress Cataloging-in-Publication Data**
The Twilight saga : exploring the global phenomenon / edited by Claudia Bucciferro.
pages cm
Includes bibliographical references and index.
ISBN 978-0-8108-9285-9 (cloth : alk. paper) -- ISBN 978-0-8108-9286-6 (electronic)
1. Meyer, Stephenie, 1973- Twilight saga series. 2. Young adult fiction, American--History and criticism. 3. Vampires in literature. I. Bucciferro, Claudia, editor of compilation.
PS3613.E979Z97 2014
813'.6--dc23
2013033315

∞ ™The paper used in this publication meets the minimum requirements of American National Standard for Information Sciences Permanence of Paper for Printed Library Materials, ANSI/NISO Z39.48-1992.

Printed in the United States of America

# Contents

Acknowledgments                                                              v

Introduction                                                                 1
    *Claudia Bucciferro*

**I: Contextualizing *Twilight*'s Appeal**                                  **15**

  **1** Mythic Themes, Archetypes, and Metaphors: The Foundations
    of *Twilight*'s Cross-Cultural Appeal                17
    *Claudia Bucciferro*

  **2** Manifest Destiny Forever: The *Twilight* Saga, History, and a
    Vampire's American Dream                              33
    *Michelle Maloney-Mangold*

  **3** Reading *Twilight*: Fandom, Romance, and Gender in the Age of
    Bella                                                 47
    *Barbara Chambers and Robert Moses Peaslee*

**II: *Twilight* Audiences**                                                **63**

  **4** "Twilight Moms" and the "Female Midlife Crisis": Life
    Transitions, Fantasy, and Fandom                      65
    *Laura K. Dorsey-Elson*

  **5** *Twilight* and Twitter: An Ethnographic Study             79
    *Michelle Groover*

  **6** *Twilight* Anti-Fans: "Real" Fans and "Real" Vampires     93
    *Victoria Godwin*

**III: Characters and Their Cultural Referents**                 **107**

 7  Renesmee as (R)omantic Child: A Glimpse into Bella and
    Edward's Fairy Tale Cottage                                    109
    *Lisa Nevárez*

 8  Isabella Swan: A Twenty-First-Century Victorian Heroine?       123
    *Gaïane Hanser*

 9  "Doesn't He Own a Shirt?": Rivalry and Masculine
    Embodiment in *Twilight*                                       139
    *Nicole Willms*

**IV: Issues of Gender, Sex, Class, and Race in *Twilight***     **153**

10  Chastity, Power, and Delayed Gratification: The Lure of Sex in
    the *Twilight* saga                                            155
    *Brynn Buskirk*

11  Alice, Bella, and Economics: Financial Security and Class
    Mobility in *Twilight*                                         169
    *Paul A. Lucas*

12  "I Know What You Are": A Philosophical Look at Race,
    Identity, and Mixed-Blood in the *Twilight* Universe           181
    *Michelle Bernard*

**V: Beyond the *Twilight* Universe**                            **195**

13  Mainstream Monsters: The Otherness of Humans in *Twilight*,
    *The Vampire Diaries*, and *True Blood*                         197
    *Emma Somogyi and Mark David Ryan*

14  Individuality and Collectivity in *The Hunger Games*, *Harry
    Potter*, and *Twilight*                                         213
    *Lisa Weckerle*

15  From *Twilight* to *Fifty Shades of Grey*: Fan Fiction, Commercial
    Culture, and Grassroots Creativity                             227
    *Sonia Baelo-Allué*

Closing Thoughts                                                   241
    *Claudia Bucciferro*

Index                                                              245

About the Editor and Contributors                                  249

# Acknowledgments

First of all, I would like to express my gratitude to our excellent contributors, who brought to the table a variety of fields of expertise, thus making this book a better volume than I would ever have been able to write on my own. They patiently went through several rounds of revision, as we worked together to create an insightful, unique, and cohesive final product. Behold the power of communication technologies, which allow us to coordinate work among people living in faraway places!

Secondly, thank you to Chris Nasso, who helped refine the original concept for this project and brought it to the attention of Scarecrow Press, and to Stephen Ryan, who made it come to fruition and become an actual book. As always, I am indebted to all the staff at Rowman & Littlefield who contributed to the process.

Early versions of chapters included in this volume were presented at the Popular Culture/American Culture Association national conferences in Boston and Washington DC, and I thank the conference attendees and fellow presenters who shared valuable insights and raised relevant questions. Special thanks to Mary Findley, chair of the Vampire in Literature, Culture, and Film division of PCA, for first inviting me to one of these meetings.

A thank you also goes to the students in my upper-division courses at Gonzaga University—especially in Intercultural/International Communication, Interpersonal Communication, and Communication Theory. The discussions that took place in our classes got me started on this project and continue to provide much of the fuel for my research on popular culture. Additionally, I am indebted to Maura Troester Nuñez and Anders Bengtsson, who introduced me to their research on metaphors and marketing and brought me into some of their industry-related projects. Our collaboration shaped my perspective on the relationship between audiences and products.

Finally, a heartfelt thank you goes to my family and friends, who patiently listened to my theoretical reveries and accompanied me in some of my research adventures. Special thanks to Maria Bucciferro, my mother-in-law, for her useful comments regarding the Introduction.

Creating this book has been a fun journey, from start to finish. I hope the readers find as much insight and enjoyment in it, as those of us who worked on it did.

C. B.

# Introduction

## Claudia Bucciferro

My first encounters with *Twilight* were anecdotal: I heard the buzzword during casual conversations. I watched Jay Leno on the *Tonight Show*, interviewing the young actor who played a vampire heartthrob—Robert Pattinson. I found articles about *Twilight* featured in some magazines and stumbled upon related merchandise at different stores. I saw the media hype around the saga steadily increase, and its young stars become celebrities. I also noticed the strong reactions that the series inspired, from fascination to hate. As all this happened, I became intrigued. I was a doctoral student at the time, and my main fields of research were media and international communication—but I was so busy reading theories *about* media, working on other research projects, and raising two young children that I had little time to engage *with* the actual content of popular media. So, for a while, I observed the *Twilight* phenomenon from afar, without watching the movies or reading the books.

Then, one sunny evening shortly after finishing school, my neighbors and I were gathered around two picnic tables for our weekly potluck. We were a strikingly diverse group, with people of different nationalities, ages, and academic interests, but all somehow affiliated with the University of Colorado at Boulder. A couple from South Korea had just arrived to town, and they were invited to join us. The husband was working for the school, so he was eager to mingle, but his wife, Jin, was very shy and spoke little English, so she mostly smiled. The conversation turned to movies, and I said that I wanted to know what was up with *Twilight*. "Has anyone seen it?" I asked.

"No. Why?" someone answered.

"I don't even know much about it, but I just got *Vanity Fair* in the mail, and this guy Robert Pattinson is on the cover *again*. It seems that women are crazy about him."

Suddenly, I felt a little tap on my shoulder. Jin was standing next to me, staring intently.

"Did you just say Robert Pattinson?" she asked.

"Yes."

"Ahhhh," she sighed, bringing her hands to her heart and lifting her eyes to the sky, then letting out a giggle.

People stood there for a moment, waiting.

"He is a good-looking guy," I explained, and Jin nodded in agreement.

Jin's gesture spiked my curiosity, so I asked her if the movies were well known in Korea.

"Oh, yes!" she replied, opening her eyes big.

"You see?" I said. "This movie series is famous all over the world. I need to know what's going on!"

"You haven't seen it?" she asked.

I shook my head.

"I'll get it for you," she offered, and later, she did.

That was the first interaction I had with Jin. English was challenging for her, and it was hard to break the ice in a new social environment, but hearing the name of a famous actor motivated her to join the conversation. That is the power of global popular culture, I thought: It can create a virtual space where people from diverse backgrounds can coalesce and interact on the basis of common interests.

In countries located outside the major centers of global power, the impact of American popular culture is greater because people try to keep up with the information coming from the center. This I know from experience because I grew up in Chile, watching Hollywood movies such as *Terminator* and *Star Wars*, listening to U2 and Madonna, and reading books by Edgar Allan Poe, Mark Twain, and J. R. R. Tolkien. My friends and I were all in tune with American and European cultural products then, even though we lived far away. So, Jin being into *Twilight* was not surprising to me but got me thinking about people's perception of transnational cultural products—a topic that I had researched earlier and wanted to revisit.

Back in 1999, I conducted a quantitative study in Chile that inquired into children's perceptions of the characters from the movie *The Lion King*, getting interesting results. Despite its charm, the film had been criticized for containing a message that validates racial discrimination and stresses the importance of borders (Humanick 2011). But I wondered: how much of this could be really perceived by kids? And how much was relevant for audiences in South American countries such as Chile? After showing the movie to a random sample of fifth-grade classes, I gave the kids a questionnaire.

The survey results showed that children perceived the characters in a stereotypical way, attributing only positive values to those playing good roles and only negative values to those appearing in bad ones. This was expected, but when asked about how they imagined each character would look like "if it were human," children tended to associate good characters with white people (light-skinned, light-colored eyes and hair) and bad characters with people of color (dark-skinned, dark-colored eyes and hair). The differences were statistically significant and ran across variables such as gender, socioeconomic status, and age. However, when directly asked about their opinions of people of different racial backgrounds, the kids didn't express a bias, evaluating them all in positive terms. This suggested that they perceived the racial stereotyping in the movie, but it didn't directly affect their everyday beliefs (Martínez 2000). This work made me wonder about the level of engagement that Chilean children had with an American film, and about their sophistication in processing a cultural product. Basically, the kids knew *The Lion King*, loved the film, and understood it well—even to the level of decoding its nuanced racial undertones—yet they didn't let it directly influence their views of real people.

In 2010, with all the media attention that surrounded the release of the third *Twilight Saga* film, it became clear that this was more than just a popular series. Not only American girls were into it, but also career women, moms, and many men, all over the world—even in Korea and Chile (Em and Lo 2009; *La Tercera* 2011). *Twilight* could no longer be labeled "just another teen movie." It was an intriguing phenomenon, worthy of study. The question was and still is: what is in it that made it so successful? It had to be something more than an actor's good looks because plenty of movies with handsome people become box-office flops. It had to be more than a good marketing strategy because advertising alone won't sell a product that people dislike. This could not simply be another romantic story made to entertain teenagers, featuring manufactured superstars created for profit. But what was it? Despite everything that had been written about the series, nobody seemed to have a good answer. Later on, as I watched the films and read the books, I went back to the same fundamental issue: what was in *Twilight* that made it appealing to so many people all over the world? And on the other hand, what made it so hated by many others?

The following semester, while talking about rhetorician Kenneth Burke (1969) and his dramatistic pentad in one of my classes, my students and I used *Twilight* to illustrate its major points. The pentad is an analytical tool that can be used for understanding different kinds of discourses and even real-life scenarios. It focuses on five key aspects, as Burke says: "act, scene, agent, agency, and purpose" (1969, xv). *Twilight*'s story fit the pentad well—which showed that it lent itself to this kind of rhetorical analysis. But I wanted to go beyond that, having been schooled in media studies and knowing the worldwide reach of American popular culture. So the idea for researching the intercultural appeal of *Twilight* was formed. At the annual meeting of the Popular Culture/American Culture Association in 2012, I chaired a panel on this and was joined at the table by two scholars who were also looking at the series in terms of how it relates to contemporary issues. The idea for this book stems from there.

## ZEROING IN ON *TWILIGHT*

This volume presents an analysis of the *Twilight* saga in relationship to the larger cultural and social trends of our global world. The main goal is to address basic questions that are often brought up but have not been satisfactorily answered yet: How does *Twilight* relate to other popular culture phenomena? What is in it that speaks to people? What does the worldwide success of the series tell us about larger cultural trends? What are the ties between the saga as an entertainment product and the realities experienced by its audiences?

These questions run across this book, although each chapter looks at the franchise from a different perspective. The work presented is interdisciplinary, although the overarching framework is cultural studies and media studies (Hall 1996). Therefore, *Twilight* is not considered a free-floating text but a "cultural artifact"—a product of its time and place. As such, it is analyzed in relationship to the social, cultural, and economic processes that surround it, not in isolation from them (Schiller 1996; Peters and Simonson 2004). In this sense, the chapters consider both the books and the movies and explore their links to larger issues. Special attention is given to the interconnections between *Twilight*—understood as a text and a pop culture product—and the different audiences it reaches. In looking at this, we go beyond *Twilight* and present deeper insights regarding the relationship between media and society in our global world.

Overall, the goal of this book is to understand the *Twilight* phenomenon from a scholarly, yet accessible, perspective. It is not our intention to either champion *Twilight* or defend it against its critics—enough of that has been done already, within both mainstream and scholarly circles (Click, Aubrey, and Behm-Morawitz 2010; Wilson 2011). Instead, our purpose is to make sense of it in terms of how it fits within larger contexts, while exploring the tensions that arise as different aspects of it are brought into focus. This book was being written while the *Twilight* fandom was in full bloom and the five-part movie series was reaching completion. So, we were able to take into account its development arc and even explore its links to new franchises, such as *The Hunger Games* and *Fifty Shades of Grey*.

Novels and films such as the *Twilight* saga are sometimes easily dismissed as irrelevant by "serious" people, but popular culture products are a powerful aspect of contemporary societies (Fowkes 2010; Couldry 2003). In fact, an extensive study conducted by the Kaiser Family Foundation found that the amount of time spent consuming media has notably increased in recent years, especially among people younger than eighteen years old (Blodget 2011). The social impact of media has long been a topic for debate (De Moraes 2007; Gurevitch et al. 1982). Yet it seems that people don't passively absorb media content but *do* things with it that influence how they conceptually manage the real world (Alasuutari 1999). For example, issues that are difficult to address directly—such as gender, sexuality, race, and class—get represented within pop culture, and audiences actively negotiate their meaning (Gauntlett 2002). The media both reflect and help shape the dominant discourses of a society, and "easy" content that holds a broad appeal is more impactful than highly specialized content that reaches only a few (Fiske 1989). At any rate, the worldwide relevance of the American entertainment industry—and the very real economic aspects associated with it—can't be denied (Hjarvard 2003).

So, why does *Twilight* matter? It does, for a variety of reasons: First, it is not just fantasy; it has ties to reality on a global scale. This is so both in terms of the economic impact of the series and its capability for representing issues (such as notions of femininity and masculinity) that are important for society at large (Wilson 2011; Hanser, Willms, both in this volume). Second, many people—especially young people—become profoundly engaged with these movies and books, and studying them gives us a glimpse into their lives (Erzen 2012; Click, Aubrey, and Behm-Morawitz 2010; Dorsey-Elson, Groover, this volume). Third, *Twilight* matters because it is not an isolated phenomenon, but has things in common with other global franchises that have recently been developed (Fowkes 2010; Grossman 2008; Weckerle, Baelo-Allué, this volume). Fourth, *Twilight* reframed the vampire as a character and brought along a new wave of popular fascination with it (Jones 2009; Somogyi and Ryan, this volume). It spearheaded the supernatural romance genre and helped to make it mainstream (Nevárez, Chambers and Peaslee, this volume). Finally, the *Twilight* phenomenon constitutes an emblematic example of the rise of global fan culture, which is, as a topic of study, relatively new and fascinating (Godwin, this volume).

The film adaptations have greatly contributed to the saga's prominence, although the novels had a strong fan base by the time the first *Twilight* movie was made. In the United States, Edward Cullen, the sparkling vampire protagonist, had plenty of infatuated followers, even before Robert Pattinson lent him his face (Peretz 2009). However, it was after the first movie's release that things began to move quickly, and within a matter of months, *Twilight* became a blockbuster that surpassed all initial expectations. Writer Stephenie Meyer says she never could have imagined that her books would have such an impact (*Time* 2008). Therefore, it is useful to review how the films shaped the *Twilight* phenomenon.

## OUTLINING THE *TWILIGHT* FILM FRANCHISE

The first film, released in 2008, was done largely *by* and *for* women. Based on a book written by a young stay-at-home mom, Stephenie Meyer, it was adapted for the big screen by a trio of women: director Catherine Hardwicke, screenwriter Melissa Rosenberg, and executive producer Karen Rosenfelt (Vaz 2008). The story is told through the eyes of a seventeen-year-old girl, so the target audience for the movie was teenagers and young adults. It was a small-budget film ($37 million) and was produced by what was then a relatively small studio, Summit Entertainment (The Numbers 2012).

Catherine Hardwicke had directed the indie film *Thirteen*, which presented an uncommon—yet troublesome—inside look at teen culture. She brought to *Twilight* not only an understanding of teens but also the ability to convey the story in a manner that seemed real for the viewers—a key aspect for the movie's success. The film was shot using a "documentary style" approach to camera movements, settings, and action sequences, with plenty of natural locations. Even the special effects were mostly staged and shot in reality instead of being digitally introduced (Vaz 2008). The main actors were little known back then, so they fully embodied their characters in the eyes of the audience.

Upon its release, *Twilight* became an unexpected box-office success, grossing $70.6 million during the first weekend (Wong 2008). Later on, with nearly $398 million in worldwide ticket sales, it was the highest grossing film directed by a woman (The Numbers 2012). While the movie involved teens and vampires, this was not what made it controversial—it was the fact that it dealt with themes such as sexual tension and restraint that really got public attention (Grossman 2008).

Plans for a sequel were quickly made, and *New Moon* was released in 2009. It was a movie done in a rush, having gone from screenwriting to postproduction in roughly a year. While it was assumed that Catherine Hardwicke would direct the sequel, she was soon replaced by another director appointed by the studio. The reasons for this were never fully explained but apparently involved disagreements over the accelerated schedule (Itzkoff 2008). This matters because it is a turning point for the series: producing a sequel so soon was part of an effort to turn *Twilight* into a profitable international franchise. Summit Entertainment didn't want to lose the momentum that had been created among the fans and the media, so production was carried through at a fast pace. Consequently, a new sequel was released every year until the completion of the series and was accompanied by a steady stream of publicity, advertising, and all types of merchandise.

Another important aspect is that *New Moon*'s director, Chris Weitz, is male—as are the other three people who went on to direct the different films of the franchise. Weitz had to his credit *The Golden Compass* (2007), a visually interesting fantasy production. He brought to the *Twilight* saga a different visual schema and a more standard way of shooting. The colors were warmer, and elements such as the weather were less intense; soundstages were used, and digital special effects abounded. Bella Swan's character became sexier and was the object of the male gaze. All this made *New Moon* more aligned with the fantasy genre, which has been traditionally considered "masculine" territory.

The story, however, presented the beginning of the love triangle between Edward, Bella, and Jacob Black, delving into themes such as the power of love, disappointment, and suicide. Interestingly, Jacob was developed into a character that is not often seen in Hollywood films (Rollins and O'Connor 1998)—a Native American teenager who is handsome, trustworthy, funny, charming, and a legitimate love interest for a white heroine. *New Moon* was accompanied by the first Team Edward/Team Jacob marketing campaign, which divided the fans and called for their overt identification, while featuring all kinds of merchandise, from key chains to pillowcases. Actors Robert Pattinson, Kristen Stewart, and Taylor Lautner were catapulted to global fame, and their faces became emblematic within teen culture. The movie went on to garner gross revenues of $709 million during the first year (IMDb 2011), a sum that would be roughly matched by each one of the sequels that followed.

Screenwriting and preproduction for the third installment of the series, *Eclipse*, began before *New Moon* premiered in theaters. According to the studio, the overlap between the projects demanded bringing in yet another director: David Slade. He had directed films such as *Hard Candy* (2005) and *30 Days of Night* (2007), as well as several music video clips, so he brought a good understanding of the male youth audience and a taste for suspense. *Eclipse* was released in the summer of 2010 and presented the cusp of the love triangle between the main characters, focusing on Bella's need to make a choice, therefore addressing the implications of romantic commitment. However, by using parallel storytelling and playing up the threat posed by an army of hostile vampires, Slade was able to turn the movie into a fast-paced thriller with plenty of action sequences and special effects. As a result, *Eclipse* appealed to a wider audience—not just teenage girls but also young men and adults. It went on to reach gross revenues of $698 million during the first year (IMDb 2011).

The last book of the series, *Breaking Dawn*, was split into two movies that were released separately—in 2011 and 2012. While the studio said that this was to fully develop the story (Vilkomerson 2011), it also served to stretch out profits. Both films were directed by Bill Condon, who was known for more adult-themed movies, such as *Dreamgirls* (2006), *Kinsey* (2004), and *Chicago* (2002). Condon took the second-to-last installment of *Twilight* away from the three genres previously explored—teen romance, fantasy, and suspense—and turned it squarely into a drama. The change was attributed to the characters' entering into adulthood and dealing with grown-up themes, such as marriage and family (Vilkomerson 2011). Yet it can't be denied that Condon, as a middle-aged male, brought his own lens to Bella's coming-of-age story.

The shooting for *Breaking Dawn Part 1* and *Part 2* was done simultaneously and under the highest level of security, although that did not prevent the fans' assiduous watch and the leakage of material onto the Internet. Thus, the movies were mostly filmed in soundstages, which created an atmosphere that percolated to the story—*Breaking Dawn Part 1* feels almost claustrophobic. International locations such as Vancouver and Rio de Janeiro were occasionally used to add a global flair, which contrasts with the authentic American Northwest locations featured in the first movie. Another big difference was the project's budget of $110 million, about three times that of the original *Twilight* (IMDb 2012).

The release of *Breaking Dawn Part 1* was accompanied by a sense of anticipation fueled by global marketing. The movie opened simultaneously around the world, and its young stars traveled to several countries to promote it. The effort paid off—the film became the fifth biggest box-office debut, earning $283.5 million during the first weekend (Germain 2011). The worldwide gross revenue during the first year was $712 million, not including the income generated by DVD rentals/sales and associated merchandise (IMDb 2012). This was not a small feat for a movie that ended without closure and received lukewarm reviews: its purpose was to serve as a link between *Eclipse* and *Breaking Dawn Part 2*, which was already scheduled for release.

Youth franchises that capitalize on the teen market have much in common, despite their respective fans' reported animosity (Weckerle, Godwin, both in this volume). In fact, *Breaking Dawn Part 2*'s trailer debuted during the opening week of *The Hunger Games*—while the trailer for *The Hunger Games* had been shown during screenings of *Breaking Dawn Part 1*. By then, Summit Entertainment was no longer a small studio, and much of its economic success was tied to the *Twilight* franchise. It would soon be bought by Lionsgate—the company behind *The Hunger Games* films—for $412.5 million (Fritz 2012).

However, the media hype surrounding *Twilight* was too big to be sustainable, and some wariness was evident among the films' young actors. Rumors of an off-screen romance between Robert Pattinson and Kristen Stewart lead to constant speculation. Pattinson spent years living in hotels and moving constantly to avoid public harassment—although dealing with assiduous fans and paparazzi is a common task for celebrities, he could not relate to it and kept trying to maintain a low profile (Sales 2011). *Twilight*'s fan base remained steady despite the passing of time, and Pattinson's persona was overshadowed by Edward Cullen's lasting presence.

Then, in the summer of 2012, came the scandal that would appear on tabloid covers and Internet sites around the world: Kristen Stewart acknowledged her romantic involvement with Pattinson, just as photos of her affair with director Rupert Sanders, a married father of two who was also twice her age, were being released (*US Weekly* 2012). In the weeks that followed, the conflation of Pattinson/Edward and Stewart/Bella, as well as their relationship, became fractured, much to the dismay of some *Twilight* fans. Robert Pattinson stayed tight-lipped until it was time to promote his next movie, *Cosmopolis*, and even then he refused to comment on the issue. Dressed in elegant suits, like his character in David Cronenberg's movie, he came off as a gentleman. Thus, the film—and somehow, the scandal—gave him a platform for moving beyond Edward's role and proving himself as an actor (Mackinley 2012).

The last installment of the *Twilight* series, *Breaking Dawn Part 2*, was released in November 2012 and was accompanied by a waning of the frenzy, even though box-office profits remained high (IMDb 2013). The film deviates slightly from the book, including amped-up action sequences and a full-blown battle between the Cullens and the Volturi. It ended the saga on a high note, presenting a relevant theme to the audience: empowerment. After being literally "transformed" by the power of love, motherhood, childbirth, and vampire venom, Bella becomes a vampire. The opening credits shift from red to white as a metaphor for her transformation, and she wakes up as a beautiful, athletic, strong, confident woman. The girl-next-door from the first movie has turned into a sexy heroine who plays a key role in saving everyone at the end. But even as the story seems to come to a close, plenty of loose ends remain. What will happen between Jacob and Renesmee? Will the Volturi come back? Will the Cullens rise as the dominant clan within the vampire world? The fans wonder, and the story continues to expand within fan fiction posts and homemade videos shared on the Internet.

In general terms, the *Twilight* saga changed over time: it went from a low-budget first movie to a money-making franchise and from the highest-grossing film directed by a woman to four sequels directed by men. At first, it was a relatively independent project, but it soon became mainstream. The audience expanded from American teenage girls to different kinds of people, worldwide. The themes delved into adult issues, going beyond the original portrayal of a teen romance. *Twilight* is an excellent example of how the entertainment industry creates cultural products that become representative of their time and place, yet transcend local boundaries (Fowkes 2010). In this sense, media both reflect and influence social trends (Couldry 2003; Gauntlett 2002).

*Twilight* could not have been merely "manufactured" to become popular, yet once its profitability became clear, actions were taken to ensure that it was so. To millions of fans, this didn't matter—they felt they had a personal connection with the story and its characters. *Twilight* captured people's imagination and influenced many other cultural products, some of which— like *A Discovery of Witches*, written by Deborah Harkness, and *Fifty Shades of Grey*, by E. L. James—are in the process of becoming franchises of their own, with film productions underway. In this sense, the *Twilight* phenomenon is here to stay, and comparative analyses of it are timely (see Weckerle, Baelo-Allué, Somogyi and Ryan, all in this volume).

## WHAT'S NEXT?

The rest of this book examines *Twilight* from various angles, considering both the novels and the films, paying special attention to their audiences, and analyzing their links to other cultural products and larger social trends. Most of the scholarly books published on *Twilight* to date focus mainly on the novels (Housel and Wisnewski 2009), are written by a sole author (Wilson 2011; Erzen 2012), are informed by a religious framework (Jones 2009), or were published before the movie series was completed (Click, Aubrey, and Behm-Morawitz 2010; Larsson and Steiner 2011). This book seeks to make a contribution by providing an overarching view of the *Twilight* phenomenon, seeking to understand it from a perspective that addresses its multifaceted character.

The chapters included are written by an international group of scholars who work within different disciplines, including communication, history, philosophy, sociology, literature, linguistics, fan studies, film theory, and more. The women and men who contributed to this book represent various age groups, ethnic backgrounds, stages in career development, and professional affiliations. They come from all over the United States and also France, Spain, Chile, and Australia. Some consider themselves *Twilight* fans, others do not. Overall, this volume benefits from the variety of the perspectives featured, while consistently engaging with fundamental aspects of the saga.

The book contains fifteen chapters organized according to sections: it begins by *contextualizing Twilight's appeal* and then presents research on different types of *audiences*. The two sections that follow focus more directly on the texts, analyzing *characters and their cultural referents* and then topics pertaining to *gender, sex, class, and race*, which are very prominent within *Twilight*. The last section, *beyond the Twilight universe*, explores the saga's links to other popular series such as *The Hunger Games*, *True Blood*, and *Fifty Shades of Grey*, advancing a cutting-edge discussion of newer franchises.

Within these general sections, each chapter is different: chapter 1 discusses core aspects that underlie *Twilight*'s appeal, considering them in cross-cultural terms. Chapter 2 analyzes the *Twilight* saga in light of foundational narratives, such as the American dream. Chapter 3 discusses *Twilight*'s links to the larger category of romance literature, bridging existing theoretical concepts with new insights.

The next section presents research findings that directly involve different audiences. Chapter 4 focuses on the famous "Twilight Moms," while chapter 5 reveals interesting data regarding women who are active on Twitter. Chapter 6 adds another dimension to the analysis of fan behavior by zeroing in on anti-fans.

In the following section, chapters 7 through 9 present an analysis of *Twilight*'s main characters, considering them in relationship to larger cultural referents. Thus, chapter 7 focuses on the unique figure of Renesmee; chapter 8, on Bella; and chapter 9, on the masculine portrayals of Edward and Jacob.

Then, chapters 10 through 12 present new perspectives on some of the most controversial social issues represented in *Twilight*: gender dynamics and sexual power play (chapter 10), portrayals of class and social mobility (chapter 11), and conflicts involving identity, boundaries, and interracial relationships (chapter 12).

The last section presents comparative analyses of *Twilight* vis-à-vis other successful popular culture products. Chapter 13 pays attention to the figure of the vampire in *True Blood* and *The Vampire Diaries*, while chapter 14 considers the individual versus the collective in *Twilight*, *Harry Potter*, and *The Hunger Games*. Finally, chapter 15 traces *Twilight*'s transformation into *Fifty Shades of Grey*, which was originally a piece of fan fiction.

Overall, it is our hope that this volume will be an enjoyable and informative read for the diverse kinds of people that the *Twilight* phenomenon has reached. There is something here for media scholars, students of communication, industry professionals, and *Twilight* aficionados. There is even something for those who may not care much about *Twilight* in particular but who would like to better understand the role that media and popular culture play in today's world.

## REFERENCES

Alasuutari, Pertti, ed. 1999. *Rethinking the Media Audience: The New Agenda*. London: Sage.
Blodget, Henry. 2011. "The Amazing Media Habits of 8–18 Year-Olds." *Business Insider*, April. Accessed May 15, 2012. http://www.businessinsider.com/how-kids-consume-media-2011-4.
Burke, Kenneth. 1969. *A Grammar of Motives*. Berkeley: University of California Press.
Click, Melissa A., Jennifer Stevens Aubrey, and Elizabeth Behm-Morawitz, eds. 2010. *Bitten by "Twilight": Youth Culture, Media, and the Vampire Franchise*. New York: Peter Lang.
Couldry, Nick. 2003. *Media Rituals: A Critical Approach*. London and New York: Routledge.
De Moraes, Denis, ed. 2007. *Sociedad Mediatizada*. Barcelona: Editorial Gedisa.

Em and Lo. 2009. *"Twilight*, Take Me Away! Teenage Vampires and the Mothers Who Love Them." *New York Magazine*, November 15. Accessed November 12, 2011. http://nymag.com/movies/features/62027/.

Erzen, Tanya. 2012. *Fanpire: "The Twilight Saga" and the Women Who Love It*. Boston: Beacon Press.

Fiske, John. 1989. *Understanding Popular Culture*. Boston: Unwin Hyman.

Fowkes, Katherine. 2010. *The Fantasy Film*. West Sussex: Wiley-Blackwell.

Fritz, Ben. 2012. "Lions Gate to Acquire Summit." *Los Angeles Times*, January 14. Accessed February 10, 2012. http://articles.latimes.com/2012/jan/14/business/la-fi-ct-lionsgate-summit-20120114.

Gauntlett, David. 2002. *Media, Gender, and Identity: An Introduction*. London: Routledge.

Germain, David. 2011. "Weekend Box Office: 'Breaking Dawn' rises to $283.5M Worldwide Debut." *DJournal.com*, November 20. Accessed March 25, 2012. http://nems360.com/view/full_story/16502000/article-WEEKEND-BOX-OFFICE---Breaking-Dawn--rises-to--283-5M-worldwide-debut-.

Grossman, Lev. 2008. "Stephenie Meyer: A New J. K. Rowling?" *Time*, April 24. Accessed April 20, 2012. http://www.time.com/time/magazine/article/0,9171,1734838,00.html.

Gurevitch, Michael, et al., eds. 1982. *Culture, Society, and the Media*. London: Methuen.

Hall, Stuart. 1996. *Critical Dialogues in Cultural Studies*. Ed. David Morley and Kuan-Hsing Chen. London: Routledge.

Hjarvard, Stig, ed. 2003. *Media in a Globalized Society*. Copenhagen: Museum Tusculanum Press.

Housel, Rebecca, and J. Jeremy Wisnewski, eds. 2009. *"Twilight" and Philosophy: Vampires, Vegetarians, and the Pursuit of Immortality*. Hoboken, NJ: Wiley.

Humanick, Rob. 2011. "The Lion King: Movie Review." *Slant Magazine*, September 12. Accessed May 15, 2012. http://www.slantmagazine.com/film/review/the-lion-king/5750.

IMDb. 2010. *The Twilight Saga: New Moon*. Accessed April 5, 2012. http://www.imdb.com/title/tt1259571/.

———. 2011. *The Twilight Saga: Eclipse*. Accessed April 5, 2012. http://www.imdb.com/title/tt1325004/.

———. 2012. *The Twilight Saga: Breaking Dawn, Part 1*. Accessed May 25, 2013. http://www.imdb.com/title/tt1324999/business?ref_=tt_dt_bus.

———. 2013. *The Twilight Saga: Breaking Dawn, Part 2*. Accessed May 30, 2013. http://www.imdb.com/title/tt1673434/business?ref_=tt_dt_bus.

Itzkoff, Dave. 2008. *"Twilight* Sequel Loses Its Director." *New York Times*, December 9, C2.

Jones, Beth. 2009. *Touched by a Vampire: Discovering the Hidden Messages in "The Twilight Saga."* Colorado Springs, CO: Multnomah Books.

Larsson, Mariah, and Ann Steiner, eds. 2011. *Interdisciplinary Approaches to "Twilight": Studies in Fiction, Media, and a Contemporary Cultural Experience*. Lund, Sweden: Nordic Academic Press.

Mackinley, Page. 2012. "Cosmopolis Teaser Seismically Shifts Critics' Perceptions about Robert Pattinson." *Movie Vine*, March 26. Accessed May 8, 2012. http://www.movievine.com/movies/cosmopolis-teaser-seismically-shifts-critics-perceptions-about-robert-pattinson/.

Martínez, Claudia. 2000. "Cómo Perciben los Niños a los Personajes de la Película *El Rey León*?" Undergraduate thesis. University of Concepción Archives, Chile.

The Numbers. 2012. *Twilight*. Accessed May 30, 2012. http://www.the-numbers.com/movies/2008/TWLIT.php.

Peretz, Evgenia. 2009. *"Twilight*'s Hot Gleaming." *Vanity Fair*, no. 592, December, 210–21.

Peters, John Durham, and Peter Simonson. 2004. *Mass Communication and American Social Thought: Key Texts, 1919–1968*. Lanham, MD: Rowman & Littlefield.

Rollins, Peter, and John O'Connor, eds. 1998. *Hollywood's Indian: The Portrayal of the Native American in Film*. Lexington: University Press of Kentucky.

Sales, Nancy. 2011. "Escape from the *Twilight* Zone." *Vanity Fair*, no. 608, April, 138–91.

Schiller, Dan. 1996. *Theorizing Communication: A History*. New York: Oxford University Press.

*La Tercera.* 2011. "El Secreto de *Crepúsculo.*" *La Tercera Cultura*, December 4. Accessed April 10, 2012. http://terceracultura.cl/2011/12/el-secreto-de-crepusculo/.

*Time.* 2008. "Ten Questions for Stephenie Meyer." Aug. 21. Accessed May 10, 2012. http://www.time.com/time/magazine/article/0,9171,1834663-2,00.html.

*US Weekly.* 2012. "Robert Pattinson Cancels Press Appearance Post Kristen Stewart Cheating Scandal." July 31. Accessed June 6, 2013. http://www.usmagazine.com/celebrity-news/news/robert-pattinson-cancels-press-appearance-post-kristen-stewart-cheating-scandal-2012317.

Vaz, Mark. 2008. *"Twilight": The Complete Illustrated Movie Companion.* New York: Little, Brown.

Vilkomerson, Sara. 2011. *"The Twilight Saga: Breaking Dawn Part 1."* *Entertainment Weekly*, August 19/26, 32–37.

Wilson, Nicole. 2011. *Seduced by "Twilight": The Allure and Contradictory Messages of the Popular Saga.* Jefferson: MacFarland.

Wong, Stephen. 2008. "'*Twilight* Dazzles with $70.6m Bow, November 21–23, 2008." *The Weekend Gross*, November 23. Accessed May 10, 2012. http://weekendgross.blogspot.com/2008/11/*Twilight*-dazzles-with-706m-bow-november.html.

*I*

# Contextualizing *Twilight*'s Appeal

*Chapter One*

# Mythic Themes, Archetypes, and Metaphors

*The Foundations of* Twilight*'s Cross-Cultural Appeal*

## Claudia Bucciferro

The *Twilight* saga has captured the imagination of millions of people world-wide, transcending cultural, national, and linguistic barriers. But how can this extraordinary popularity be explained? Over the years, the question has been posed often, and although the series has been analyzed from various perspectives, there is still no clear answer (Wilson 2011; Click, Aubrey, and Behm-Morawitz 2010; Jones 2009; Housel and Wisnewski 2009). An argument commonly put forth states that *Twilight*'s success is the result of large marketing campaigns tailored to fit the sensibilities of "vulnerable" populations, such as women and teens. Yet, as Melissa A. Click, Jennifer Stevens Aubrey, and Elizabeth Behm-Morawitz (2010) say, this answer is biased and overly simplistic.

A basic premise of cultural studies is that people are not "dupes"—they are not passive beings that consume media content indiscriminately (Hall 1996). From this perspective, *Twilight*'s success can't be merely the result of marketing—although the inscription of the series within a profit-driven entertainment industry is obvious. Looking beyond promotional campaigns, I propose that the *Twilight* saga's cross-cultural appeal is related to the *texts* themselves (in all formats) and what they *do* for audiences. This can be analyzed by focusing on three fundamental aspects: core themes, characters, and overarching metaphors.

Therefore, this chapter argues that the main themes found in *Twilight* have mythic roots, and they resonate with people because they engage with issues that overstep local boundaries. The characters are archetypal, yet imperfect, which enables audience identification. Their struggles involve transcendental concepts, such as love, hate, trust, fate, and mortality, connecting them to a long storytelling tradition. Furthermore, the overarching metaphors present in the story can be understood around the world.

The *Twilight* saga is not the first popular series to have these characteristics—for example, *Star Wars* and *The Lord of the Rings* do, too (Deyneka 2012; Fowkes 2010). Yet, discursively, *Twilight* is often set apart from other fantasy works. Going beyond the surface, this chapter focuses on core aspects of the *Twilight* texts, examining why they appeal to audiences across cultural contexts. The analysis draws from works in communication and media studies and involves qualitative text analysis as a methodology (Hesse-Biber and Leavy 2004).

## SENSUALITY, LOVE, COMMITMENT, AND OTHER THEMES

Five core themes run throughout *Twilight*, connecting the story to myths and fables that are known to surpass cultural contexts. These topics have been found in world literature for centuries, but maintain a contemporary appeal (Hamilton 1999). Although the social dynamics associated with late modernity bring along a reduced engagement with traditional narratives, these narratives don't disappear—instead, they are reformulated within media discourses (Couldry 2003; Hall 1996; Deyneka 2012). Their themes relate to complex and enduring issues, so novel representations usually involve a negotiation between old and new social understandings (Hollis 1995).

The *Twilight* texts reflect this, lending themselves to multiple readings and conflicted explanations, and inviting readers/viewers to navigate them as they please (Wilson 2011; Click, Aubrey, and Behm-Morawitz 2010). Despite their apparent simplicity, they succeed at drawing the audience into their world—and this is partly due to people connecting directly with the core aspects of the story.

### Sensuality and Choice

The *Twilight* series persistently explores the sexual tension between its main characters. In fact, Robert Pattinson and Kristen Stewart were cast for the films' main roles partly because their mutual attraction transpired on-screen (Peretz 2009; Vaz 2008). However, in *Twilight*, sensuality is tied to chastity, choice, and other tropes (Jones 2009). Edward and Bella share an intense bond but postpone intercourse until marriage—and it is him, not her, who establishes sexual boundaries. This subverts typical power dynamics, even though it could represent a masculine attempt to control a woman's sexuality (Diamond 2011; Buskirk, this volume).

In any case, the topic of teenage sex is relevant—and conflictive—both within the social realm and media productions (Shalit 2007; Thornham 2007). Many teen media discourses offer highly sexualized characters and overtly erotic plotlines, and it is usually the girls who are objectified the most (Thornham 2007). Within this context, *Twilight* is different, featuring chaste characters involved in an old-fashioned romance with lots of talk and little touch. The appeal of the sensuality contained therein lies in its undertones.

Choice appears in the main couple's need to negotiate rationality versus instinct, desire versus restraint, agency versus domination—something that everyone must do. Edward chooses not to drink human blood and not to have intercourse. Bella chooses Edward over Jacob and, with it, a vampire life for herself. Hence, choice involves the right to agency and validates various pathways (Bernard, this volume). Even when Bella "chooses" to continue a dangerous pregnancy, the *Twilight* texts make no direct allusions to the key-word that has been used within feminist discourse for decades (Thornham 2007; Wilson 2011). Thus, in its ambiguity, *Twilight* addresses, but doesn't sanction, broader social debates.

## The Impossible Relationship

This core theme has been widely featured in world literature and folklore, yet still holds appeal (Hamilton 1999). *Twilight* portrays the story of a mixed union—a human and a vampire united by a love they can't resist—so the links to *Romeo and Juliet* or *Beauty and the Beast* are notable (Diamond 2011). But *Twilight* goes further: Edward is perceived by Bella as too hand-some, rich, smart, *and* supernatural to be with a girl like her, while Edward feels *he* is a monster not worthy of *Bella*, who is pure and good. To each other, they embody the forbidden fruit (Buskirk, this volume). Conflict en-sues, and many people are troubled by their relationship.

Bella and Edward's yearning for each other, despite the forces that pull them apart, can be understood around the world because—cliché as it sounds—love is a universal language (Sternberg 1998). People everywhere develop relationships and struggle to accommodate social norms, while negotiating unity versus individuality. Thus, *Twilight* functions as a meta-phor for a cross-cultural relationship, since Bella and Edward come from different worlds and make an effort to be together (Bernard, this volume).

This impossible relationship is inherently dangerous—and, some say, at times almost abusive (Jones 2009; Wilson 2011). Bella lies to her parents, Edward tries to control her every move, and intimacy is perilous. Yet people identify with this because it is difficult to navigate the realm of romantic relationships: to negotiate power, define boundaries, maintain a healthy sense of self, and make proper decisions. The characters' behavior contributes to the story's resonance, even though it is not ideal. In this sense, pop culture products may be more effective at portraying social issues than offering paths for solving them. Violence and abuse are cross-cultural characteristics, too (Kenrick 2011). The fact that they are undesirable doesn't neutralize the relevance of their ambivalent portrayal within media.

## Unconditional Love

Bella and Edward's relationship encounters multiple difficulties, but their love endures. They experience it as a mysterious force that they can't deny, repress, or ignore. They lose themselves in their bond and sacrifice endlessly for each other; everything else in the world pales in comparison with this love (Jones 2009; Clasen 2010). Bella and Edward love each other like only teenagers and fools do—without fearing disappointment or pushing an agenda. Romantic poets of the nineteenth century would have found this perfectly acceptable, and *Twilight* has plenty of romantic roots (Nevárez, this volume). But in today's world, it seems almost irresponsible. Still, people yearn for a love that goes beyond measure and pardons all faults. The great stories of old, from Greek mythology to masterworks of Western literature, are full of accounts of reckless loving.

The theme taps onto powerful emotions and fills a need for people—even if it's just the need to believe that such love exists (Chambers and Peaslee, this volume). Adult *Twilight* fans, for example, say that the texts remind them how it was to be young and caught up in a whirlwind of infatuation (Dorsey-Elson, this volume). There is appeal in the story of an all-consuming, passionate, and enduring love—especially within the context of a fragmented social realm, where relationships are sometimes disposable. As other fantasy tales, *Twilight* bridges imagination and reality, challenging common assumptions and providing virtual satisfaction to unspoken needs (Fowkes 2010).

## Taming the Monster

"I am a monster," says Edward in a famous scene of the first film. "You won't hurt me," replies Bella. She should run, but she stays and gives him a chance. The danger involved is what makes *Twilight* a thriller that crosses boundaries of genre. "I never thought of *Twilight* as a vampire movie," says producer Greg Mooradian, and Catherine Hardwicke adds that if Edward wasn't a vampire, he would be a biker (Vaz 2008, 16). As Paul Trout (2011) and Jonathan Maberry and David Kramer (2009) state, the vampire stands for something else: the *Other*, danger, desire, predatory instincts, and an obscure side of the human psyche. Ultimately, it also stands for power.

The monsters populating fantasy stories are not just *out there* but also *within*—in Trout's words, they are a "projection of the greedy, aggressive impulses at the core of what Carl Jung called the Shadow" (2011, 171). And according to Jung (1976b), everyone has a Shadow. In *Twilight*, the monster/Shadow is a moving target: it is James, Victoria, and the Volturi, but also, potentially, Edward, Paul, and even Renesmee. All the characters have issues of their own—for example, Jacob has to control his impulsivity, and Bella deceives and manipulates while berating herself for it. Everyone has to deal with their demons in order to grow.

Trout proposes that people's fascination with monsters is related to the history of our species. Over thousands of years, humans went from being vulnerable scavengers, to hunters and herders—and the transition was marked by our ability to mimic the behavior of natural predators. Indeed, Trout says "we became efficient killers by watching and imitating efficient killers—which is to say that we 'performed the predator' in more ways than one" (172). We internalized the tactics used by predators in order to compete with them, and traces of this are with us still (Kenrick 2011). Since our evolution ensured our survival, we couldn't simply get rid of the adaptive responses that developed along the way. But we learned to deal with them symbolically—hence the role of myths and stories featuring monsters that need taming (Hollis 1995).

Legends from around the world have plenty of monsters in them (Hamilton 1999; Bader, Mencken, and Baker 2010). With some variations, tales of vampires and werewolves appear in all cultures and date back to ancient times (Maberry and Kramer 2009). Contemporary accounts of horrendous behavior—such as abusing or killing innocent victims—abound in the media, and research suggests that violent impulses are more common than people think (Kenrick 2011). Subjugating the evil side of human nature is a necessity and is also a theme found in religious texts. Considering that Stephenie Meyer is Mormon, this topic's presence in *Twilight* may not be casual, yet its relevance goes beyond any single religious tradition.

## Commitment and Restraint

Marriage and abstinence—commitment and restraint—are important within *Twilight* and highly controversial (Diamond 2011; Wilson 2011). Unlike teen fiction that frames youthful romance as casual and exploratory, the saga depicts an intense bond between the protagonists, validating the depth of their experiences. *Twilight* conjures up the emotional whirlwind that comes along with the first love—which is powerful for everyone. And the characters talk openly about their feelings, creating a strong connection with the audience (Jones 2009).

The saga also suggests that young lovers can wait until marriage to have sex and should exercise self-restraint. Its take on commitment goes against other popular teen media discourses: it advocates for an early marriage and lays out the expectation that it would last "forever." Nevertheless, Bella has second thoughts about this, while Edward is eager to commit. This subverts gender stereotypes and brings up contemporary dilemmas regarding love and commitment (Buskirk, this volume). The texts function as a mirror for larger social debates.

With its plot of "girl meets boy, girl gets boy, and they live happily ever after," *Twilight* fits within traditional romance literature (Clasen 2010). And as such, it has been criticized (Godwin, this volume). Yet romance fills a need for its audience, as Janice Radway (1984) first pointed out and others confirm (Click, Aubrey, and Behm-Morawitz 2010; Chambers and Peaslee, this volume). Women who sacrifice daily for their families, for example, appreciate the reaffirming message of texts that value love, commitment, and restraint (Dorsey-Elson, this volume). From old chivalric tales to today's paperbacks, the endurance of the romance genre is a testament to its relevance—regardless of its literary attributes. Over time, its stories have been representing and often redefining the romantic ideal for new generations (Clasen 2010). The ideal has been contested by feminist authors (Thornham 2007; Radway 1984), but that does not make it any less relevant for the general public.

## HEROES AND MAIDENS: ARCHETYPAL CHARACTERS

The three main characters in *Twilight* are archetypal, standing for the hero, the restless youth, and the redeeming maiden. These characters appear all over the world and relate to a long storytelling tradition —for example, the Archive for Research in Archetypal Symbolism (2012) contains thousands of images that document their pervasive presence. In the saga, they are made to fit the social landscape of the twenty-first century, so their inner struggles convey the need to redefine their identities within this context. Hence, Edward and Jacob represent two different types of contemporary masculinity (see Willms, this volume), and Bella must choose what kind of woman she will become (see Hanser, this volume). Archetypes are cross-cultural and share fundamental traits, even though their representations change according to specific cultural environments (Campbell 2008).

In his foundational work on archetypes, Jung (1976a, 1976b) proposes that they are stored in the collective unconscious, which contains images and perceptions that are passed down through the generations (Salman 1997). He argues that this mental archive is like a repository of shared knowledge, carrying forth the memory of our common history. Thus, Jung says, archetypes are "patterns of instinctual behavior" (1976a, 61), embodying characteristics that are associated with certain states of being and that relate to fundamental human experiences (hence, "the maiden," "the mother," etc.). Because of this, they are understood everywhere.

Jung (1976b) says that the two major archetypes are the animus and the anima—which are abstract representations of the female and male principles (152). As such, they can be called forth, projected, enacted, and even embodied by people in certain situations. They attract each other, and their relationship is also archetypal. In his words:

> The language of love is of astonishing uniformity, using the well-worn formulas with the utmost devotion and fidelity, so that once again the two partners find themselves in a banal collective situation. Yet they live in the illusion that they are related to one another in a most individual way. (1976b, 154)

This is why people connect with *Twilight*'s main characters and become involved in their relationships—the underlying aspects are universal, but they feel personal.

## The Troubled Hero: Edward

Edward Cullen is a Byronic hero (Peretz 2009; Greydanus 2008). He is handsome, mysterious, and gifted, but lonely and troubled. When faced with an ethical dilemma, he does "the right thing," yet he has made mistakes in the past. He finds no meaning in life until he encounters love. All this makes him attractive and connects him to other literary and mythic characters (Hamilton 1999; Nevárez, this volume). It also defines his relationship with Bella, the maiden/heroine: as a hero, he is the rescuer, but by the power of love, he is rescued from despair (Greydanus 2008).

In folklore, vampires have been usually represented as horrible, devilish creatures that destroy whomever they encounter, but in contemporary media, they have undergone a deep change (Maberry and Kramer 2009). From Polidori's *The Vampyre* (published in 1819) to Anne Rice's *Interview with the Vampire* (1976), they went from being incarnations of evil to handsome characters with tortured souls, who mesmerize not only their lovers, but also their audiences. The transformation of the vampire into a "dark prince" accompanied its mainstreaming within popular culture, and its heightened eroticism took him away from the horror genre and moved him closer to romance (Somogyi and Ryan, this volume).

The males in *Twilight*'s Cullen clan epitomize the representation of this "good vampire," yet Edward is far from a perfect man—or a straightforward hero. His behavior is often questionable, and plenty of people dislike him (Wilson 2011; Godwin, this volume). He is a troubled hero, so his story is one of redemption.

## The Redeeming Maiden and the Selfless Mother: Bella

As the story's narrator and main female character, Bella is *Twilight*'s anchor. But she is as controversial as the saga itself—some find that she is too weak, lacks assertiveness, and has low self-esteem; others say that she is too reckless and does dubious things (Jones 2009; Hanser, Buskirk, both in this volume). Many consider her to be inadequate as a heroine, yet Bella's character is interesting because she is imperfect. As a seventeen-year-old falling in love and figuring out who she really is, Bella is full of conflicts. She does not have the beauty, wealth, or attitude that young female protagonists often possess, so she departs from the poised and sexy ideal typically portrayed in teen media (Thornham 2007; Hanser, this volume). She is the girl-next-door, and young women relate to her.

Bella's self-sacrificing nature connects her with the archetype of the redeeming maiden, whose quiet strength enables the hero's quest, and with the mother, who is caring and forgiving (Campbell 2008). Bella is domestic and dutiful. She cooks for her father and protects her mother, even at her own risk—which is more noticeable in the *Twilight* books than films. She is mature for her age and very nurturing, so when she has a baby—and dies in childbirth, only to be reborn as a vampire—the transition from maiden to mother is complete.

The maiden is associated with purity and desire, the mother, with nurturance, selflessness, and life. The mother's power is linked to transformative love, which is a recurring theme that also appears across cultures. She is a prominent character within literature and folklore (Campbell 2008), perhaps because motherhood is a fundamental experience for many women, all over the world.

## The Restless Youth: Jacob

Jacob is spontaneous, young, and hotheaded, with a witty sense of humor and a sharp tongue. Warm and loyal, he represents Bella's connection with the earth—which is further indicated by his being a werewolf. There is much of the hero in Jacob, but he better embodies the restless youth, who ventures off into the world in a process that brings growth and self-discovery, even as his sense of duty tempers his desire for freedom (Gresh 2009). While Bella's fascination with Edward represents erotic love, her feelings for Jacob are deep but fraternal. Her dilemma not only involves two different types of males, but also different ways of loving.

Jacob is Quileute, which has been interpreted in different ways. On the one hand, it is rare for male American Indians to appear in film as charming men courting the main heroine (Rollins and O'Connor 1998). On the other hand, his portrayal as a brown, working-class male contrasts sharply with

Edward's undisputed upper-class whiteness (Willms, this volume; Wilson 2011). However, Jacob is no less attractive than Edward—and he is just as much of an archetype, albeit in a different form.

Moreover, as a werewolf, Jacob's character has links to the shape-shifting beings that often appear in folklore stories (Maberry and Kramer 2009; Campbell 2008). And in *Twilight*, the werewolves—just as some of the vampires—are good people, not scary monsters.

## The Characters' Journey

The power of the archetypes lies in their ability to represent human experiences that, though symbolic, are connected to aspects that are real (Jung 1976b; Salman 1997). As the stories develop, they often portray journeys that are also archetypal (Campbell 2008; Hollis 1995). Hence, Edward, the hero, has to make peace with his past and learn to surrender control. Bella, the maiden/mother, must choose her path and discover her inner strength. Jacob, the youth, has to deal with rejection and become a leader. Throughout the saga, all the characters have to wrestle with themselves and others, facing both inner struggles and outside challenges. These involve fundamental concepts such as love, hate, knowledge, trust, fate, and mortality—all of which are timeless and cross-cultural (Hamilton 1999; Housel and Wisnewski 2009).

As they struggle, *Twilight*'s characters learn about intimacy, establish their independence, raise and destroy boundaries, develop commitments, and create alliances. Their identities are challenged, and they have to make choices. Their relationships are complicated, and their behavior is not ideal, but in the end, they surpass all challenges and triumph over their opponents. In this sense, the *Twilight* texts—as other fantasy films and literature—present an alternative world in which issues of "real" relevance can be represented and addressed, although not solved (Fowkes 2010; Deyneka 2012).

Lois Gresh (2009) says that Meyer's vampires and werewolves are unique because "they care about humans. They don't want to hurt people, and indeed, they will sacrifice themselves to protect their human loved ones" (2009, 1). They are monsters with a conscience, and they are archetypal but imperfect—so their struggles make them seem real. This matters because, as Trout (2011) argues, "myths about heroes defeating primordial monsters are less history than therapy, helping us manage our fear" (181). It is in the face of adversity that we discover our power, so the struggles portrayed in mythic stories are full of meaning (Campbell 2008; Hamilton 1999).

Although circumstances change, the core of human nature is remarkably similar (Kenrick, 2011). The maiden, the mother, the hero, and the youth are characters that cross boundaries, their importance given by our common experiences. The monster is also a timeless signifier, and its inscription within the supernatural allows for a conceptual flexibility that heightens its appeal (Bader, Mencken, and Baker 2010). Some say that we "love our monsters," to which Trout (2011) adds: "At any rate, we need them" (181).

## TRANSFORMATION, JOURNEY, AND OTHER DEEP METAPHORS

Metaphors have been used within oral and written literary traditions for centuries and are also found in everyday language (Pinker 2007; Lakoff 1987). Humans' ability to think metaphorically is related to our capacity for abstract thought, enabling us to conceptually manipulate our world without engaging in "real" action. Considering "what if . . ." scenarios and talking about them before making risky moves is a useful adaptive trait and is linked to our capacity for inventing stories (Trout 2011; Lakoff 1987). This has been crucial for the survival of the species, and it is still fundamental for people's success in navigating the intricacies of modern life (Kenrick 2011).

Research done on metaphors indicates their cross-cultural character (Lakoff 1987). People everywhere *use* metaphors, and *the same* metaphors are found to be in use in different cultures. People *relate to the world* in a metaphorical way, while at the deepest level, the metaphors that come up are often the same. From a cognitive perspective, this is indicative of the universal structure of the human mind and the fundamental characteristics of human experience (Lakoff 1987; Pinker 2007). Despite apparent cultural differences, our common evolutionary history implies that people across the globe are more alike than they may believe (Kenrick 2011).

Gerald Zaltman and Lindsay Zaltman (2008) propose a link between metaphors and marketing, exploring the way people relate to various products. Although the possibilities for metaphorical thinking are many, they say there is a limited number of "deep metaphors" that underlie the way people experience events, relationships, and things. Metaphors are not rare; in fact, people use them every day—they may say they are "filled with joy," "swamped with work," or in a relationship that is "going nowhere." Because of their widespread use, metaphors may be connected to deep levels of the psyche. The unconscious mind is "like the pied piper," Zaltman and Zaltman say: the deep metaphors are the tunes, and we all dance to them (2008, xxi).

The authors argue that people don't just *use* a product but *experience* it in a way that imbues it with meaning. This is relevant for popular culture products, such as *Twilight*, that call for a deep and personal engagement with the texts. Zaltman and Zaltman (2008) identify seven deep metaphors that recurrently appear all over the world: transformation, journey, balance, container, connection, resource, and control. Interestingly, they are found throughout the saga and provide a plausible explanation for its success.

## Transformation

Transformation is the strongest metaphor in *Twilight*—most clearly expressed in humans turning into vampires or werewolves and in the looming danger of injury and death. It is also evident when characters grow and change as the story unfolds. Before Bella is "changed" into a vampire, she is transformed by the intensity of her relationship with Edward and the experiences that come with it. Edward and Jacob are, too, transformed by love. Katherine Fowkes (2010) proposes that transformation is a central theme within the fantasy genre and one that not only appears within the text but also is found in the way audiences relate to it. She says: "Fantasy's appeal may lie in its insistence on engaging us in imaginative experiences that invite us to temporarily transcend our sense of what is possible" (9). Fans say that they feel different when reading or watching *Twilight* (Chambers and Peaslee; Dorsey-Elson, both in this volume). Hence, transformation expands from the text onto reality.

## Journey

Journey is also found recurrently in the saga. First, physical journeys are part of the story, as the characters travel to Forks, Arizona, Alaska, Brazil, Italy, and so forth. Then, Bella and Edward's love story is a journey that goes from meeting to dating and marriage, overcoming challenges all along. Each one of the characters is embarked on a journey of self-discovery and atonement: Bella must choose her future, Edward must make peace with his past, and Jacob has to become a responsible adult. People often experience relationships as stories or journeys that lead to personal growth (Sternberg 1998). In this sense, the metaphor's appearance in *Twilight* is "in tune" with the way many people already perceive the events in their life.

## Balance

Balance appears throughout *Twilight* as a precarious goal that the characters strive for. At first, the relationship between Edward and Bella is *not* balanced—hence, her wish to become a vampire and relate to him as an equal. Bella also wants to be one of the Cullens, while keeping some ties to the human world. The treaty that maintains peace between vampires and werewolves in Forks implies balance, but Jacob's involvement with Bella and the Cullens disrupts it. Conceptually, balance is related to "home," and as Fowkes (2010) points out, home is a relevant theme in fantasy works (11). In *Twilight*, as in many other tales, at the end, the protagonists feel they have found their place in the world, their home—things come full circle, and balance is achieved. In the "real" world, people often strive for balance. It is a metaphor of particular importance to women, who are often asked to fulfill multiple social roles.

## Container

Zaltman and Zaltman (2008) say that, metaphorically, container relates to "inclusion, exclusion, and other boundaries" (99). It appears under many different guises in *Twilight*: vampires live among humans, but humans are excluded from their secret world—hence, the problems brought along by Bella's involvement with Edward. Boundaries between vampires and were-wolves are clearly drawn and presumably must be kept. On a different level, sexual boundaries are important for Bella and Edward's relationship. The body and the mind can be also considered containers, and Bella is both—her human body contains her blood (which, when spilled, can change the course of events), and her mind is a "shield" that nobody can penetrate. In the real world, as in the saga, boundaries are common, for good or bad—they are built up, torn down, challenged, manipulated. Many situations are managed through containment.

## Connection

"Humans have a basic need for affiliation," say Zaltman and Zaltman (2008, 121). In *Twilight*, connection (and lack thereof) is present in all its dimensions—emotional, mental, and physical. Bella and Edward are attracted to each other, yet sometimes they don't "connect," which leads to angst. Bella has an emotional connection with Jacob. In *New Moon*, Bella feels cut off from both humans and vampires and even from her own feelings. Edward and Alice, given their special abilities, share a special bond. *Twilight* fans say that they feel connected to its characters and to other fans (see Groover, this volume). The purchase of merchandise is also a way to establish, by means of a tangible product, a sense of connection with *Twilight*'s fantasy world.

## Resource

A resource can be either physical or intangible (Zaltman and Zaltman 2008, 141), and *Twilight* has links to both. The Cullen family has resources, such as money, cars, and designer clothes; they also have social contacts, experience, knowledge, and supernatural abilities (Lucas, this volume). Bella doesn't own much but is very resourceful and usually finds a way to get what she wants. The final confrontation with the Volturi is determined by each party's available resources. On a different level, fans say that they *use* the *Twilight* series as a resource that helps them connect with other people and manage their moods (Groover, Dorsey-Elson, this volume). Being a profitable franchise, the saga also constitutes a resource within the entertainment industry.

## Control

The last deep metaphor involves control over the self, others, and the environment, and it appears frequently in *Twilight*. Carlisle has great self-control, being able to "change" people without killing them and remaining unfazed by blood. Edward strives for self-control and sexual restraint, while often trying to control Bella. Bella is vulnerable as a human, but as a newborn vampire, she has an unnatural sense of control. Jasper can influence people's emotions. Werewolves, on the contrary, are unstable, sometimes losing control. Victoria manipulates her newborn army. The Volturi oversee the vampire world. In sum, issues of power and control are everywhere, and they also permeate the "real" world. People want to feel in charge of their lives and their behavior; they want to manage what happens in their immediate environment. When this is not possible and they are overwhelmed, they may turn to fantasy as a way to cope. Some people even write fan fiction to gain control over a story (Baelo-Allué, this volume).

Overall, deep metaphors are fundamental in attracting audiences because they define how people "experience" certain products, in both symbolic and tangible ways (Lakoff 1987; Zaltman and Zaltman 2008). Their cross-cultural character is related to the universality of fundamental aspects of human cognition and experience. Engaging with a fictional world that presents these powerful metaphors can be a profound experience for people—and this is key for understanding the global appeal of not only *Twilight* but also other series, such as *Harry Potter* and *Star Wars*.

## CONCLUSION

*Twilight*'s worldwide success is not due simply to girls loving handsome actors and reading easy novels as a way to escape more serious matters. That may happen, too, but it does not account for the broad pop-culture phenomenon that the series has become. This chapter argues that we need to look deeper into what the texts present, how they function, and how they establish meaningful links to audiences across cultural contexts. Hence, *Twilight*'s popularity should be considered in terms of the relationship between the *texts* and what they *do* for people, and also in light of how this is part of larger social processes.

Despite the apparent simplicity of *Twilight*'s story, it appeals to various audiences because its themes, characters, and metaphors can be understood across boundaries. The core themes found in it connect to mythic tropes that have been fascinating people for centuries. The characters' archetypal natures relate to beings that populate tales around the world. The challenges faced by *Twilight*'s characters involve the big questions of all time—the meaning of love, death, and transcendence—which matter to people everywhere (Housel and Wisnewski 2009). *Twilight* also raises contemporary issues, such as the importance of personal choices and the value of commitment. Beth Jones (2009) says that the saga is about romance, love, sex, desire, family, and life, and it approaches all these "from *a girl's perspective*" (2, emphasis in the original). Therefore, as Click, Aubrey, and Behm-Morawitz (2010) note, the debate surrounding *Twilight* is not neutral, but gendered.

From a rhetorical perspective, *Twilight*'s narrative is effective because, as Kenneth Burke (1969) argues, drama is an intrinsic part of life and is charged with emotional content, so people relate to fictional representations of it. Within a modern world that highly values reason, emotions are often overlooked. Yet, as Elster says, "Emotions matter because if we did not have them nothing else would matter" (cited by O'Shaughnessy and O'Shaughnessy 2003, 4). People respond to stories that allow them to work through their feelings within a fictional—hence, safe—realm. *Twilight* does this well, pulling the audience into an emotional journey so strong that it is often unsettling, as indicated by fans and critics alike. Emotions can be powerful and may even influence people's decisions—including economic ones (O'Shaughnessy and O'Shaughnessy 2003). People establish both emotional and conceptual relationships with things, and much of the process is mediated by metaphors.

Furthermore, *Twilight* has many ties to storytelling, which has traditionally contributed to the creation and maintenance of culture. Trout (2011) proposes that a "mythmaking mind" developed historically and shaped our cultural constructs. He says, "The ability to think mythically . . . brought about the transition from mimetic culture to *mythic culture*" (130, emphasis in original). Over the course of human evolution, storytelling tied the development of language, narrativity, mythmaking, and creativity with the rise of a sophisticated mind. Although we don't usually acknowledge it, the adaptive features that helped us survive through millennia are still with us and influence the way we perceive the world (Pinker 2007; Kenrick 2011). Moreover, people interpret their own experiences as stories, and love stories fit within predictable patterns. *Twilight* represents a "fantasy story," which, according to Robert Sternberg (1998), is "perhaps the most classical love story," involving a charming prince and a prospective princess whose love will last forever (165).

In contemporary societies, issues such as identity and boundaries are relevant and are often represented in media discourses (Couldry 2003). Love stories between people who are "different" have always existed, yet in a global world, they matter more, because as traditional boundaries change, mixed relationships become more common. People "want to believe" that true love is real, that heroes exist, and that mysterious events take place—however they may be defined to fit individual taste (Bader, Mencken, and

Baker 2010). Conceptually, monsters stand for the *Other* and the unknown, and tales of the paranormal have always been popular.

The last question is: Are these stories bad? Do they just enable "escapism"? Fowkes (2010) argues that fantasy creates a space of "cultural interdiction," a pause that lets us look at reality with fresh eyes (7). This is because the fantasy's alternative universe is not altogether different but has things in common with reality—it is familiar enough for people to relate to it but distinct enough to engage their imagination. In the story's ability to create this kind of space lies the "pleasure offered the viewer" (Fowkes 2010, 7), which also shapes the commercial success of any cultural product. *Twilight* has several characteristics that make it meaningful for people across cultures. The fundamental plot of two people whose love transcends all barriers is not new, so *Twilight* is a reincarnation of an old—and cherished—tale. Fowkes (2010) says that "fantasy tends to favor happy endings, and eschews not only tragedy, but cynicism, providing solace and redemption in a world of evil and violence" (6). As J. R. R. Tolkien knew well, people want—and perhaps also need— stories that give them hope.

## REFERENCES

Archive for Research in Archetypal Symbolism. 2012. "About ARAS." Accessed March 20, 2012. http://aras.org/aboutaras.aspx.

Bader, Christopher, F., Carson Mencken, and Joseph Baker. 2010. *Paranormal America: Ghost Encounters, UFO Sightings, Bigfoot Hunts, and Other Curiosities in Religion and Culture.* New York: New York University Press.

Burke, Kenneth. 1969. *A Grammar of Motives.* Berkeley: University of California Press.

Campbell, Joseph. 2008. *The Hero with a Thousand Faces.* 3rd ed. Novato, CA: New World Library.

Clasen, Tricia. 2010. "Taking a Bite out of Love: The Myth of Romantic Love in the *Twilight* Series." In *Bitten by "Twilight": Youth Culture, Media, and the Vampire Franchise,* ed. Melissa A. Click, Jennifer Stevens Aubrey, and Elizabeth Behm-Morawitz, 119–34. New York: Peter Lang.

Click, Melissa A., Jennifer Stevens Aubrey, and Elizabeth Behm-Morawitz, eds. 2010. Introd. to *Bitten by "Twilight": Youth Culture, Media, and the Vampire Franchise,* ed. Melissa A. Click, Jennifer Stevens Aubrey, and Elizabeth Behm-Morawitz, 1–17. New York: Peter Lang.

Couldry, Nick. 2003. *Media Rituals: A Critical Approach.* London: Routledge.

Deyneka, Leah. 2012. "May the Myth Be with You, Always: Archetypes, Mythic Elements, and Aspects of Joseph Campbell's Heroic Monomyth in the Original *Star Wars* Trilogy." In *Myth, Media, and Culture in "Star Wars": An Anthology,* ed. Douglas Brode and Leah Deyneka, 31–46. Lanham, MD: Scarecrow.

Diamond, Fleur. 2011. "Beauty and the Beautiful Beast: Stephenie Meyer's *Twilight Saga* and the Quest for a Transgressive Female Desire." *Australian Feminist Studies* 26, no. 67 (March): 41–55. DOI: 10.1080/08164649.2010.546327.

Fowkes, Katherine. 2010. *The Fantasy Film.* West Sussex: Wiley-Blackwell.

Gresh, Lois. 2009. *The "Twilight" Companion, Completely Updated: The Unauthorized Guide to the Series.* New York: St. Martin's Griffin.

Greydanus, Steven. 2008. *"Twilight* Appeal: The Cult of Edward Cullen and Vampire Love in Stephenie Meyer's Novels and the New Film." *Decent Films Guide.* Accessed January 10, 2013. http://www.decentfilms.com/articles/*Twilight*.html.

Hall, Stuart. 1996. *Critical Dialogues in Cultural Studies*. Ed. David Morley and Kuan-Hsing Chen. London: Routledge.

Hamilton, Edith. 1999. *Mythology: Timeless Tales of Gods and Heroes*. New York: Warner Books.

Hesse-Biber, Sharlene, and Patricia Leavy, eds. 2004. *Approaches to Qualitative Research: A Reader on Theory and Practice*. New York: Oxford University Press.

Hollis, James. 1995. *Tracking the Gods: The Place of Myth in Modern Life*. Toronto: Inner City Books.

Housel, Rebecca, and J. Jeremy Wisnewski, eds. 2009. *"Twilight" and Philosophy: Vampires, Vegetarians, and the Pursuit of Immortality*. Hoboken, NJ: Wiley.

Jones, Beth. 2009. *Touched by a Vampire: Discovering the Hidden Messages in "The Twilight Saga."* Colorado Springs, CO: Multnomah Books.

Jung, Carl. 1976a. "The Concept of the Collective Unconscious." In *The Portable Jung*, ed. Joseph Campbell, 59–69. New York: Penguin Books.

———. 1976b. "Aion: Phenomenology of the Self." In *The Portable Jung*, ed. Joseph Campbell, 139–62. New York: Penguin Books.

Kenrick, Douglas. 2011. *Sex, Murder, and the Meaning of Life: A Psychologist Investigates How Evolution, Cognition, and Complexity Are Revolutionizing Our View of Human Nature*. New York: Basic Books.

Lakoff, George. 1987. *Women, Fire, and Dangerous Things: What Categories Reveal about the Mind*. Chicago: University of Chicago Press.

Maberry, Jonathan, and David Kramer. 2009. *They Bite: Endless Cravings of Supernatural Predators*. New York: Citadel Press Books.

O'Shaughnessy, John, and Nicholas O'Shaughnessy. 2003. *The Marketing Power of Emotion*. Oxford: Oxford University Press.

Peretz, Evgenia. 2009. "*Twilight*'s Hot Gleaming." *Vanity Fair*, no. 592, December, 210–21.

Pinker, Stephen. 2007. *The Stuff of Thought: Language as a Window into Human Nature*. New York: Viking.

Radway, Janice. 1984. *Reading the Romance: Women, Patriarchy, and Popular Literature*. Chapel Hill: University of North Carolina Press.

Rollins, Peter, and John O'Connor. 1998. *Hollywood's Indian: The Portrayal of the Native American in Film*. Lexington: University Press of Kentucky.

Salman, Sherry. 1997. "The Creative Psyche: Jung's Major Contributions." In *The Cambridge Companion to Jung*, ed. Polly Young-Eisendrath and Terence Dawson, 52–70. Cambridge, UK: Cambridge University Press.

Shalit, Wendy. 2007. *Girls Gone Mild: Young Women Reclaim Self-Respect and Find It's Not Bad to be Good*. New York: Random House.

Sternberg, Robert. 1998. *Love Is a Story: A New Theory of Relationships*. New York: Oxford University Press.

Thornham, Sue. 2007. *Women, Feminism and Media*. Edinburgh: Edinburgh University Press.

Trout, Paul. 2011. *Deadly Powers: Animal Predators and the Mythic Imagination*. New York: Prometheus Books.

Wilson, Natalie. 2011. *Seduced by "Twilight": The Allure and Contradictory Messages of the Popular Saga*. Jefferson: MacFarland.

Vaz, Mark. 2008. *"Twilight": The Complete Illustrated Movie Companion*. New York: Little, Brown and Company.

Zaltman, Gerald, and Lindsay Zaltman. 2008. *Marketing Metaphoria: What Deep Metaphors Reveal about the Minds of Consumers*. Boston: Harvard Business Press.

## Chapter Two

# Manifest Destiny Forever

*The* Twilight *Saga, History, and
a Vampire's American Dream*

## Michelle Maloney-Mangold

Midway through *Eclipse*, the *Twilight* saga's heroine, Bella Swan, sits with her boyfriend, Edward Cullen, and his family, who are all desperately trying to understand what kind of force the evil vampire Victoria is using to attempt to kill Bella. Jasper, Edward's brother, first realizes what Victoria has done because, as he explains to Bella, "We immortals have our histories, too," a history he lived in his early vampire life in the 1860s (Meyer 2007, 290). As we will see, Jasper's unique knowledge of this history becomes crucial, both for the Cullens' victory over Victoria at the end of *Eclipse* and for their growing knowledge of the duplicity of the Volturi. As Victoria and the Volturi comprise the two most threatening villains of the series, we can see how important knowledge and an understanding of history are to the outcome of the *Twilight* saga.

And yet the importance of history has often been overlooked in the critical conversation about the series. While several critics have examined the British literary influences on the series, few have yet explored the ways in which Stephenie Meyer belongs in the American literary tradition. In this essay, I situate the *Twilight* saga in the genre of the American historical romance, and I argue that Meyer draws from two dominant themes in American history and literature: American exceptionalism and Manifest Destiny. The Cullens' victories over Victoria and the Volturi recreate the teleological mythology of America, wherein a liberty-loving underdog overthrows the tyrannical oppressor and embarks upon a journey across the frontier. The tiny town of Forks, where much of the series takes place, becomes a kind of vampire "city upon a hill" to which the rest of the vampire world can turn for inspiration, leadership, and freedom. And, though these two themes have often justified expansionism and imperialism throughout American history, the saga erases any implication of untoward intentions; we are instead left with a conservative, feel-good assessment of this new vampire nation (the Cullen family) and its role in the world.

## READING THE *TWILIGHT* SAGA AS AN AMERICAN HISTORICAL ROMANCE

I first came to the realization of *Twilight*'s place in the American Historical Romance tradition while considering a much different story, Sir Walter Scott's *Waverley* (2012). In György Lukács's landmark study, *The Historical Novel*, he writes this about Edward Waverley, the hero of Scott's novel:

> The "hero" of a Scott novel is always a more or less mediocre, average English gentleman. He generally possesses a certain, though never outstanding, degree of practical intelligence, a certain moral fortitude and decency which even rises to a capacity for self-sacrifice, but which never grows into a sweeping human passion, is never the enraptured devotion to a great cause. (1963, 33)

To an avid *Twilight* fan, the resemblance in this description to Bella Swan is striking. Like Waverley, Bella frequently describes herself as "ordinary" and unremarkable; indeed, a great deal of her anxiety about her relationship with Edward stems from her belief that she falls far short of his extraordinariness. Likewise, Bella displays great "moral fortitude," which Edward laments as Bella's almost supernatural stubbornness. Moreover, Bella serves the most crucial purpose of the Waverley figure; she "bring[s] the extremes whose struggle fills the novel, whose clash express[es] artistically a great crisis in society, into contact with one another" and brings "the extreme, opposing social forces . . . into a human relationship with one another" (Lukács 1963, 36). While we may have to expand our definition of "human" in this case, Bella clearly fits the "wavering hero" model that Scott created in Waverley, as one of her greatest roles in *Twilight* is to bring together the feuding werewolf and vampire clans. As we will later see, this alliance is crucial to the outcome of the series and to this chapter's argument.

While there are other similarities between *Twilight* and the American historical romance,[1] it is the American and the historical aspects of the saga that interest me most. At first glance, *Twilight* might seem to have little to do with history or historical representation. Meyer sets the story in present-day Washington, and it spans a roughly two-year period in the mid-2000s, though there are few markers that ground the series in any sort of historical or cultural moment. I contend, however, that *Twilight* is inextricably linked with history; because vampires are immortal, they are simultaneously contemporaneous and historical figures. They must negotiate the present while they process and remember the past.

In this way, then, the vampires in the *Twilight* saga are much more rooted in a time and a historical moment than any of the humans are. The year 2005, Bella's time, is never explicitly stated in the series, but Meyer assigns each of the Cullens a specific rebirth year, thus securely situating them in a particular time and historical moment. Unlike historical figures in a typical historical romance, however—Prince Charles in *Waverley* (Scott 2012), General Montcalm in *The Last of the Mohicans* (Cooper 2009), or the pseudonymous historical characters in romances like Nathaniel Hawthorne's *Blithedale Romance* (2009) or Henry James's *The Bostonians* (2009)—the vampires can and must transcend their time of origin and infiltrate all of history from that time forward. While Prince Charles cannot exist much beyond the 1740s, Carlisle Cullen must exist in the 1640s, when he was born; the 1660s, when he was turned into a vampire; and in every other historical epoch from that point forward. This complex but undeniable relationship to history situates the *Twilight* saga securely within the framework of the American historical romance, while the saga simultaneously adapts the romance genre to the realities of its universe.

Just as the vampires are more rooted in time than are the humans, Meyer also emphasizes vampire history over human history, and the narrative of this history reflects a particularly American notion of history and progress. Though romance primarily drives *Twilight*'s emotional affect, politics and an emphasis on democracy drive the series' action. Each novel effectively has at least two villains, one "local" or emotional threat and one "global" or outside, violent villain: in *Twilight*, Edward is the former and James, the latter; in *New Moon*, Edward again serves as a kind of threat, while Victoria, who wishes to avenge her mate's (James) death, and the Volturi fill the roles of the violent villain. In *Eclipse*, Victoria and her vampire army again appear as the outside villains, while Edward and Jacob's battle for Bella occupies the local concern; finally, in *Breaking Dawn*, Bella's unborn child, who slowly kills Bella from within her, is the first danger, while the Volturi prove to be the series' ultimate and most serious global threat to the Cullens and their alternative lifestyle.

Critics tend to focus on the local villains, and thus on the romance, of the series, but it is the global villains that belie the series' debt to American history and politics. In each of these villains, Bella and/or the Cullens struggle with a tyrannical and unjust force that wishes to revoke individual liberty and free will, to silence them from expressing dissent—in short, to oppress them, physically and psychologically. The series' two most important villains, Victoria and the Volturi, then, are ultimately enemies of democracy and to the traditional American values of individualism and freedom. For the remainder of this essay, I will explore the influences of two important national myths, American exceptionalism and Manifest Destiny, on the *Twilight* saga.

## "THE DEVELOPMENT OF THE GREAT EXPERIMENT OF LIBERTY": MANIFEST DESTINY, EXCEPTIONALISM, AND THE (VAMPIRE) AMERICAN REVOLUTION

Few beliefs have had as sustained an influence on American history than the twin myths of American exceptionalism and Manifest Destiny. The concept of American exceptionalism is often traced back to John Winthrop's 1630 sermon "A Model of Christian Charity." Allegedly delivered the night before the Massachusetts Bay Company sailed to the New World, the governor imagines that one day, "men shall say of succeeding plantations: the Lord make it like that of New England: for we must consider that we shall be as a City upon a Hill, the eyes of all people are upon us" (1996, 10). At the core of this theme is the notion that America is fundamentally different from other nations: more pure, more fair, more prosperous—in short, more blessed by God than any other nation in the world. These blessings compel the rest of the world to look to the United States for leadership, protection, and inspiration.

Closely related to American exceptionalism (Madsen 1998, 124), the idea of Manifest Destiny is rooted in a religious belief that America is destined to spread democracy, freedom, and prosperity to the rest of the world. We normally associate Manifest Destiny with the expansionist impulses of the nineteenth century: the explorations of Lewis and Clark or Pike and subsequent acquisition of far western territories, the Homestead Act, the annexation of Mexican territory, and, finally, the United States' altercations with Spain in Cuba, Puerto Rico, Guam, and the Philippines. The journalist John O'Sullivan coined the term in 1845, first in an essay entitled "Annexation" and later again that year when he wrote in the *New York Morning News* that it is the United States' "manifest destiny to overspread and to possess the whole of the continent which Providence has given us for the development of the great experiment of liberty and federated self-government entrusted to us" (1845b, 2). This larger belief encompasses many others, most notably the belief that God is on America's side, that America is synonymous with freedom, and that it is God's wish and America's destiny to take possession of the entirety of North America in order to do its good work.

Taken together, these two ideas form the backbone of the American imaginary. To many Americans, the United States invented the very concept of freedom, and its remarkably fast journey from creation to dominance provides ample evidence of its exalted place in God's favor. Such a conviction requires a belief in the linear progression of history and, of course, in destiny: since its inception, America was destined for greatness, and it has been simultaneously working toward and demonstrating that greatness step by step, spreading its good news of liberty and opportunity along the way. Fundamental to this belief is the notion that we have something that others do not: we have freedom while others have tyranny; we have the opportunity to rise above even the humblest beginnings while others are locked into a rigid class system; we win hearts and minds, liberate the subjugated, and spread democracy while others oppress and scheme. In this version of the story, Americans did not "steal" anyone's land because it was always meant to be ours in the first place. Indeed, John L. O'Sullivan's first use of the term "manifest destiny" was, remarkably, in response to those "nations [which] have undertaken to intrude" into the United States' affairs in Texas "for the avowed object of thwarting our policy and hampering our power, limiting our greatness and checking the fulfillment of our manifest destiny to over-spread the continent allotted by Providence for the free development of our yearly multiplying millions" (1845a, 6). The fact that these nations—in this case, Britain and France, although he might as well have included the First Nations—held territory on the North American continent before America even existed does not matter: Americans have Providence on their side, and it is their fate and their right to possess the entirety of the continent.

Of course, some of the most important and uncomfortable moments in American history must be left out of this teleology. Though, as Godfrey Hodgson argues, "The history of the United States ought to be seen as only one part of a broader history" of "vast international historical processes, from the expansion of Europe and the African slave trade, through the Reformation and the Enlightenment, the global competition between the European powers, especially Britain and France, and the industrial revolution," and Americans often learn their history as if they were the only important partici-pant in it (2009, 155). The horrifying events of Indian removal or extermina-tion, the institution of slavery itself, the unlawful annexation of foreign terri-tory, and the ugly processes of imperialism are either ignored or recast as America's "settling" a vast and empty frontier, "saving" savages from god-lessness and squalor, claiming land that God meant Americans to have, and "liberating" the oppressed from their oppressors. Though popular historians like Howard Zinn (2005) and James Loewen (2008) have published best-selling books that attempt to reframe American history, the conservative Right still insists upon a revised, nationalistic story of America's exception-alism, benevolence, and hospitality.

The *Twilight* saga solves this problem in its retelling of American history. The series closely mirrors the unfolding of American history, and yet it does so without the unfortunate genocide, xenophobia, and imperialism of actual events. The Cullens, like the United States, wish to spread the message and truth of democracy and freedom around the world, but they do so almost reluctantly, as they simply endeavor to protect their own family and way of life. They so inspire others in the supernatural world, however, that these foreign vampires and werewolves pledge their loyalty and their physical might to the Cullens in the hopes of overthrowing the tyranny of the Volturi. The Cullens do not coerce or threaten; instead, the truth and righteousness of their beliefs and actions shine through plainly, winning the allegiance of all who believe in good. In what remains, I will show how Meyer accomplishes this subtle yet thorough revision of American history.

The Cullens' story begins in seventeenth-century England, just as part of America's story does. Carlisle Cullen was born in London in the 1640s, the son of an Anglican pastor whom Edward describes as "an intolerant man." Carlisle comes of age during a tumultuous time in English history, but his thoughtful, patient personality does not mesh with the extreme times. Edward explains Carlisle's upbringing to Bella as follows:

> As the Protestants came into power, [Carlisle's father] was enthusiastic in his persecution of Roman Catholics and other religions. He also believed very strongly in the reality of evil. He led hunts for witches, werewolves . . . and vampires. . . . They burned a lot of innocent people—of course the real creatures that he sought were not so easy to catch. (Meyer 2005, 331)

Even for American readers unfamiliar with the particularities of English history, this context will not be so different from the stories told by American history textbooks—indeed, religious intolerance and persecution are the very conditions that drove the Pilgrims to escape the Old World. Meyer casts Carlisle as an enlightened but dutiful man and thus only a reluctant participant in the literal witch hunt; he takes up his father's mantle out of filial obedience, not out of violent intolerance or fanaticism: "At first Carlisle was a disappointment; he was not quick to accuse, to see demons where they did not exist" (Meyer 2005, 331). Regardless of Carlisle's motivations, however, his actions are punished in the end; in a raid on a vampire coven, Carlisle is bitten and transformed into a vampire himself. Fearing his father's certain wrath, he flees his home forever and begins his second life as the thing his father hated the most.

Carlisle's rebirth catapults him to the status of legend in *Twilight* mythology. In his new body with its unbelievable power and incessant thirst, we might expect Carlisle to abandon his former principles and give justification to his father's hatred, but he does the opposite: first, he tries to kill himself, and, when that fails, he discovers that he can survive on the blood of animals, erasing any fears he had of taking human life. With this realization, Carlisle chooses his life's work and becomes a physician in an attempt to make amends to the universe for the sins of his species. In Meyer's telling, Carlisle becomes a kind of saint; when Edward recounts Carlisle's story to Bella, "[h]is expression bec[omes] awed, almost reverent" (2005, 339), marking Carlisle's willpower and compassion as inspired or, at least, exceptional. Carlisle's capacity for benevolence knows no bounds and eventually takes him to the New World, where he "dreamed of finding others like himself," others who would shirk human blood and share his respect for human life (Meyer 2005, 341). Once there, he practices medicine, which is how he eventually finds the individuals he will transform into his family members. Carlisle "saves" them all from mortality and then instills in them his "vegetarian" values.

Carlisle's motivations for creating a family for himself are nearly never questioned. Though two of his family members, Edward and Rosalie, detest their vampirism and constantly pine for their long-dead humanity, neither seems to fault Carlisle for what they might consider to be his selfish decisions. Indeed, Edward even expresses admiration for his "father," both at the restraint Carlisle showed when biting Edward to infect him with transformative venom and at Carlisle's impulse to save humans from death: when Bella asks Edward if one must be dying to become a vampire, Edward responds with "respect in his voice," "No, that's just Carlisle. He would never do that to someone who had another choice" (Meyer 2005, 288). Carlisle's decisions to sire new vampires are always characterized as a gift, not a curse, and though they are explicitly selfish—Edward twice mentions that he created companions out of loneliness—his family accepts his reason without question or anger because they trust his innate goodness. Unlike the bloody intentions and history of U.S. expansionism, we as readers feel confident that Carlisle always intends to raise his family to hold his value for human life dear. Indeed, Edward's ability to read minds reassures us—and him—of Carlisle's "perfect sincerity" about compassion and humanity (Meyer 2005, 342). When a family member strays from that path, as Edward does ten years after his transformation, Carlisle shows compassion, not wrath, and when Edward realizes his mistake, Carlisle "welcome[s him] back like the prodigal" (Meyer 2005, 343). He does not wish to command or rule them or to build some sort of regime; he simply wishes to love and to share his life of compassion and service.

Over and over again, the Cullens' rejection of the traditional vampire diet sets them apart from the rest of their kind. As a family, they move west in 1936 to settle in Forks, Washington, as far west as one can go in the contiguous United States. As destiny would have it, they settle on land directly adjacent to the Quileute tribe's ancestral land. The Cullens make a treaty with the Quileutes that establishes a firm boundary between their two territories and also forbids the Cullens from biting (not just killing) any humans. It is difficult to overstate how important and remarkable this treaty is in Quileute history. In *Eclipse*, Bella joins Jacob at a Quileute meeting in which the tribe elders recount the origins of the Quileute ability to shape-shift. Their history includes a great deal of hatred for and war with vampires, but when an elder comes to the Cullens' arrival, the tone shifts slightly:

> A bigger coven came, and your own great-grandfathers prepared to fight them off. But the leader spoke to Ephraim Black *as if he were a man*, and promised not to harm the Quileutes. His strange yellow eyes gave some proof to his claim that they were not the same as other blood drinkers. The wolves were outnumbered; there was no need for the cold ones to offer a treaty when they could have won the fight. (Meyer 2007, 259; emphasis mine)

To the Quileutes, the difference between the Cullens and all other vampires is the difference between human and demon—between good and evil itself. As vampires who have no intention to destroy any humans, the Cullens represent a completely new paradigm to a tribe with a more than one-thousand-year-old memory. Unlike those who might attempt to deceive the Quileutes, the Cullens' restraint gives the tribe pause: their yellow eyes, earned with the sacrifice of their animal diet, provide instant proof of their regard for human life, while their reluctance to wreak violence on the tribe, which would surely result in their victory, ultimately assures the Quileutes of the family's righteousness and exceptionalism.

The Cullens do not test the treaty until Bella's pregnancy requires Edward to bite her in order to turn her and save her life, and by that point, they are under Jacob's new pack's protection. Even if Jacob had not granted Edward permission to change Bella, the birth of Renesmee cancels the wolves' retribution, as Quileute code dictates that the object of a wolf's imprinting must never be harmed. We might conclude, then, that the Cullens never actually break the 1936 treaty until it is dissolved in 2006. Going forward, we know that Renesmee and Jacob's relationship will guarantee the good graces between the coven and the tribe, so no future treaties or understandings will be necessary.

In a nation that even still breaks treaties with native tribes, this bloodless, optimistic story revises, and improves, a great deal of American history. Others (Burke 2011; Jensen 2010; Wilson 2010) have commented on the Cullens as representatives of wealthy, European colonialists and the Quileutes as stereotypes of superstitious, natural natives, but such criticism overlooks the revision of American history that takes place here. The major amendment lies in the Cullens' intentions, which are as pure as Carlisle's were when he was expanding his family. The Cullens simply want to live in peace; when they make a treaty with the tribe, they keep it for seventy years, and it is only void when the two factions find a way to truly coexist as equals. And though there is a great deal of animosity on both sides, readers do not hold one species above the other: the wolves match the Cullens in strength, while the Cullens rival the wolves in virtue. In short, the *Twilight* saga is a new-and-improved retelling of westward expansion, one in which anyone is free to move about the country and no one needs to commit genocide to explore and "settle" new land.

Indeed, the Cullens explicitly disapprove of imperialism, as we learn in *Eclipse*. As established above, Jasper deduces that Victoria has created an army of newborn vampires because of his personal involvement in one of the most important events in vampire history: the Southern Wars. After decades fighting in these wars, Jasper realized the immorality in the southern pursuit and abandoned his post. His new family shares his disgust with the Southern Wars and, therefore, with imperial intervention.

Victoria, of course, has no such qualms against creating an army ostensibly to achieve her own goals and disposing of the newborns after she has used them. Because of Jasper's personal experience with vampire history, he immediately understands Victoria's reasons for creating the newborn army and the strategies she will use to try to defeat the Cullens. Using Jasper's story, Meyer primes the reader to associate Victoria with Maria, and Victoria thus becomes not just a woman seeking revenge for her partner's death but an immoral dictator who will create and destroy lives in order to achieve her own goals. Maria plucked young humans from the prime of their lives and placed them in a brutal war only to dispose of them when they ceased to be useful. Though we do not see this happen in *Eclipse*, *The Short Second Life of Bree Tanner* (Meyer 2010) confirms this reading. Victoria and her second-in-command, Riley, lie to the newborns in order to ensure their loyalty to the mission, telling them that they will burn in the sun so that they would not venture out in the daylight and that the Cullens are a threat to them. Riley kills Diego after he discovers Victoria's lies, and Bree dies after the battle with the Cullens and the Quileutes. The vampire–werewolf coalition wins the battle with the newborns, and Edward kills Victoria; the compromising democratic coalition defeats the crazed tyrant, and the Cullens and Quileutes live to fight another day.

The Cullens' ability to build coalitions proves to be the key to their survival. As we have seen, the alliance between the Cullens and the Quileutes culminates in the battle with Victoria's army and grows further when Carlisle visits the Quileute reservation—normally forbidden territory—to treat Jacob's extensive wounds. Even more strikingly, in *Breaking Dawn*, the Cullens spread out beyond the United States' sea-to-shining-sea borders as they make appeals to vampires all over the world to stand with them in defiance of the Volturi. When they learn that the Volturi mistakenly believe that Renesmee is an immortal child and will travel to Forks to destroy them, Emmett argues for gathering witnesses that can simply stand beside them to make the Volturi pause before doling out punishment. When Carlisle protests, unwilling to risk the lives of his friends, Emmett reassures him, claiming, "Hey, we'll let them decide," and "We'd do it for them" (Meyer 2008,

550). The Cullens immediately spring into action, reaching out to their friends to convince them of Renesmee's true origins and to save themselves from the Volturi's retribution. They win the hearts and minds[2] of more than twenty who travel from places as far as Ireland, Romania, Egypt, and the Amazonian jungle to witness for the Cullens' goodness.

The parallels to—and revisions of—American mythology are obvious here. As stated above, the Cullens' story is a story of expansion: first with Carlisle's travel from England to the New World, then his creation of a new family, then their move from east to west, and finally their spreading influence from the United States to the rest of the world. We might consider the culmination of this expansion—the Cullens' ideological overthrow of the Volturi—to be their Manifest Destiny and the destiny of the entire vampire species. Moreover, when the Cullens recruit for their vampire League of Nations, they do so not to win sovereignty over other vampires, nor do they force their worldview or beliefs on them. The vampires are free to decline the Cullens' invitation and to leave if at any time they change their minds, and, in fact, a few do. As Edward tells one of his Alaskan cousins, however, "It's difficult to doubt our story when you see it for yourself" (Meyer 2008, 592). The Cullens' virtue cannot be denied, especially with Renesmee's gift of communicating her thoughts, feelings, and memories to anyone she touches; every character in the novels, friend or foe, believes in the Cullens' cause.

As we will see, nothing short of total belief would do, as no *Twilight* villain could rival the Volturi, the representatives of the Old World in the series. As such ancient figures—Aro, Marcus, and Caius form their coven between 1400 and 1200 BCE (*Twilight* Lexicon 2012)—they inspire the same kind of awe, fear, and respect that historical figures such as Alexander the Great or Genghis Khan might inspire in a contemporary person today. Indeed, Jasper speaks of them with the utmost respect when recounting the history of the Southern Wars. Because of their immortality, however, they continue to exist as very real threats in the vampire world; as simultaneously towering historical and contemporary figures, Meyer renders them doubly terrifying, doubly impressive. In short, the Volturi are integral to vampire society. They are judge, jury, and executioner for all vampire offenders and thus serve as the only legal and judicial apparatus in the vampire world.

They are also a monarchy. When Edward first tells Bella about the Volturi, he describes them as a "very old, very powerful family of our kind . . . the closest thing our world has to a royal family" (Meyer 2006, 19). They live in a castle in Volterra, Italy, one complete with stone walls, turrets, and thrones, and it is in this throne room that the three brothers dole out their particular version of justice. As early as *New Moon*, Edward begins to doubt the Volturi's intentions, as he could hear Aro's thoughts in his mind: "There was also the thought of you, Carlisle, of our family, growing stronger and larger. The jealousy and the fear: you having . . . not *more* than he had, but still, things that he wanted. He tried not to think about it, but he couldn't hide it completely. The idea of rooting out the competition was there" (Meyer 2007, 305). His judgments are confirmed in *Bree Tanner* when we learn that, as Edward suspects, the Volturi know about the newborn army but do nothing; they prefer instead to let Victoria destroy the Cullens herself rather than dirty their own hands (and reputations) with the task (Meyer 2010, 78–80). Aro has little experience with not getting his way, and his desire both to possess Edward and Alice and to rule the vampire world with absolute sovereignty become his compass, pointing him toward the verdicts that will ensure his preferred outcome. As monarchs, he and his brothers answer to no one, no matter how twisted their logic or sense of justice; ordinary vampires have no recourse once they have reached a decision. As tyrants, they provide the perfect foil to the Cullens, the champions of liberty and free will.

By the end of the series, the parallels to (and revisions of) American history become almost transparent. The Cullens, the upstarts with the British Founding Father, join their allies from around the world to challenge their Old World oppressors. They do this peacefully, even reluctantly, but they are willing to fight for their freedom if necessary. Staggeringly, they even have a soldier from the American Revolution in their ranks, who whispers, "The redcoats are coming, the redcoats are coming" as the Volturi approach (Meyer 2008, 680). Indeed, it is Garrett, an American nomad turned during the Revolutionary War, who finally delivers the plain truth about the Volturi to the dozens of gathered vampires. In his speech, aimed at the forty witnesses the Volturi have gathered, he asks, "Who rules you, nomads? Do you answer to someone's will besides your own? Are you free to choose your path, or will the Volturi decide how you will live?" (Meyer 2008, 719). Though as readers we already know these truths to be self-evident, Garrett boldly states them for all the representatives of the vampire world to hear. Garrett is a free spirit and thinker, but it is the Cullens who bring him to his realization about the Volturi. The Cullens' "life of sacrifice" astounds and impresses Garrett, and because of this sacrifice, he knows that the Cullens have "no thought for domination"—the very thing that Garrett detests the most (Meyer 2008, 718). The Volturi's actions confirm Garrett's concerns after his speech, as their guard works to incapacitate them while they "counsel"; as we know, the coalition is only saved by Bella's ability to shield them from supernatural attacks and then by Alice's evidence about vampire-human hybrids. The Volturi retreat, ideologically overthrown if not physically defeated, and a New World Order begins. As Carlisle's friend Siobhan prophesies, "Perhaps the time will come when our world is ready to be free of the Volturi altogether." Carlisle replies, "If it does, we'll stand together" (Meyer 2008, 743).

## CONCLUSION

A fervent belief in destiny dominates the *Twilight* saga; by the time we reach the opening of *Breaking Dawn*, it seems unthinkable that Bella and Edward could ever do anything but live happily ever after, literally. As I show in this essay, readers yearn not just for Bella and Edward's destiny but for the destiny of the vampire nation as well, and, indeed, these destinies are inextricably intertwined. In this way, the romance and the politics of the series work together and are inseparable from one another. Over and over again, it is the Cullens' exceptionalism that saves them and enables them, and the new vampire nation that is to come, to flourish: Carlisle's exceptional self-control and compassion kept him from being discovered by his father's angry mob when he was turned, and that same self-control allows him to create a family for himself without succumbing to the temptation of their blood. Edward's exceptional love for Bella prevents him from killing her, even when he must actually taste her blood. The Cullens' collective exceptionalism and virtue wins over more than twenty vampires who rally to their side, and in the end, Bella's incredible talent protects all she loves from the Volturi's duplicitous attacks. Indeed, Bella—through her transformation from an ordinary teenager to a flawless, extra-supernaturally powerful vampire, wife, mother, and possible national matriarch—lives out the vampire version of the American Dream. Without these exceptional skills and values, Bella and Edward's relationship would be doomed but so would the lives of those vampires who seek to change the world and desire to make it better, freer.

This story—of exceptionalism, democracy, and good intentions—is the story that Americans, and many around the world, wish to tell and be told about themselves. In its retelling of American history, the *Twilight* saga retains the nation's most favorable characteristics while discarding its most unfortunate moments—the slave trade, Indian removal, and imperial interventions around the world. The Cullens honor their treaty with the Quileutes until they eventually become allies and then family; they earn international allies by winning hearts and minds with the righteousness and purity of their mission. And when they ideologically overthrow the Volturi, it is with a bloodless revolution, as the Cullens are always reluctant to fight and kill. When at so many points in its history the United States has more closely resembled the domineering, imperial Volturi and not the Cullens, it is unsurprising that so many want to hold on to the centuries-old story of American exceptionalism that the Cullens so perfectly embody. In the *Twilight* saga, at least, we never have to fear that we are rooting for the bad guys.

## NOTES

1. These similarities include competing "light" and "dark" love interests (represented in the saga by Edward and Jacob) and a conservative, more or less happy ending.

2. Elizabeth Dickinson quickly traces the use of the term "hearts and minds" in order to show how it has "become indelibly associated with the challenges of an interventionist U.S. foreign policy" (Dickinson 2009).

## REFERENCES

Burke, Brianna. 2011. "The Great American Love Affair: Indians in *The Twilight Saga.*" In *Bringing Light to "Twilight": Perspectives on a Pop Culture Phenomenon*, ed. Giselle Liza Anatol, 207–19. Gordonsville, VA: Palgrave Macmillan.

Cooper, James Fenimore. 2009. *The Last of the Mohicans.* Reprint., ed. John McWilliams. New York: Oxford University Press.

Dickinson, Elizabeth. 2009. "A Bright Shining Slogan." *Foreign Policy*, October. http://www.foreignpolicy.com/articles/2009/08/13/a_bright_shining_slogan.

Hawthorne, Nathaniel. 2009. *The Blithedale Romance.* Reprint. New York: Oxford University Press.

Hodgson, Godfrey. 2009. *The Myth of American Exceptionalism.* New Haven, CT: Yale University Press.

James, Henry. 2009. *The Bostonians.* Reprint, ed. R. D. Gooder. New York: Oxford University Press.

Jensen, Kristian. 2010. "Noble Werewolves or Native Shape-Shifters?" In *The "Twilight" Mystique: Critical Essays on the Novels and Films*, ed. Amy M. Clarke and Marijane Osborn, 92–106. Critical Explorations in Science Fiction and Fantasy (CESFF) 25. Jefferson, NC: McFarland.

Loewen, James W. 2008. *Lies My Teacher Told Me: Everything Your American History Textbook Got Wrong.* Rev. ed. New York: New Press.

Lukács, György. 1963. *The Historical Novel.* Boston: Beacon.

Madsen, Deborah L. 1998. *American Exceptionalism.* Edinburgh: Edinburgh University Press.

Meyer, Stephenie. 2005. *Twilight.* New York: Little, Brown.

———. 2006. *New Moon.* New York: Little, Brown.

———. 2007. *Eclipse.* New York: Little, Brown.

———. 2008. *Breaking Dawn.* New York: Little, Brown.

———. 2010. *The Short Second Life of Bree Tanner: An Eclipse Novella.* New York: Little, Brown.

O'Sullivan, John L. 1845a. "Annexation." *United States Magazine and Democratic Review* 17 (1): 5–10.

———. 1845b. "Editorial." *New York Morning News*, December 27.

Scott, Walter. 2012. *Waverley.* Reprint. Penguin Classics.

*Twilight* Lexicon. 2012. "Timeline." Accessed December 1, 2012. http://www.twilightlexicon.com/the-lexicon/timeline/.

Wilson, Natalie. 2010. "Civilized Vampires versus Savage Werewolves: Race and Ethnicity in the *Twilight* Series." In *Bitten by "Twilight": Youth Culture, Media, and the Vampire Franchise*, ed. Melissa A. Click, Jennifer Stevens Aubrey, and Elizabeth Behm-Morawitz, 55–70. Mediated Youth 14. New York: Peter Lang.

Winthrop, John. 1996. *The Journal of John Winthrop, 1630–1649.* Ed. Richard S. Dunn and Laetitia Yeandle. Cambridge, MA: Harvard University Press.

Zinn, Howard. 2005. *A People's History of the United States: 1492 to Present.* Rev. ed. New York: Harper Perennial Modern Classics.

## Chapter Three

# Reading *Twilight*

*Fandom, Romance, and Gender in the Age of Bella*

## Barbara Chambers and Robert Moses Peaslee

In the November 19, 2009, issue of the *Washington Post*, Monica Hesse (2009) notes how "good, smart, literary women tried to resist the vampire phenomenon, and then, alas, they bit."[1] Hesse laments in her article that while Stephenie Meyer's *Twilight* books and films "came for the tweens, then for the moms of tweens, then for co-workers who started wearing those ridiculous Team Jacob T-shirts," these literary women resisted because they were too "literary . . . they didn't do vampires . . . they were feminists" (2009). Thus, while the *Twilight* series was intended for a female teenage audience, the crossover appeal to adult women has made it even more successful. This phenomenon begs analysis to examine the study of gender representation in popular culture and among female audiences.

Carol Stabile (2011) suggests, "Despite changes in production, distribution, and consumption that have revolutionized fan practices and visibility, feminist fan studies really have not advanced beyond [Janice] Radway's *Reading the Romance* [1984]," and "as a field, feminist media studies need to collectively revisit its premises, methods and practices" (61). This study explores these questions by comparing and contrasting findings from focus-group research with *Twilight* fans in different life stages to the subjects explored in Radway's canonical work. Using Radway's study as a foundation, we hope to advance the understanding of romance readership, *Twilight* fandom, and how fans attribute meaning to these texts in a twenty-first-century "postfeminist" world.

## TWILIGHT "MANIA": FANDOM, ROMANCE, AND FEMINISM

There is no doubt *Twilight* has developed a devoted fan following. Meyer's success as an author has also translated onto the big screen where, with a five-film production budget of approximately $385 million, Summit Entertainment and its partners have seen total worldwide box-office receipts of over $3.2 billion and counting.[2] In addition, in 2008, the *Twilight* franchise had one of the most successful licensing programs in the United States (Lisanti 2009). This is interesting since neither Summit Entertainment, who manages the books and films, nor Striker Entertainment and Most Management, who manage the merchandise and licensing, were even listed among the top one hundred licensor or agents in 2008 (*License! Global* 2009a, 2009b; Linsanti 2009). It is clear that such successes are driven in large part by an avid fan base.

Fandom, or participatory culture (Jenkins 1992), has received considerable popular and academic attention in the past twenty years, particularly in the age of networked electronic communication. Early in fan scholarship, fandom was depicted as "a result of psychological or cultural dysfunction" (Smith, Fisher, and Cole 2007, 84). This stereotypical treatment that belittled fans and placed them on the fringes of society was slowly supplanted by a more careful examination of fannish practices influenced by the cultural turn in media studies (Sandvoss 2005). Cornel Sandvoss (2005), in his review of the fandom literature, describes fandom as being the "regular" and "emotional" act of consuming texts. Scott Smith, Dan Fisher, and S. Jason Cole (2007) note literature that defines fanaticism as "deep commitment" and the pursuit of activities not proportionate to the average consumer (81).

Much research in the area of fandom focuses on subcultures within these broad constructs and fannishly affiliated groups that resist dominant discourses (Bacon-Smith 1992; Gray, Sandvoss, and Harrington 2007; Hills 2002; Jenkins 1992; Penley 1991; Radway 1984). Given this diversity, fandom is more rigorously theorized as practices unfold at different levels of intensity. John Fiske (1992) initially suggests three such levels: the "semiotic" fan, or one that creates "meaning in the process of reading" (29); the "enunciative" fan that takes part in social interaction with others as they consume various fan sources; and the "textual" fan, characterized by productivity resulting in fan-created and fan-distributed content. Both Nicholas Abercrombie and Brian Longhurst (1998) and Sandvoss (2005) present similar taxonomies that essentially reproduce a continuum from some level of passionate but largely unproductive audiencehood on one end to a contributory, heavily invested one on the other.

Accordingly, the Internet has helped fuel the growth of *Twilight* fandom communities. According to Sarah Summers (2010), http://www.twilightsaga.com, the official *Twilight* fansite, has more than 75,000 registered members.

The fansite http://www.twilightmoms.com had 45,391 members as of December 2012 (TwilightMOMS.com). Sites such as these and http://www.twilightlexicon.com have been sources of fan information since the beginning of the franchise. While some *Twilight* fan activity has been characterized as excessive, Nancy Baym counters that *Twilight* fandom could be interchangeable with the passion many men have for sports, wherein men may "stay up late at night looking at statistics and playing fantasy football," and that this is similar to a female searching online for *Twilight* news and trivia (Spines 2010). Both *Twilight* and sports fans passionately engage with these topics, and both could be considered dysfunctional if taken too far. Baym thus notes what seems to be a societal double standard with regard to avidly engaged female audiences.

## Vampires, Women, and Romance

While the gender of book buyers is difficult to discern, *Twilight* film fans first trended toward the young female with 60 percent of the first film's audience being made up of teenage girls (Schuker 2009). For the latest film, *Breaking Dawn Part 2*, females still made up 79 percent of the film's audience (Stewart 2012). Franchise fans over the age of thirty, otherwise known as "Twilight Moms," helped compose nearly 40 percent of the overall female fan base that is over twenty years of age (Goodale 2010). That *Twilight* is both a vampire tale and a romance contributes to its popularity with women.

Molly Williamson (2005) notes how "the vampire is one of the most enduring of popular fictions in modern Anglo American culture" (45) and that, in the twentieth century, a new type of vampire has emerged: "morally ambiguous and sympathetic . . . luring audiences with the pathos of their predicament and painful awareness of outsiderdom" (29). The new vampires are portrayed as either "attractive rebel figures" or as more domesticated characters that develop friendships and families (31). Anne Rice's literary *Vampire Chronicles* and the television series *Buffy the Vampire Slayer* best portray this new vampire generation, whose melodramatic stories are reminiscent of the gothic novel. Rice's character Louis is the epitome of the melodramatic figure who "depicted misrecognized and persecuted innocence" while living as a "vegetarian bloodsucker" (40–41). This restraint—the hesitation or refusal to feed—is a key characteristic of this new sympathetic portrayal of vampires. In Williamson's research of female vampire fandom, she finds females actually identify with the male vampire rather than his female victims. The vampire fan cultures she explores are focused on narratives where the main vampire in the story is sympathetic and expresses "intense emotional states such as passion and feelings for life" (64). While characters like Dracula are seen as predators, the readers of Rice's series find themselves caring for characters like Louis and Lestat, especially since "they did not choose to become a vampire but had it thrust upon them" (63).

The *Twilight* series is a catalyst for, and perhaps the most prominent symptom of, a larger societal interest in the vampire genre, and its subsequent academic study is found in edited volumes (Anatol 2011; Click, Aubrey, and Behm-Morawitz 2010; Housel and Wisnewski 2009; Parke and Wilson 2011; Reagin 2010), monographs (Erzen 2012), and countless book chapters and peer-reviewed articles. The foci of this literature are predictably diverse but usually include gender representation and the implication of the romance genre. According to the Romance Writers of America (2010), in order for a story to be considered as a romance, there must be a central love story and an emotionally satisfying and optimistic ending. In 2008, romantic fiction generated sales of $1.37 billion with 74.8 million readers (Romance Writers of America 2010). Kristin Ramsdell (2004) lists multiple subgenres for romantic fiction, and vampire and shape-shifting tales such as those in *Twilight* fall into the alternate reality romance or paranormal romance genres.

## Radway Revisited

Romantic novels have in general been, as Elana Levine (2010) points out, the "ultimate objects of scorn" (281). In some cases, this ridicule has emerged from both paternalist and feminist concerns about romance's potential for spilling over into the realm of the pornographic (Driscoll 2006), a realm from which women have historically been both ideologically and spatially discouraged (Juffer 1998). Janice Radway's (1984) *Reading the Romance* and Tania Modleski's (1982) *Loving with a Vengeance*, however, both make great strides in presenting a non-stereotypical approach to women's popular culture in an attempt to "resist the double standard which operates to condemn or dismiss women's genres and to 'rescue' feminine forms as worthy of attention" (Gill and Herdieckerhoff 2006, 491).

While Modleski psychoanalyzes soap operas, gothic novels, and Harlequin romances and the pleasure women receive from them, Radway's canonical work attempts to understand the "economic, cultural, ideological, and pleasurable phenomenon" of romantic fiction (Gill and Herdieckerhoff 2006, 492). Unlike previous feminist scholars, Radway used an oral interview method to evaluate romance reading, allowing her to understand readers from an emic perspective and not just from an academic or feminist point of view. According to Helen Wood (2004), Radway presents one of the first "ethnographic explorations of popular culture consumption" (147). Her goal is to understand not only why women are drawn to romance literature but also what types of sense-making strategies they use when reading.

Ien Ang (1996) suggests, because of Radway's feminist stance and disapproval of the romantic texts' ideology, she finds reading romances a way in which women nurture themselves "within the demands and power relationship of family life" and from "within the oppression of the patriarchal family dynamic" (Wood 2004, 149, 151). The women in the study—the Smithton women—were primarily married women living with children in a suburb of a large city in the midwestern United States. Ang (1996) finds Radway's conversations with the Smithton women have an "empowering effect on them in that they were given the rare opportunity to come to a collective understanding and validation of their own experiences" (101). Radway's interactions with these women provide intriguing insight in how they dealt with gender and power issues on their own terms. She notes that the women "insistently and articulately explained their reading was a way of temporarily refusing the demands associated with their social role of wives and mothers" (Radway 1984, 11) and declaring "themselves temporarily off-limits to those who would mine them for emotional support and maternal care" (12). The women did not want to shirk their roles as wives and mothers but instead used romance reading as a way to replenish themselves from the strains of everyday life.

Though the act of reading provided escape, the women often reported feeling a sense of guilt about spending money on books, especially when being criticized by those around them. Radway notes how Dot Evans, a bookseller and resource for the Smithton women, often encouraged them to feel proud of their reading and to question critiques by asking if it is "any different from their husbands' endless attention to televised sports" (54). Radway's participants also felt guilty for taking part in something that brought them so much pleasure but took them away from their children and husbands; they felt the need to "hide the evidence of their self indulgence" and felt shame about their "hedonist behavior" (90). Part of this stemmed from their intense desire to continue reading until they "experienced the resolution of the narrative" (59).

The Smithton women valued "strong, fiery heroines . . . capable of defying the hero, softening him, and showing him the value of loving and caring for one another" (54). They saw these stories as tales of female empowerment and expected the heroine to demonstrate intelligence, independence, and a sense of humor (77). The hero, meanwhile, was to be masculine and strong, but "capable of unusual tenderness, gentleness, and concern for her pleasure" (81). They did not see the heroine as falling prey to the whims of a man but instead felt the characters' mutual dependence on each other was evidence of a "mutuality in love" that required some sacrifice on the part of each character (81). As Radway summarizes:

> It must be emphasized that this group finds it possible to select and construct romances in such a way that their stories are experienced as a reversal of the oppression and emotional abandonment suffered by women in real life. For Dot and her customers, romances provide a utopian vision in which female individuality and a sense of self are shown to be compatible with nurturance and care by another. (55)

Radway, thus, is one of the first cultural studies scholars to take romance seriously as a literary form and its engagement by women as a practice of ideological resistance, subtle as that resistance may seem to feminist audiences.

## Pleasure and "Third-Wave" Feminism

While Radway is empathetic to the views of the Smithon women, her own academic feminist stance means she analyzes the women's experience as "an activity of mild protest and longing for reform necessitated by those institutions' failure to satisfy the emotional needs of women" (Ang 1996, 213). The work relies upon a feminist assumption that romance reading might remove the need to seek out real social change against patriarchal oppression. In fact, Radway expresses the need to create a world "where the vicarious pleasure supplied by its [romance] reading would be unnecessary" (Radway 1984, 222). Ang (1996) critiques this positioning of feminism as the "superior" solution for all women's problems, however, as if feminisms automatically possessed the relevant and effective formulas for all women to change their lives and acquire happiness (103).

Ang's primary concern is the absence in Radway's account of the pleasureableness of romance reading. While Radway may dismiss this pleasure as temporary or vicarious, Ang believes Radway also dismisses the possibility that romance reading pleasure is real, belying an assumption on Radway's part that other forms of pleasure would be more authentic, lasting, and "more real" (Radway 1984, 104). While the Smithton women knew what type of heroine they preferred, Radway is concerned that the women could not describe a typical heroine in their stories or admit their books had a standard plot. Ang (1996) counters this concern by noting that perhaps pleasure is found in the "subtle, differentiated texture of each book's staging of the romantic tale that makes its reading a 'new' experience even though the plot is standard" (105). Another area that bothers Radway is the need for the women to know in advance if the book will have a happy ending, which she saw as the failure of the women to accept "the threat of the unknown" (Radway 1984, 205). Ang (1996) suggests instead that if the reader is assured of a happy ending wherein the hero and heroine are united, then "she can concentrate all the more on how they will get each other" (105). Ang further points out that the reader is not required to be part of any conflict that comes after the happy ending but instead chooses to start another book to "maintain the feeling of romance" no matter if it is temporary or lacking in real life (107). Ang does not deny the importance of the gap between feminism and romance reading but states that this "should not invalidate the significance of the craving for and pleasure in romantic feelings that so many women have in common and share" (107).

Ang's critique is more easily understood in the sociohistorical context of a changing notion of feminism. The feminist movement is typically categorized into three waves (Kaplan 1990; Happel and Esposito 2010; Botkin-Maher 2007; Catterall, Maclaran, and Stevens 2005; McRobbie 2008; Orbach 2008). In short, the first wave took place between 1850 and 1919 and focused on women's voting rights (Happel and Esposito 2010, 527). Following victory at the polls, the second wave is believed to have started with the publication of Betty Friedan's *The Feminine Mystique* in 1963 and to have caught momentum as white, educated, middle-class mothers countered the normative discourse of suburban familial happiness (Botkin-Maher 2007, 194). The second-wave feminists campaigned for equal opportunities in employment and choices in reproduction (Aronson and Buchholz 2001). According to E. Ann Kaplan (1990), the 1980s and 1990s saw a paradigm shift to what is known as the third wave, where a new generation of "postfeminists" enjoyed the benefits derived from the activism of their mothers and grandmothers and believed they could have it all since there were "numerous opportunities for females to achieve positions of power without perceiving a loss of their femininity" (Catterall, Maclaran, and Stevens 2005, 490). Angela McRobbie (2008) finds in the third wave an impression that since the goals of feminism had been reached, and since young women were employed, there was no need for a renewed or revitalized feminist agenda (240). This shift could be characterized as one from activism to consumerism, where feminism today is marketed and repackaged as a "quest for freedom, choice, and opportunity" through consumption and pleasure (Catterall, Maclaran, and Stevens 2005, 490). This celebratory feminism allows women to return to pleasure while picking and choosing participation based upon their enjoyment.

Authors have contextualized *Twilight* in a postfeminist culture (Shachar 2011), and numerous critiques have been leveled against *Twilight* from feminist scholars (Schau and Thompson 2010; Happel and Esposito 2010; Bode 2010; Summers 2010). While many of the critiques are aimed at Bella Swan's dependent nature, Jennifer Botkin-Maher (2007) advocates being suspicious of "representational 'empowerment' discovered via female characters who can run in high heels, fire a gun, and bed the boss" (195). Hope J. Schau and Margo Buchanan-Oliver (2012) find that *Twilight* causes fans to think "often for the first time about the compromises and tradeoffs of being a contemporary woman" (35) and that the *Twilight* brand is used by fans to negotiate feminism and role expectations. Levine (2010) states that *Twilight* provides another opportunity to add to the debate of the meaning of feminism in a contemporary society, especially since many of its fans only "lived in a world changed by the women's liberation movement" (282). This brief review shows that there remains a strong academic ambivalence toward the attraction for women of what appears to be a text of strong gender conservatism.

Despite academic ambivalence, the blockbuster success of the *Twilight* franchise is evidence of its attraction for audiences across the globe. The purpose of this research is to ask why. Using Radway's findings and critique of the romance genre as a foundation for comparison, the goal was to engage qualitatively with female consumers of the *Twilight* books and films, to tease out their feelings of the series' content and characters, their practices of engagement with the texts, and the meanings they derive from their consumption.

## METHOD

Four separate focus groups were conducted in February 2010, with a total of seventeen females ranging in age from seventeen to forty-five. Focus groups were chosen to enhance the quality of data in dynamic social interaction though the discussion of texts in a safe environment in which to share feelings (Patton 2002; Lunt and Livingstone 1996). This safe environment is especially important for *Twilight* fans who often face ridicule from non- or anti-fans. Participants were recruited using a snowball sampling methodology. The criteria for participating in the focus groups required each person to have read at least one of the books in the *Twilight* series. Those that had only seen the movies were not asked to participate.

## FINDINGS

The transcripts were analyzed based on segmenting the participants into groups based on life experience. The Adult category consisted of seven women between the ages of twenty-five and forty-five and was made up of working moms, stay-at-home moms, and working singles. The second group of six female participants, referred to as Collegiates, included undergraduate and graduate students between the ages of nineteen and twenty-four. The third group, Teens, consisted of high school seniors between the ages of seventeen and eighteen.

The topics in Radway's study guided our categorization of participants' discussions. We also examined these areas through the lens of our participants' life stage.

## Romantic Escape

As with Radway's (1984) Smithton women, the participants in this study repeatedly noted the *Twilight* books to be a means of escape through romance. Adult reader Monica stated, "You can't help be caught up in the romance . . . I remembered back to when I first met my husband." Collegiate reader Heather stated, "I just love to read and be in a different world because I don't have to deal with reality." Adult Brandi explained the importance of the escape: "Normally, it's work and young children. It's giving a lot. I could read in my little corner without taking care of anybody. I was just doing something for me."

There was significant discussion among the Adults about how *Twilight's* romance was written especially for women. Samantha suggested that "[*Twilight*] is going to be forever. . . . It's *Star Wars* for the females of this generation."

## Relationships, Devotion, and Emotion

Teens reported that *Twilight* had the greatest meaning for them on the level of relationships with others. They related to how people get along in high school and develop bonds with family and friends. Marla pointed out: "[Charlie] was a really good dad. . . . Bella also loved Charlie and wanted to keep him safe so she kept things from him." Similarly, Courtney suggested, "It's relatable back to high school since you are loyal to your clique. It's human nature."

Other discussions related to both the competition and alliances between different social groups in the story. The Teens discussed how the different packs (i.e., the vampires and the werewolves) were in competition but had to work together to fight for Bella. This reiterated the importance of relationships for those in high school and the challenges and opportunities presented by cliques. Teens consistently referenced the teamwork and loyalty in the various relationships throughout the story.

The Adult women noted the devotion in the story. Monica sated, "You want someone to be like [Edward] with you; you want them to want to keep you safe and happy and worry about your soul." Another appeal for the Adult group was the emotional maturity shown in Edward and Bella's romance. Rhonda noted, "There is more than just sex as you get older. . . . I was able to relate more with the emotional connection they had."

## Conflict, Community, and Time

The groups pointed out within the emotional ties of any relationship, there is often conflict. Adult participant Rhonda commented: "There was a battle between good and evil with the internal struggle Edward feels. There's how he wants to be and his nature, especially with Bella around. He is in love with her, but doesn't want to change her or she might lose her soul." Ann agreed: "There is so much conflict. . . . the conflict they all feel when Bella bleeds, when Carlisle works on patients, how Bella likes Jacob but is in love with Edward. The main conflict through the whole book is whether Bella is going to be changed."

All of these themes seemed to connect *Twilight* fans in a community. Collegiate Heather noted the community appeal, "I think that [the appeal] is because everyone likes it. Everyone wants to know why others are so enthused? What's going on? Why is it so great?" Adult participant Megan noted this community is based more on life experiences than merely age: "The books are mentally satisfying at my current age. . . . You love them no matter what age we are, but what we take away from them is different."

While Radway interviewed a homogenous group of women, this study examined *Twilight* fans at three different life stages in order to identify perspectives from which each generation viewed the story. The Adults in this study were more likely to view the story through the lens of the past. They were nostalgic and philosophical about the text, often remembering when first love was new. Patricia noted, "Emotions start flooding through again, and you start remembering that time." The Collegiates were cognizant of the present, though sometimes thinking back to high school. Teens seemed to be more focused on the future and finding a significant other that would be a friend like Jacob or a husband like Edward.

## Reluctance and Dissonance

Despite the participants' love of the story, there was reluctance by some to admit their fandom. Radway's Smithton women expressed discomfort being the target of criticism from outside sources, which compelled them to hide their romance reading. Because *Twilight* was written for a young adult audience and had received criticism from non- and anti-fans, this question was asked to ascertain the level of reluctance each generation felt when consuming the texts. The Adults most clearly reflected the anxieties of the Smithton women in this regard. One woman mentioned she was an adult and should have more self-control. Several referenced how they should be reading classic literature or paying more attention to their family, work, or studies. Overall, they were embarrassed by their obsession. When asked if she was embarrassed by reading *Twilight*, Brandi replied, "Heck yeah. . . . I'm a grown woman, and this was some little teeny bopper book!" Those that weren't embarrassed said it helped that they had friends or daughters reading the books.

Most of the Collegiates, meanwhile, had no problems being known as fans. Those that mentioned some discomfort noticed that any criticism they received was mostly from non-fans. While they were aware criticism existed, they did not feel it held merit.

Predictably, Teens had the least problem with being known as *Twilight* fans. Teen participant Kyra said: "I'm in high school, and I'm sure there are some people there that think Edward really exists. So it's not an issue."

One of the most surprising findings was the level of compulsion and subsequent dissonance each group felt when reading. Most admitted they could not put the books down. Gina, a Collegiate, "wanted to read everything so I know the complete story and what is going to happen. . . . I just want closure." Radway's Smithton women also commented on how once they were immersed in the story, they felt compelled to continue reading until they reached the happy ending. While the typical romance novel is not usually in serial format, the *Twilight* series had some resolution in each book, but the unfinished storyline stretched over four books with cliffhangers at the end of each one. Many of the participants also began reading the books after the entire series had been released, so there was no reason for them to wait.

Overwhelmingly, the Adults seemed to experience the most dissonance about their inability to put down the books. Samantha relates:

> My husband said it's like watching somebody at an all-you-can-eat buffet gorge themselves on food. . . . I was ready for it to be over because of how much of my life it was manipulating. I was sitting there reading a 600-page book going, "I really gotta do the laundry, I need to do the dishes. . . . It's 7:00 and I didn't make dinner!"

Brandi, another Adult participant, said she knew it was bad when, "I was sitting in the bathroom because that was the only light that wouldn't disturb my husband. I'm sitting on the bathroom floor reading the book, and I was like, 'Wait a minute, what am I doing?'" Rhonda agrees:

> I'm 34 with kids and couldn't even put the books down to interact with my in-laws. . . . I told them I had to be upstairs with the baby in case she cried, and I sat on the floor in the bathroom and read each book. My husband came in one time and caught me. I was like, "Oh, well I couldn't sleep and I didn't want to wake the baby." And you know I was totally lying!

These comments provide compelling parallels to what Radway found; many of the Smithton women had to seek out resolution of the story and often had to lie to cover up their love of reading.

## Interpreting the Characters

Radway explores how the Smithton women felt about various romance roles. The women had specific opinions concerning the traits they felt were important for the hero and heroine to possess. In the current study, there were differences among the groups with the way they related to the central characters in the books. The younger females were more connected to Jacob and impressed he was always there for Bella. They felt he was someone they could befriend. The Collegiates felt Jacob was used by Bella as a "rebound" relationship. The older females felt Jacob was to blame since he continued to pursue Bella despite knowing her feelings about Edward. The Adults were more connected to Edward and his maturity, wisdom, and respect for Bella. The Collegiates saw Edward as chivalrous while also being possessive and even "creepy" when he snuck into Bella's room to watch her sleep. Many of the Teens admitted wanting to find their own Edward. The teens sympathized with Edward, because it was difficult for him to show Bella how much he loved her due to her fragile mortality.

Of all the characters, Bella was the most divisive. It was more difficult for the groups to separate the movie portrayal of Bella from the book character. Most felt their view of Bella was tainted by their general dislike of Kristen Stewart's performance in the movies.

The Adults saw Bella's character in the book as quirky, simple, intelligent, funny, and independent. Patricia noted how Bella lost her independence when she met Edward. Samantha disagreed, "I think she gave it up, or exchanged it for being able to be in his world." Overall, they felt this was often a necessary tradeoff in marriage.

All of the groups had the most problem with Bella's overly depressed self after Edward left her in *New Moon*:

> Ann: She couldn't do anything without Edward.
> Megan: Bella was so codependent, and it drove me crazy.
> Rhonda: It's not healthy to wake up screaming every night . . . not normal . . . what is that like to read as a 14 year old?
> Monica: Breakups are devastating and you are sad, but you have to get up and move on.

While Adults were concerned about the influence of this codependence on young girls, Teens seemed more concerned that Bella ignored her human friends when she began dating Edward and then after he left. They felt that had she been more involved with her friends, her breakup with Edward might have been more manageable. Courtney, a Teen participant, noted, "I get so wrapped up in friend relationships like Bella that it takes every ounce of me if anyone leaves. . . . I'm so devastated." Most participants did not see Bella as being emotionally strong. When the Teen group was asked why they still liked the story, even though they did not particularly see Bella as a strong heroine, Brittney quickly responded, "Because I am the perfect heroine. . . . You insert yourself in the story as Bella."

It is in this area the current research differs most from Radway's findings. While the Smithton women seemed to value the typical romantic heroine's strength, intelligence, and independence, the *Twilight* participants largely found Bella to be lacking strength and independence, yet they enjoyed the story anyway. This supports Molly Williamson's (2005) findings that female fans of vampire texts most often identify with the male vampire instead of the vampire's female victims.

## FINAL THOUGHTS

The *Twilight* fans in this study discussed very similar themes and appeals to those outlined thirty years ago in Radway's (1984) *Reading the Romance*. For example, reading as an escape from daily life or to evoke particular feelings from the past were mentioned by respondents in both studies, as was the experience of guilty feelings for spending money and taking time away from family obligations. There were also many similarities between the two studies in the characteristics women valued in storyline. For example, loyalty, devotion, and romance not based solely on sex were important characteristics. Another important similarity was the audiences' parallel needs to see the resolution of the narrative or to get to the happy ending.

One of the biggest differences from Radway's findings, however, was the importance of a strong, independent heroine. While Radway finds this is critical to the enjoyment of romance for the Smithton women, this study finds the series could be enjoyed even without identification with a strong heroine. What is puzzling about this is that Bella is portrayed as the hero in the fourth book, *Breaking Dawn*, and saves everyone she loves. This fact was not discussed by any of the participants, and it is downplayed in the film versions of the saga.

There were also differences in the current study among the various life experience categories wherein each group had its own view of the role of family and friends. The Teens focused on relationships as central themes in the story and felt Bella should have done more to stay connected to her friends. The Collegiates, perhaps due to the inherently transitional nature of their lives, were more comfortable with the changes Bella went through in developing a relationship with the person who would be her life partner. The Adults also felt family was central to the story and were glad Bella found a family that she could relate to with the Cullens. There were group differences in the relationships with the characters as well as temporal views. Edward was the favorite of most of the older participants, while Jacob was the favorite of the younger participants. The Adults reflected on the past, while the Collegiates saw their present, and the Teens looked to their future.

Overall, Radway's *Reading the Romance* provides an excellent foundation for examining the romance genre through a feminist lens. But since almost thirty years have passed since that seminal work, the time has come to conduct more research into new practices in female romance reading, a new view of feminism, and a new type of fan.

## NOTES

1. The success of Meyer's books and Summit Entertainment's film adaptations, described in the introduction to this volume, needs no reiteration here.
2. Budget and box-office figures referred to in this article are derived from http://www.boxofficemojo.com.

## REFERENCES

Abercrombie, Nicholas, and Brian Longhurst. 1998. *Audiences: A Sociological Theory of Performance and Imagination*. London: Sage.

Anatol, Giselle Liza. 2011. *Bringing Light to "Twilight": Perspectives on a Pop Culture Phenomenon*. New York: Palgrave Macmillan.

Ang, Ien. 1996. *Living Room Wars: Rethinking Media Audiences*. London: Routledge.

Aronson, Kimberly M. Rodman, and Ester Schaler Buchholz. 2001. "The Post-Feminist Era: Still Striving for Equality in Relationships." *American Journal of Family Therapy* 29 (2): 109–24.

Bacon-Smith, Camille. 1992. *Enterprising Women: Television Fandom and the Creation of Popular Myth*. Philadelphia: University of Pennsylvania Press.

Bode, Lisa. 2010. "Transitional Tastes: Teen Girls and Genre in the Critical Reception of *Twilight*." *Continuum* 24 (5): 707–19.

Botkin-Maher, Jennifer. 2007. "The Post-Feminist Mystique." *College Literature* 34 (3): 193–201.

Catterall, Miriam, Pauline Maclaran, and Lorna Stevens. 2005. "Postmodern Paralysis: The Critical Impasse in Feminist Perspectives on Consumers." *Journal of Marketing Management* 21 (5/6): 489–504.

Click, Melissa A., Jennifer Stevens Aubrey, and Elizabeth Behm-Morawitz, eds. 2010. *Bitten by "Twilight": Youth Culture, Media, and the Vampire Franchise*. New York: Peter Lang.

Driscoll, Catherine. 2006. "One True Pairing: The Romance of Pornography and the Pornography of Romance." In *Fan Fiction and Fan Communities in the Age of the Internet*, ed. Karen Hellekson and Kristina Busse, 79–96. Jefferson, NC: McFarland.

Erzen, Tanya. 2012. *Fanpire: "The Twilight Saga" and the Women Who Love It*. Boston: Beacon.

Fiske, John. 1992. "The Cultural Economy of Fandom." In *The Adoring Audience: Fan Cultural and Popular Media*, ed. Lisa A. Lewis, 30–49. New York: Routledge.

Gill, Rosalind, and Elena Herdieckerhoff. 2006. "Rewriting the Romance: New Femininities in Chick Lit?" *Feminist Media Studies* 6 (4): 487–504.

Goodale, Gloria. 2010. "Twilight Moms: Why Women Are Drawn to Teens' 'Eclipse.'" *Christian Science Monitor*, June 28.

Gray, Jonathon, Cornel Sandvoss, and C. Lee Harrington. 2007. *Fandom: Identities and Communities in a Mediated World*. New York: New York University Press.

Happel, Alison, and Jennifer Esposito. 2010. "Vampires, Vixens, and Feminists: An Analysis of *Twilight*." *Educational Studies* 46 (5): 524–31.

Hesse, Monica. 2009. "*Twilight*, 'The Love That Dare Not Speak Its Shame.'" *Washington Post*, November 19. Accessed March 27, 2010. http://www.washingtonpost.com/wp-dyn/content/article/2009/11/18/AR2009111804145.html.

Hills, Matthew. 2002. *Fan Cultures*. New York: Routledge.

Housel, Rebecca, and J. Jeremy Wisnewski, eds. 2009. *"Twilight" and Philosophy: Vampires, Vegetarians, and the Pursuit of Immortality*. Hoboken, NJ: Wiley.

Jenkins, Henry. 1992. *Textual Poachers: Television Fans and Participatory Culture*. New York: Routledge.

Juffer, Jane. 1998. *At Home with Pornography: Women, Sex, and Everyday Life*. New York: New York University Press.

Kaplan, E. Ann. 1990. "Sex, Work and Motherhood: The Impossible Triangle." *Journal of Sex Research* 27 (3): 409–25.

Levine, Elana. 2010. Afterword to *Bitten by "Twilight": Youth Culture, Media, and the Vampire Franchise*, ed. Melissa A. Click, Jennifer Stevens Aubrey, and Elizabeth Behm-Morawitz, 281–86. New York: Peter Lang.

*License! Global*. 2009a. "Best Retail Exclusive: *Twilight* at Hot Topic." January 1. http://licensemag.com.

*License! Global*. 2009b. "Excellence in Retail: Hot Topic's Romance with *Twilight*." May 1. http://licensemag.com.

Lisanti, Tony. 2009. "Behind the Numbers: *License! Global* Ranks the Top Licensors and Agencies Shaping the Industry and Building the Bottom Line." *License! Global*, April 8.

Lunt, Peter, and Sonia M. Livingstone. 1996. "Rethinking the Focus Group in Media and Communications Research." *Journal of Communication* 46, 79–98.

McRobbie, Angela. 2008. "A Response to Susie Orbach: On Generation and Femininity." *Studies in Gender and Sexuality* 9 (3): 239–45.

Modleski, Tania. 1982. *Loving with a Vengeance: Mass Produced Fantasies for Women*. Hamden, CT: Archon Books.

Orbach, Susie. 2008. "Chinks in the Merged Attachment: Generational Bequests to Contemporary Teenage Girls." *Studies in Gender and Sexuality* 9 (3): 215–32.

Parke, Maggie, and Natalie Wilson, eds. 2011. *Theorizing "Twilight": Critical Essays on What's at Stake in a Post-Vampire World*. Jefferson, NC: McFarland.

Patton, Michael Quinn. 2002. *Qualitative Research and Evaluation Methods*. Thousand Oaks, CA: Sage.

Penley, Constance. 1991. Introd. to *Close Encounters: Film, Feminism, and Science Fiction*, ed. Constance Penley, Elisabeth Lyon, Lynn Spigel, and Janet Bergstrom, vii–xi. Minneapolis: University of Minnesota Press.

Radway, Janice A. 1984. *Reading the Romance: Women, Patriarchy, and Popular Literature*. Chapel Hill: University of North Carolina Press.

Ramsdell, Kristin. 2004. "Love That Is out of This World!" *Library Journal* 129 (9): 70.

Reagin, Nancy, ed. 2010. *"Twilight" and History*. Hoboken, NJ: Wiley.

Romance Writers of America. 2010. "The Romance Genre Overview." Accessed March 19, 2010. http://www.rwanational.org/cs/the_romance_genre.

Sandvoss, Cornel. 2005. *Fans: The Mirror of Consumption*. Cambridge, UK: Polity.

Schau, Hope J., and Margo Buchanan-Oliver. 2012. "'The Creation of Inspired Lives': Female Fan Engagement with *The Twilight Saga*." In *Gender, Culture, and Consumer Behavior*, ed. Cele C. Otnes and Linda Tuncay-Zayer, 33–58. New York: Taylor.

Schau, Hope J., and Katherine Thompson. 2010. "Betwixt and Between: Liminality and Feminism in the *Twilight* Brand Community." *Advances in Consumer Research* 37: 91–92.

Schuker, Lauren A. E. 2009. "Harry Potter and the Rival Teen Franchise." *Wall Street Journal*, July 10, eastern edition, W1–W12.

Shachar, Hila. 2011. "A Post-Feminist Romance: Love, Gender and Intertextuality." In *Theorizing "Twilight": Critical Essays on What's at Stake in a Post-Vampire World*, ed. Maggie Parke and Natalie Wilson, 147–64. Jefferson, NC: McFarland.

Smith, Scott, Dan Fisher, and S. Jason Cole. 2007. "The Lived Meanings of Fanaticism: Understanding the Complex Role of Labels and Categories in Defining the Self in Consumer Culture." *Consumption, Markets and Culture* 10 (2): 77–94.

Spines, Christine. 2010. "When *Twilight* Fandom Becomes Addiction." *Los Angeles Times*, June 27. Accessed December 26, 2012. http://articles.latimes.com/2010/jun/27/entertainment/la-ca-twilight-addiction-20100627.

Stabile, Carol. 2011. "Review Essay: 'First He'll Kill Her Then I'll Save Her': Vampires, Feminism, and the *Twilight* Franchise." *Journal of Communication*, 61 (1): E4–E8.

Stewart, Andrew. 2012. "Fans Flock to Finale in Record Global Bow." *Daily Variety* 317 (36): 1–28.

Summers, Sarah. 2010. "'*Twilight* Is So Anti-Feminist That I Want to Cry': *Twilight* Fans Finding and Defining Feminism on the World Wide Web." *Computers and Composition* 27 (4): 315–23.

TwilightMOMS.com. 2012. Forum statistics. Accessed December 26, 2012. http://forums.twilightmoms.com/.

Williamson, Molly. 2005. *The Lure of the Vampire: Gender, Fiction, and Fandom from Bram Stoker to Buffy*. London: Wallflower.

Wood, Helen. 2004. "What *Reading the Romance* Did for Us." *European Journal of Cultural Studies* 7 (2): 147–54.

*II*

*Twilight* Audiences

*Chapter Four*

# "Twilight Moms" and the "Female Midlife Crisis"

*Life Transitions, Fantasy, and Fandom*

Laura K. Dorsey-Elson

David Letterman: The fan base [for the *Twilight* saga] seems to be teenage girls . . .
Robert Pattinson: It's not just so much teenage girls . . . it's older than people realize . . .
David Letterman: Older women . . . ?
Robert Pattinson: And the *older ones* are the more . . . far more . . . passionate fans . . .

The truest of "Twi-hards" (the most zealous fans of the *Twilight* books and films) know the conception story of the series well. When Stephenie Meyer began to write *Twilight*, she was a stay-at-home mother and wife, writing in between the constant needs of three young children and the daily demands of married/family life. Her writing became a refuge, mainly at night when all were asleep. She reflects on her website (Meyer 2013) and blog that when she began to write the first book in the series, she hadn't written anything for nearly six years. What had been a core part of her identity had understandably lain dormant while she attended to the equally important nest-building years. She says that writing was "something I hadn't done in so long, I wondered why I was even bothering" (Meyer 2013). But she pushed herself, night after night, and, in doing so, enlivened a part of her that in turn enlivened millions of others.

It is this experience of enlivenment that Meyer herself admits to having while writing *Twilight* that provides the initial inspiration for this book chapter. In her blog, Meyer tells about how the story of Edward and Bella came to her in a dream; a dream so vivid and interesting that when she awoke she had no choice but to write to see where this improbable relationship between a human teenage girl and a handsome vampire might go. With this, it could be realistically argued that one of the reasons that she wrote so passionately about such an intense pair as Bella and Edward and the passionate world they existed in was as a way to reconnect and reintroduce herself to her own passions. In other words, her effort became a vicarious way to also see the improbable places she could go with one of her passions: writing and story-telling. And it is this idea, the reinvigoration of dormant passions, in oneself, in one's relationship, in one's career, that many fans of the series connect to in a fervent and powerful way. Therefore, the runaway phenomenon of millions of "older women" who are referred to at times with affection, and at times in parody, as "Twilight Moms," who repeatedly read and watch the *Twilight* saga books and films, emerged.

## DEFINING THE "TWILIGHT MOM"

By all accounts, the term "Twilight Mom" was originally coined around 2007 by Lisa Hansen, creator of the official "Twilight Moms" website, www.TwilightMOMS.com. Lisa, a wife and mother, became obsessed with the book series and wanted to find other women near her age and in the midst of the same experience. It took her some time, but when she linked up with a few older, female *Twilight* fans, she began to refer to this initial group as "Twilight Moms." Today, "Twilight Moms" include women from around the world and from a plethora of backgrounds and life stories. Some are married, some are not. Some have children, some do not. The age of a "Twilight Mom" seems to begin at thirty, but the ending age is not precisely estab-lished. I, the author of this chapter, attended a *Twilight* convention in the fall of 2011 and had the opportunity to ask a TwilightMOMS.com website repre-sentative, in front of a room of about three hundred other "Twilight Moms," to be clearer on what defines us as a unique group. The answer given was purposely vague and a conscientious attempt to include as many women as possible. What stood out the most was that a "Twilight Mom" is a woman thirty or above who is a self-proclaimed lover of all things *Twilight*. With this, Stephenie Meyer considers herself a "Twilight Mom" and is quoted on the group's website, saying, "It's just so cool that I'm not the only 30+ mom and wife in love with fictional underage vampires and werewolves" (Twi-lightMOMS.com 2013). Although there are plenty of casual references to "Twilight Moms" in the media, to date, only three publications on this group exist (Taylor and Sharkey 2009; Goodale 2010; Hayes 2010).

## MIDDLE-AGED "TWILIGHT MOM" THESIS

This chapter explores the question of why there is a *Twilight* obsession for forty- to fifty-year-old women specifically. Why does the saga take over this subgroup of "Twilight Moms," and why can it be so intense? Is there something about the particular stage of life of these women that makes the rabbit hole of the *Twilight* saga so compelling? This chapter further examines the question of the *female midlife crisis* from the stance that the forty- to fifty-year-old "Twilight Mom" finds sanctuary in the *Twilight* saga books and films as she navigates the very real issues that can come with "middle age." Of course, there may be some similarities between the life issues that forty- to fifty-year-old women face and those faced by their younger counterparts, but the theoretical premise operating here is that these *older* "Twilight Moms" deserve special attention.

This chapter is written from the stance that women in their forties to fifties are biologically and chronologically nearing what is described as "midlife" and are no longer "young" but hardly "old." These women are indeed *older* and have accrued a fair share of life experiences: like fifteen-plus years of a career, starting and sustaining a family, managing marriages and partnerships, raising children, handling divorce, nurturing long-term friendships over decades, surviving health scares, the death of parents, and more. This older group of "Twilight Moms" is often navigating very serious life issues—issues associated with the Western cultural notion of a "midlife crisis." Concern with mortality, attainability of life goals/dreams, sustained attractiveness, the legacy one will leave behind, and more come into serious question at this time. Drastic actions are taken, life-changing decisions are sometimes made and are often erratic, and perceivably comical choices are acted upon in an effort to alleviate the tremendous anxiety that this stage of life can bring.

It is these same *older* women who upon discovering *Twilight* reportedly relegate their work, family, real-world responsibilities, and stage-of-life concerns as mere second-tier priorities to the tale of Edward and Bella and the mystical world they fell in love with—women, who in the midst of all of the heaviness and responsibility of life, become "Twilight Moms." Coupling auto-ethnographic anecdotal thematic data from the author, with a selection of discussion posts by older women on the TwilightMOMS.com popular website, this chapter sheds some light on why they obsess with the series and how this might be connected to managing the middle of life.

## THE "WHY" OF THE OLDER "TWILIGHT MOM"

Although there are probably many reasons that explain why older women become so engrossed with the *Twilight* saga, four salient explanations are presented below because of their connection to specific midlife issues for women in their forties to fifties. Each explanation is then supported by selected postings from older "Twilight Moms" taken from the Twilight-MOMS.com website discussion boards.

### 1. The *Twilight* saga offers middle-aged women an opportunity to feel a much-needed vicarious sense of youth and immortality.

A woman in her middle years faces aging in both intellectual and manifestly physical ways. The prospect of growing old and eventually dying as well as the experience of her body changing with age can bring uncomfortable feelings. When a middle-aged woman reads of Edward, his family, and eventually Bella's immortality as vampires, it can help her momentarily escape the worry of her own real aging issues/thoughts and wonder of her own imaginary immortality in a relieving way.

> Posting 1: While our bodies may be getting older, our minds do not, and they still are able to crave these experiences as though we were 18 and having them for the first time. In fact, they make us feel as if we were 18 again, which is reinforcing in and of itself for those of us who wish we were not aging so quickly.
>
> Posting 2: For one [when answering the question of why she loves the *Twilight* series] . . . all the vampires are really decades/centuries old but trapped in youthful bodies (who wouldn't want to be "trapped" in a youthful body??).

### 2. The *Twilight* saga invites a welcomed regression (sometimes after long periods of dormancy) to all-consuming eros love in a middle-aged woman's long-term committed relationship and/or encourages the seeking of such a type of love/relationship in its absence.

At the heart of the series lies a passionate love story between Edward and Bella. For some middle-aged women, the type of angst-ridden, obsessive "can't live without you" love found between Edward and Bella is not as present (if present at all) in their own relationships. The memory of it is distant, and the desire for its return is strong. The series can allow a middle-aged woman to regress into this type of love both in her mind and sometimes in her reality, which can be exciting, renewing, and reaffirming.

Posting 1: I appreciate these books so much because they really brought back the love and passion in my relationship (married 16 years), feeling like a giddy teenager all over again! Love to be in Love!

Posting 2: After I read Twilight, I felt more in love with my husband! I had forgotten those butterflies, falling in love feelings from long ago. Ah young, romantic love.

Posting 3: The whole fantasy was very awesome! I had a similar experience in my marriage in that, my interest and obsession in the books brought out more lust and romance and sexual desire for my husband because I wanted him to be my Edward. And I'm happy to say that he understood and our romantic life could never be better!

## 3. The *Twilight* saga invokes fantasies for a middle-aged woman of being the center of someone else's universe that serve as an escape from the other-centered (for children, aging parents, life partners) stance she must predominantly hold in her real life.

Life for middle-aged women can be filled with the demands others place on their time and energy. One of the most endearing qualities of Edward is his unwavering devotion to Bella and to Bella only. For most of the series, he will not leave her side and is willing to literally give up his own existence for hers. Although a middle-aged woman has probably accrued enough life experience to know that this type of selfless love does not truly exist (and isn't quite healthy in the long term), the series provides a place to dream of a world where it does and where she might be the recipient of it at a time in her real life where it is greatly needed.

Posting 1: He [Edward] is caring and will do anything to make Bella happy. Wouldn't we all like to have someone in our life that thinks the sun rises and sets on you and would do anything for you?

Posting 2: When he [Edward] loves, he loves *completely*. His entire existence becomes about making her [Bella] happy. Even if it means he is going to suffer. Who wouldn't want a man like that?

Posting 3: He [Edward] is absolutely there to give her [Bella] what she wants even if it hurts him in the end.

## 4. The *Twilight* saga allows middle-aged women to temporarily engage in behaviors that remind them of their teenage girlhood, where hours of conversation and giggles about imaginary characters can feel momentarily real and ultimately therapeutic.

One of the things that can consume the lives of some middle-aged women is all of the adult responsibility: to family, to career, to children, to communities, and so forth. Idle time seems like an indulgence and is mainly nonexistent. But the series temporarily changes this experience. During the height of obsession with it, a fervent communion with friends who are "Twilight middle-years Moms" takes precedence over most other responsibilities. The ensuing endless discussion of the story brings a joyful sense of being a teenage girl again, and this can be experienced as therapeutic.

> Posting 1: I was completely amazed when I could not put them down I had to keep reading to know what would happen for me reading the saga was like time travel I was back in high school and it was like living those care free days all over.
>
> Posting 2: I am happy remembering who I was at 17 and knowing that there is much of that 17 year old girl still kicking around.
>
> Posting 3: You know when you are obsessed when it is Sunday afternoon, your husband, dog and baby are finally taking their siesta and instead of trying to sleep you are writing replies [on a discussion board] to a bunch of women like myself, absolutely in love with twilight.
>
> Posting 4: I have had such wonderful and meaningful conversations here [on a "Twilight Mom" discussion board] and LAUGHED so much too!

## DEFINING THE "MIDLIFE CRISIS"

### The History of the Term

In addition to the explanations offered, it is necessary to explore the question of whether being in the "middle of life" and potentially being in "crisis" also lends itself to understanding the older "Twilight Mom" phenomenon. The challenge is that much of the "midlife crisis" has been and continues to be studied solely from the perspective of *men* (Jacques 1965; Stein 1983; Levinson 1986; Conway 1978; Maccaro 2004; Conway and Conway 2010). One could argue from the sheer volume of publications that the male aspect of the overall midlife phenomenon has been more legitimized and culturally condoned (at least in Western cultures). It has only been since the 1990s that the female version of the midlife crisis has been conceptualized and investigated (Conway and Conway 2010; Shellenbarger 2004), and of course, this body of work does not rival in scope that of the male version.

Sue Shellenbarger (2004) provides a concise account of the evolution of the term *midlife crisis*. She writes that, for much of human history, the middle of life has been seen as a "wasteland of decline and decay" and that life after forty or fifty was "regarded as a time of decline and retirement" (Shellenbarger 2004, 239). It was during the 1950s that attitudes toward human development began to consider the idea that human beings develop throughout their entire lives. This shift primarily began with psychologist Erik Erikson, who extended all previous human development theory to include adults well into old age. He outlines eight life stages for human beings (Erikson 1950; 1959). Stage 7 is particularly germane to the argument of this chapter. In this stage, he identifies that the "mid-adult's" focus is on *children* and *community*. This is when an adult builds her career and family but does little self-reflection. As she transitions into her "late adult," years, in what Erikson calls stage 8, questions of *meaning, purpose,* and *life achievements* come into focus. Erikson's groundbreaking work led to a great advancement in human-development theorizing and opened the door for studying the plethora of development issues facing the middle-aged person.

The term "midlife crisis" was originally coined by psychologist Elliot Jacques in the 1960s (Jacques 1965; Shellenbarger 2004), when he studied the reported decline in productivity for late forty-year-olds. Daniel J. Levinson (1978) furthered the integration of the term "midlife crisis" in his published work on the stages of male development. Then, Gail Sheehy (1976) mainstreamed the term in Western culture in her bestselling book *Passages*. Sheehy redefined the denotative meaning of the word "crisis" (disaster, catastrophe, calamity) when writing about one's transition between major life stages, replacing it with the more perceivably gentle word "passages." She is credited with both normalizing the notion that all human beings must navigate poignant emotional "passages" (or crises) as they move through life—midlife being no different. She writes that the forty- to forty-five-year-old enters a stage of "reevaluating his [*sic*] own life" and is possessed by "thoughts of aging and imminent death" (375).

## The Female Midlife Crisis

A specific focus on a woman's "midlife crisis" has been limited. Levinson (1986) followed up his analysis on male development with a similar book on women. He devoted a portion of this work to a woman's midlife "transition years" but kept much of his analysis on women between ages thirty and forty-five with traditional careers. He did not study a diverse set of women in age, culture, and life experience.

There are a number of academic studies to date that have some focus on women at midlife (Moen and Wethington 1999; Wethington 2000; Wethington, Kessler, and Pixley 2004), and they can be credited with the beginning conceptualization of the female midlife crisis experience. The most comprehensive study of the female midlife crisis comes from Shellenbarger (2004), who brings her ideas to popular culture in her book *The Breaking Point: How Female Midlife Crisis Is Transforming Today's Women*. She writes that women between the ages of forty and fifty do have a period of extreme self-evaluation and drastic changes. Women at this age look at their careers, relationships, goals, and dreams much as previous work on midlife states. She distinguishes the female crisis from that of the male in several important ways:

1. Women place more emphasis on retaining their health and vigor at old age than men.
2. Women's crises are more often triggered by family events than career.
3. Women are more likely to worry more about losing their attractiveness than men.

Shellenbarger (2004) defines the specific nature of the female midlife crisis from a Jungian (Carl Jung) analytical perspective of archetypes. She writes that every woman's midlife crisis experience is driven by one (or sometimes more than one) of these archetypes, which can influence the way that she navigates it. She reviews six archetypes that are not necessarily new to social psychology life-stages literature but provide a new lens through which specific female midlife crises issues can be viewed. The archetypes are: 1) the adventurer, who seeks the catharsis of physical adventure or bold travel; 2) the lover, who seeks a soul mate at midlife—a lover who promises a chance of attaining complete psychological intimacy; 3) the leader, who wants to get past others' rules and her own people-pleasing behavior to create something new and uniquely her own; 4) the artist, who's primary joy arises from growing in creativity, manifesting her vision, and uplifting or stimulating others with her work; 5) the gardener, who has concluded that the best path to wisdom lies in tending to her own metaphorical garden and therefore strives to make the most of home, family, friends, community, and existing pursuits; and finally, 6) the seeker, who ascribes central importance on finding a set of spiritual beliefs and practices that afford her meaning and serenity.

Shellenbarger (2004) argues that the choices a woman makes in the midst of her crisis can be linked to the major characteristics of her internal unconscious archetypes. For example, the forty-four-year-old woman who suddenly begins to skydive does so from the archetype of the "adventurer," while the forty-eight-year-old who abruptly quits her job to study painting does so from the archetype of the "artist." Moreover, the forty-six-year-old woman who leaves her current life partner, takes up Spanish-style tango, and has a torrid affair with her dance instructor could be doing so from her archetype of the "lover."

Shellenbarger (2004) also says that when forty- to fifty-year-old women have their so-called crises, it need not be a time of life that only causes them embarrassment or invites ridicule from onlookers. Much of mainstream popular culture characterizes this stage of life as one of desperation and loneliness. Punch lines about "the change" are often the only answer offered for their erratic and unusual behavior, when this is not even close to what is happening to them. The full personhood of a woman is not often explored when it comes to midlife issues, and it is hardly ever portrayed as something that has positive and self-healing moments. But Shellenbarger argues that this period of time can ultimately be one of renewal, re-centering, and true attainment of happiness, even in the midst of the upheaval and chaos it can bring. She writes:

> The energies that drive midlife crisis spring from hopes, wishes, and goals that have been repressed. When these parts of ourselves reemerge, they take on great power. That we have shoved them underground for a time—to win that corner office, to raise our kids, to pay our bills, to draw about us the mantle of adult responsibility and respectability—does not diminish their potency (2004, 39).

She reminds her readers that women at this stage of their life have often navigated and compromised a lot, sometimes without awareness, encouraged by the underlying cultural pressures to be selfless and *other*-centered. It is from this standpoint that new choices, new energy, and self-focus gloriously emerge. One can find a general theme of new choices, new (or returned) energies and behaviors embedded in the postings of the older "Twilight Moms." When reading through many of the postings, one can see a desire for new ways of seeing themselves, the quest for new passions, the wish to lead themselves (and others) down new paths and to rediscover self-acceptance. As one older "Twilight Mom" wrote on the discussion boards, in her attempt to defend her love of all things *Twilight*: "I don't know about you but when I was a teen, the emotions I felt with new relationships, celebrity crushes and fandoms like this one put so much positive into my life. Why get rid of that just because we're a few years older?"

## THE CREATION OF A "TWILIGHT MOM"

The previous section offered a detailed theoretical explanation of the issues and archetypes that arise for women in their middle years. It can now be argued that there is some connection between the life experience of forty- to fifty-year-old women and the way they take so passionately to the series. The following story of how the author of this chapter came to be a "Twilight Mom" serves as a final opportunity to make the link between that experience, the female midlife crisis archetypes, and the reason why older women are part of the cultural phenomenon of *Twilight*.

So, I am a "Twilight Mom." More specifically, I am a forty-four-year-old, married, working mother of a nine-year-old girl, Imani, and six-year-old boy, Asante. How I literally (no . . . not metaphorically) became obsessed with a young adult, fictional story about a 107-year-old vampire who falls in love with a 17-year-old human girl in perpetually overcast Forks, Washington, is as compelling a mystery about myself as I have come across. But I did. And I continue to be. I have been driven to understand why ever since I read the opening words of *Twilight*: "I'd never given much thought to how I would die—though I'd had reason enough in the last few months—but even if I had, I would not have imagined it like this" (Meyer 2005, 1). As someone who is at a stage of life where mortality has more of a reality to it, an opening such as this has a special hook for me.

All "Twilight Moms" have their unique "How I came across *Twilight*" story, and I have mine. My story begins with the birth of my second child. I was thirty-eight years old with one child and still transitioning from being a person without children to being one with children. Needless to say, finding that particular way to "balance it all" was ridiculously elusive. In the midst of this time, my dear friend Barbara (another full-fledged "Twilight Mom"), sent me the book *Twilight* wrapped in a brown paper envelope with a simple note that read something like "Enjoy." It was the fall of 2006, and at the time, there was no way I was going to read anything between working, breastfeeding, trying to sleep at least three consecutive hours each night, and attempting to have some sort of relationship with my husband and myself. I put *Twilight* and my darling friend's note on my nightstand where it collected dust for three solid years. I told myself in my all-too-grown-up, responsible voice, "I was just too busy for some novel about vampires meant for teenage girls." I find commonality between myself at this time with the encumbering other-centeredness state that a lot of women reflect upon in the earlier Twi-lightMOMS.com postings. It was an exhausting time in my life; one where I felt fulfilled in very important ways but, in truth, also emptied by others.

Then one late night, the spring of 2009, woozy from folding the millionth load of laundry, bitter over having to bring work home once again, already anticipating the exhaustion I was going to feel the next day as it was too late to expect enough sleep, feeling more like an eighty-year-old than a forty-one-year-old, I tuned into one of my overpriced cable channels and an angel appeared. An angel named Robert Pattinson. I actually think little cherub children with heart-shaped bows and arrows descended from my ceiling when he graced my screen.

Prior to his appearance in the film, I vaguely knew that I was watching the film version of that book my friend had given me. "What was it called again," I said to myself. "*Twi-something?*" And, the opening was somewhat intriguing. Initially, I asked very practical and grown-up questions. "Why was Bella choosing to move to Washington from Arizona so close to finishing high school?" I thought, "It's not the smartest move for her college-prep plans . . . and why would she move so far away from her mother . . . she must have issues with her mother that she is not facing. And speaking of her mother . . . why would she just let her go?" Then I focused on the strange imagery in the first moments of the film (that accompanied Bella's voice-over), and the image of the deer frantically running through the woods really struck me. I think I actually said out loud to an empty room, "Wait, did something just attack that poor deer?"

So as my adult mind/voice was drawn into overanalyzing the film . . . thanks to the appearance of that adorable young Pattinson/Edward . . . that adult part of me was silenced . . . and I was a seventeen-year-old girl again . . . instantly . . . and all I knew was that I wanted that feeling to last forever. When the movie was over, I had to pick up that book my friend sent me, to see what the fuss was all about. So, I understand how the *Twilight* series brought me back to listening to my friends and wanting to connect with them in ways that made me feel young. I also understand why Shellenbarger argued that women in the middle of their life seek to rekindle friendships that they had neglected. My friend Barbara and I talked daily about *Twilight* for nearly three months straight. We were no different from the millions of other "Twilight Moms" on the dicussion boards. It was wonderful and a "middle life" memory that I will cherish into my old age.

After I read *Twilight*, then *New Moon*, then *Eclipse* and *Breaking Dawn*, I could not put them down. I went on and read the sole spin-off story Stephenie Meyer wrote after the series, *The Short Second Life of Bree Tanner* (2010), and guiltily tore through the unpublished partial manuscript *Midnight Sun*. I finished off my reading with *The Twilight Saga: The Official Illustrated Guide* (2011), where Meyer shares a plethora of inspirations and illustrations regarding the writing of the entire series. After my reading, I watched all of the movies that were, at the time, available (*Breaking Dawn Part 1* and *Part 2* were months away from release) . . . again and again . . . and then bought them one-by-one. I bought more of the books and films at cheap secondhand stores and gave them to friends with notes inside reading "Enjoy" (now I understood how perfect this one word captured the *Twilight* experience). Perhaps, I should have become concerned about myself when I almost bought a Spanish-translated version of *Twilight*. I'll never forget—it was called *Crepúsculo*. But I wasn't alarmed at all; I just knew that I could find some Spanish-speaking forty-year-old woman whose life would be forever changed after reading it. There's a *Twilight* saga slogan that can be found on t-shirts, mugs, magnets, and so forth that captures what I was going through—it simply reads, "Twilight: Read, Watch, Repeat."

I bought everything *Twilight* from "Team Edward" bumper stickers, to jewelry (my Bella engagement ring sat proudly on my right hand much to the chagrin of my husband for months), to blankets, journals, and postcards. I placed a huge Edward Cullen/Robert Pattinson poster right over my home office computer desk—where it still sits as I type this. I even went to a *Twilight* convention and took a photograph with some of the cast that I undoubtedly shall treasure forever.

Of course, there is more I can tell about my antics, but to sum it up, like so many other "Twilight Moms," I was blissfully lost in a world of eternal love, immortality, dangerous love triangles, risky kisses, devotion, betrayal, and the self-centered indulgences of high school all over again. In other words, the reasons why my fellow "Twilight Moms" were captured by the series were very much true in my own experience. I loved the temporary relief it gave me from the demands of my life at the time. I loved living out a fantasy of my own immortality and being someone else's obsessive focus through the evolving story of Bella and Edward. The "passion factor" with my husband of twelve years increased in a wonderful way, and although things did settle down again eventually, the injection of a sense of newness and discovery in our marriage was significant. And the resurgence of idle time with my friends quelled a loneliness that the isolation of my middle years brought. I did more laughing, storytelling, imagining, and dreaming in the midst of my *Twilight* submersion in the same ways I had when I was a teenager worshiping the 1980s rock band Duran Duran and television star Johnny Depp (the *21 Jump Street* Johnny Depp . . .).

I also link my behavior and life decisions during the intensity of *Twilight* to some of the female midlife crisis archetypes that Shellenbarger suggests. During that time and since, I have been in touch with my "lover," "leader," and "seeker" internal midlife archetypes. I have a renewed sense of passion in my marriage. I have started developing an exciting new business opportunity. And I have developed a spiritual practice that is aligned with no particular religious ideology but satisfies me and helps me know my place in the universe in a way that finally works. I am more whole now than I have been in my adult years, and I have a fictional 17-year-old teenage girl, a 107-year-old vampire, and a young-adult fiction author, Stephenie Meyer, to thank for it. In my mind, this book chapter is the ultimate way I can express my gratitude.

## CONCLUSION

This chapter set out to provide some explanation for the "Twilight Mom" phenomenon with particular attention to the forty- to fifty-year-old fan. Four primary reasons were offered: the need to escape issues of mortality, the need to feel more passion, the allure of the fantasy of being the focus of someone else's attention, and the regressive pleasure of girlhood teenage antics with other "Twilight Moms." These reasons were coupled with significant female midlife "crisis" archetype theory (adventurer, lover, leader, artist, gardener, seeker) that gave a new lens through which to understand this unique occurrence. The actual postings from TwilightMOMS.com gave the main argument of this chapter more focus while my auto-ethnographic story provided another layer of plausibility for that argument. Ultimately, the "Twilight Mom" portion of the overall *Twilight* series phenomenon is a unique form of fandom that no other modern age book/film series has brought. The paradox that a young adult fiction novel would eventually inspire a legion of loyal older women fans worldwide to find a new energy for themselves, their friendships, their relationship, their careers, and more is now in plain view. This chapter is offered with the hope that the "Twilight Mom" label can become less of a punch line so that those who question it gain greater clarity. But really, it is my guess that "Twilight Moms" are not that concerned with what the world thinks of our crazy obsession; we are too busy having the time of our lives, and we are still looking for vampires, werewolves, and the possibility of something unexpected, just around the next corner of life.

## REFERENCES

Conway, Jim. 1978. *Men in Midlife Crisis*. Wheaton, IL: Tyndale House.

Conway, Jim, and Sally Conway. 2010. *Your Husband's Midlife Crisis*. Peoria, IL: Intermedia.

Erikson, Erik. 1950. *Childhood and Society*. New York: Norton.

———. 1959. *Identity and the Life Cycle*. New York: Norton.

Goodale, Gloria. 2010. "Twilight Moms: Why Women Are Drawn to Teens' 'Eclipse.'" *Christian Science Monitor*, June 28. Accessed April 22, 2013. http://www.csmonitor.com/USA/2010/0628/Twilight-moms-Why-women-are-drawn-to-teens-Eclipse.

Hayes, Andrea. 2010. *Addicted to "Twilight": Confessions of a Twilight Mom*. Oviedo, FL: Ashlyn Group.

Jacques, Elliot. 1965. "Death and the Midlife Crisis." *International Journal of Psychoanalysis* 46:502–14.

Levinson, Daniel J. 1978. *The Seasons of a Man's Life*. New York: Ballantine Books.

———. 1986. *The Seasons of a Woman's Life*. New York: Ballantine Books.

Maccaro, Janet. 2004. *Midlife Meltdown: Spot It, Prevent It, Overcome It*. Lake Mary, FL: Siloam.

Meyer, Stephenie. 2005. *Twilight*. New York: Little, Brown and Company.

———. 2010. *The Short Second Life of Bree Tanner*. New York: Little, Brown.

———. 2011. *The Twilight Saga: The Official Illustrated Guide*. New York: Little, Brown.

———. 2013. The Official Website of Stephenie Meyer. http://www.stepheniemeyer.com.

Moen, Phyllis, and Elaine Wethington. 1999. "Midlife Development in Middle Age." In *Life in the Middle: Psychological and Social Development in Middle Age*, ed. Sherry Willis and James Reid, 3–18. San Diego: Academic.

Sheehy, Gail. 1976. *Passages: Predictable Crises of Adult Life*. New York: Ballantine Books.

Shellenbarger, Sue. 2004. *Breaking Point: How Female Midlife Crisis Is Transforming Today's Women*. New York: Henry Holt.

Stein, Murray. 1983. *In Midlife: A Jungian Perspective*. Woodstock, CT: Spring.

Taylor, Emma, and Lorelei Sharkey. 2009. "*Twilight*, Take Me Away! Teenage Vampires and the Mothers Who Love Them." *New York Times Magazine*, November 15. Accessed April 22, 2013. http://nymag.com/movies/features/62027/.

TwilightMOMS.com. 2013. http://www.twilightmoms.com.

Wethington, Elaine. 2000. "Expecting Stress: Americans and the 'Midlife Crisis.'" *Motivation and Emotion* 24:85–103.

Wethington, Elaine, Ronald Kessler, and Joy Pixley. 2004. "Turning Points in Adulthood." In *How Healthy Are We? A National Study of Well Being at Midlife*, ed. Orville Gilbert Brim, Carol Riff, and Ronald Kessler, 586–613. Chicago: University of Chicago Press.

*Chapter Five*

# *Twilight* and Twitter

## *An Ethnographic Study*

## Michelle Groover

Women worldwide have enjoyed the *Twilight* saga books and films, thus creating a cultural touchstone as many relate to the characters in the story (Memmott 2008; Puente 2009). Though Stephenie Meyer says the books were not written for a particular age group, her publisher (Little, Brown) marketed the series to the young adult audience. "Meyer didn't write *Twilight* for a specific age group or category of reader. She originally wrote the story to entertain herself. So it's perhaps not surprising that many adult women like the *Twilight* series too," says Katherine E. Krohn (2010, 8). In that vein, Carol Memmott (2008) states there is not a "typical" fan, but fans range from teenagers to young adults to adults.

As women in their twenties and older began to devour the books and the love story, many felt they did not have like-minded people with whom to discuss the books. Since they felt they could not discuss *Twilight* with friends in their real life, many turned to social media, in particular Twitter, to find like-minded individuals. For some fans of the series, the line between fantasy and reality is a thin one (Garcia et al. 2009). For others, it is an opportunity to bond with individuals who share the same level of excitement toward the series, including its characters and the actors who portray them.

This chapter will discuss an ethnographic study that was conducted to explore the experiences of female fans of *Twilight* who also use Twitter. As part of the ethnography, I conducted eighteen in-depth interviews with adult women who are fans of the saga and who use Twitter as a means to talk to other *Twilight* fans. The study investigated the relationships among these women, how they talk about the *Twilight* series, their shared experiences in this area, and the personal relationships they have formed with other fans via Twitter.

Previous studies on this topic have been conducted using virtual ethnography (Carter 2005; Underberg 2006), regarding relationships formed online and building community. Thomas R. Lindlof (1995) suggests virtual ethnography requires "adaptation of procedures traditionally associated with participant observation research roles" (Scodari and Felder 2000, 239). While Christine Hine (2000) recommends not focusing on whether the person is who she says she is but rather assessing how she is experiencing culture.

The significance of this research is that one may discover, through studying the *Twilight* subculture, how and why a series such as this has created a frenzied passion among females of all ages (Krohn 2010). Maria Puente (2009) states, "It's the moms and grandmas standing in line at theaters, reading and rereading the books, spending big bucks on the merchandise and writing reams of fan fiction." It is also important to investigate how individuals are using social media, in this case Twitter, to connect with others they may not know and to explore the amount of personal information they are willing to share.

Little to no research has been conducted on the impact of Twitter in regard to forming social connections. With a gap in this subject, this is an important area of study in which researchers need a better understanding of a phenomenon and culture-sharing group, as it can provide more depth and understanding regarding changing social dynamics.

## TWITTER AND *TWILIGHT* FANDOM

Twitter is a micro-blogging service. "Twitter is a real-time information network that connects you to the latest information about what you find interesting" (Twitter 2013). Site users can choose to receive the messages sent by selected other users by *following* those users. Users can follow anyone with a public profile and will see the messages sent by the people or organizations they are following. Each message, called a "tweet," consists of 140 characters or fewer and can include links to pictures, videos, and webpages. Tweets are distributed to an individual's followers. While the default setting for tweets is public, users can set their accounts to be private. In this case, only those followers who have been approved by a user will see the messages the user is creating. "Twitter has a directed friendship model: participants choose Twitter accounts to 'follow' in their stream, and they each have their own group of 'followers'" (Marwick and boyd 2010, 116). Individuals follow others who share their same likes or dislikes, as well as follow companies, organizations, news outlets, and celebrities.

In addition to sending a tweet, one can also send and receive direct messages (DM). A direct message is similar to an e-mail, in that it is a private conversation; however, it also has the constraints of 140 characters. Additionally, users can only send direct messages to people who follow them. While any follower can see your tweets, only the person sent a DM will see that message. In addition to tweeting and direct messaging, users can also "retweet," which is similar to forwarding an e-mail. If a user sees a message he or she likes on Twitter, the user can distribute that message to followers by clicking the retweet link on any message. Messages from private, rather than public, accounts cannot be retweeted.

Conversations between users occur through the use of usernames, preceded by the "at" symbol (i.e., @username). In a "conversation," in order to guarantee the other person will see a comment, one must use the syntax including the @username. Conversations using user names remain public and appear as messages in the Twitter feed of followers. Since conversations remain public, additional followers may join in the conversation.

Since its inception in 2006, Twitter has gained popularity. Tweets are instantaneous, and many receive news via their Twitter feed (Stassen 2010). "It may very well be that Twitter turns out to be the *app du jour* that will fade from the limelight, or it could become a staple of daily life" (Arceneaux and Weiss 2010, 1263). Twitter grows every day with the addition of new users. A blog updated by Twitter reports that, at the time of this writing, the site has more than 175 million registered users (Twitter 2013). The possibilities for how to use Twitter appear to be endless.

## FANDOM, SUBCULTURES, AND COMMUNITY

In order to understand how groups share and create culture, it is important to understand subcultures and fandom, the use of language by those using social media, and fans' incorporation of media, including social media, in their communication.

While some scholars see subcultures as being comprised of deviants (Kozinets 2001), subcultures also afford significant meanings and practices that construct consumers' characters, actions, and interactions (Hebdige 1979; McCracken 1998; Schouten and McAlexander 1995; Thornton 1997). Michael Brake (1985) states, "Subcultures exist where there is some form of organized and recognized constellation of values, behavior and actions which is responded to as differing from the prevailing set of norms" (8). Using Brake's definition, *Twilight* fans fall comfortably into this category of culture. In a fandom subculture, fans integrate what they watch into their lives and often create bonds with characters that take the place of those with people in their real lives (Davisson and Booth 2007). Fandom is one such subculture that has been described as "a vehicle for marginalized subcultural groups (women, the young, gays, etc.)" (Jenkins 1988, 87). Fandom allows individuals to transform the world and culture around them, creating a popular culture (Jenkins 1988).

Subcultures based on fandom use social media to survey, participate, and communicate within that subculture. Kate Crawford (2009) considers "listening online" to occur through a variety of social media, including Really Simple Syndication (RSS) feeds, blogs, and Twitter. "Twitter is fruitful territory, as it offers a relatively young platform (having launched in 2006), where the norms of use are nascent and contested. It also functions for many users as a continuous background presence, a steady stream of messages that can be briefly focused on then returned to the peripheries of attention" (Crawford 2009, 526). As something that is always in the background, Twitter can become part of a fan's everyday life—something that is there but not thought of every second of the day. It offers users a way to stay connected by something that is not constantly in their face.

Communities are being constructed by people online around the world. These communities share interests and use social networking to circulate information and interact with one another (Eid and Ward 2009). Social media, including Facebook, Twitter, and YouTube, "provide constant connectivity among people that is previously unparalleled" (Jansen et al. 2009, 2169). With 24/7 access to social media, it is not unheard of for conversations among users to go on for hours.

While divulging information online can be precarious, as people can never be quite sure who is truly on the other side of the conversation, online users are willing to do so every day (Simpson 2010). "People often express anger, sadness, fear and resentment. They may also misrepresent themselves and lie. Nonetheless, the disclosures made in social media spaces develop a relationship with an audience of listeners" (Crawford 2009, 528–29). Social networking is unique in the ways it allows people to meet who, under "normal" circumstances, may never have crossed paths (boyd and Ellison 2008). As relationships develop within social media, individuals will determine how they wish to "manage" their conversations (Cappella 1985). "The variety of topics, activities, and communication channels increases. People reveal more important, risky, and personal information" (Parks and Floyd 1996). As people get to know one another via social networking, they are often more willing to share intimate details of their lives.

## THEMES DISCOVERED

In order to explore the use of Twitter by *Twilight* fans and the relationships between these fans, I interviewed eighteen adult women about their experiences and interactions. The women represented thirteen different American states and three countries—Australia, Canada, and France.

The interviews found four basic themes surrounding the use of Twitter by *Twilight* fans: 1) fans used the social networking site to connect with people who were "like them" in their interest in *Twilight*; 2) fans felt they could more freely share their thoughts on Twitter than in their "real" lives; 3) the virtual relationships on Twitter lead to the creation of personal friendships among fans; and 4) those personal relationships were expected to be persistent and last well beyond the publication of the books and the release of the movies.

## LIKE-MINDED FANS

The first common theme identified among several of the women was their interest in finding like-minded fans by searching for *Twilight* on Twitter or connecting with people through introductions from their other Twitter friends. "I just typed in *Twilight* and found a few people at first, then they would 'introduce me' to their friends," said Jennifer. Each Friday, many users would tweet who they recommend their followers should follow using the hashtag #FollowFriday or #FF. Many participants found followers through the "Follow Friday," such as Denise who started following "random Twilighters" on the recommendation of her followers.

Social network sites (SNS) enable users to easily find one another. "What makes social network sites unique is not that they allow individuals to meet strangers, but rather that they enable users to articulate and make visible their social networks" (boyd and Ellison 2008, 211). Several of the women interviewed also maintain blogs dedicated to the *Twilight* saga, and many of those interviewed visit a variety of *Twilight*-themed blogs. Through these blogs, they also found followers on Twitter. On the blog she maintains, Casey explains how she gained followers on her Twitter account,

> There are a lot of people that follow the blog. I would tweet about things, give my opinion and when people started responding, I would make connections. I did contests to gain some followers and I would follow people back when they would have discussions with me.

Jenny says that many of her connections started on blogs, but "flourished" on Twitter. Stephanie believes her blog opened the door to many of her Twitter friends. She said, "It started as a connection between my blog and Twitter. I made the Twitter account so I could make posts for when my blog updates." Through these intermediary paths, these women found others who shared their interest and passion for the *Twilight* saga and the actors portraying the characters. To many fans, this also provides a break from the outside world. Casey explains how this phenomenon has impacted her life:

> If someone would have told me a couple years ago that I would pick up a book and end up where I am now, I would tell them they were crazy. I've found an escape from the stresses of the real world. And found a place that accepts me for loving *Twilight* and the characters/actors as much as I do.

Christie added, "Twitter is a place to go and escape when I need to get away from real life." Through Twitter, many women have found a place where they can be themselves, let their hair down, and be accepted without qualification (Nguyen, Bin, and Campbell 2012; Tonkin 2010).

## BUILDING FRIENDSHIPS VIA TWITTER

A second theme that emerged was how these relationships, formed via social media, evolved into close, personal friendships. Michael Sunnafrank and Artemio Ramirez Jr. (2004) state, "Most relationships form in social environments where individuals are repeatedly in close physical proximity" (362). While these women were not in the same physical space, they did share the same space electronically. Many of the women interviewed described the close friendships that formed through the electronic environment of Twitter. "Once we broke the ice, talking about everyday things comes naturally," said Denise. Friendships evolve differently on Twitter from those developed face-to-face. Nicole points out:

> You meet people in reverse on Twitter. You get to know the person without knowing what they look like, you don't know what their race is, you don't know their religion, you know nothing about them. Then you get to know them more and more, then you start to find out the personal things. Where else in the world does that happen? I have made friends with people who in real life we wouldn't even cross paths. I think it can open up your world because you're meeting those people.

As Nicole alludes, on Twitter a number of users do not use their own picture as their avatar, opting instead to use a quote, picture of a celebrity, and so forth (Scott 2010). Though a number of the women interviewed used an avatar of Kristen Stewart and/or Robert Pattinson, others use a photo of themselves. Through this perceived anonymity, they are not allowing others to make impressions based on their appearance but rather what they say. In today's world, when we meet others, we let first impressions cloud how and what we think of the individual.

For many, bonds are formed and connections are made, even if only online. Jenny describes the bond she has with her followers as special.

> It's like modern day pen pals. I don't think people understand the connections
> you have with people after having daily conversations on Twitter and blogs.
> You just reach a deep level of understanding and "knowing" with someone
> that you only correspond with through written communication.

These types of self-disclosure and sharing are not uncommon. Friendships
are able to form and develop through sharing with others, as well as creating
an understanding of who the other person is (Bargh, McKenna, and Fitzsimons 2002). With social networking sites, such as Twitter, first impressions
are left behind, and the substance of who the person is and what she shares is
what becomes important.

For many of those interviewed, these friendships (formed through Twitter) are often stronger than those they have with friends in "real life." As
Nicole said, "I have four best friends, women who if I don't talk to all four of
them in one day, then I worry about them. I talk about things that I never
would have talked about ever, things I didn't even know about before I got
here." Friendships are important for one's well-being, allowing individuals to
form bonds of companionship and support (Amichai-Hamburger, Kingsbury,
and Schneider 2013). "I have two very close friends on Twitter. I call them
my best friends. They know things about me that my boyfriend doesn't
know. Plus, they are always there for me and vice versa," Kelly shares. These
friendships provide support both emotionally and for encouragement (Carter
2005).

Alice and Nekol, who are regular contributors on Twitter, shared how
their Twitter friends are there for them when they need others to lean on. If
they "disappear" from Twitter for more than a day, their Twitter friends are
quick to email to check on their well-being. Also, if they are having a bad
day, their Twitter friends will cheer them up, whether it is via Twitter or a
phone call. Stefanie, a stay-at-home mom, cherishes her Twitter friends:

> I live in a rural area and don't have many real life friends who live close.
> When I found *Twilight*, then Twitter, I had been feeling isolated. It's been
> great to "meet" other women who feel as strongly as I do about *Twilight*. It's
> been fun and has helped me feel connected to the outside world.

No longer is one bound to his or her location to make and retain friendships.
Through social networking, individuals have the capability to engage in relationships with others regardless of their geographic location (Eid and Ward
2009).

Friendships formed on social networking sites also provide comfort for
many. Dorothy Jerrome (1984) describes the ties of these types of friendships
as an "emotional release friendship afforded from the strains and pressures of
other role performance" (709). For one "Twilighter" in particular, the friendships she formed helped her through a particularly rough patch, when her

husband's kidney failed and he was in need of a transplant. Nekol describes how these individuals became her support system. Individuals she had only corresponded with via Twitter offered to watch her children, while some went so far as to drive to Baltimore, Maryland (where the transplant was taking place), to sit with her. "People who I have never met, were willing to go far and beyond just to do something. Some of them [her twitter friends] stayed up with me all night [on Twitter] when my husband was in surgery," she said. The actions of the Twitter friends in Nekol's experience mirror age-old understandings regarding friendship, such as what Aristotle (2006) said about friends doing things for the sake of others, expecting nothing in return.

Malcolm R. Parks and Kory Floyd (1996) find relationships that begin online prove that the Internet is simply a new place to meet others. Denise Carter (2005) also states, "Because online and offline social experiences exhibit the same similarities and differences, it follows that they may also be interchangeable" (162). As several participants point out, Twitter has allowed people to meet individuals they most likely never would have met—whether it is due to physical distance, ethnicity, or other factors. The relationships of many of these women have morphed from being a fan of a book and movie series, to true friendships.

## FREELY SHARING WITH OTHERS

Twitter also provides users with anonymity or the ability to share more freely than in their "real lives." John A. Bargh, Katelyn Y. A. McKenna, and Grainne M. Fitzsimons (2002) discuss the "true self," stating there are qualities of the Internet that allow users to interact differently from face-to-face conversations. Being face-to-face with an individual and being online with that person are very dissimilar. "In live settings, we also often ask 'Who can touch or hurt me?' Indeed, one of the things that distinguishes mediated communication from live communication is the lack of risk of physical harm or involvement" (Meyrowitz 1985, 39). It appears some use the Internet as a mask in order to not show their true selves, while others willingly remove that mask to share their thoughts and feelings with others. "The Internet has become a significant social laboratory for experimenting with the constructions and reconstructions of self that characterize postmodern life. In its virtual reality, we self-fashion and self-create" (Turkle 1995, 180). With anonymity, users are able to put forth any personality they wish (Phillips 2008). The process of reconstructing one's identity and just being yourself was discussed by several participants.

"It's been a fascinating experience, crafting a persona there that I could never have the freedom to display in real life. I have found it incredibly freeing and validating," Linda states. Christie finds it freeing, saying,

—

> I find that I can be more of myself because I'm behind a name, that nobody knows it's me, not a lot of people know what I do for a living, not a lot of people know a lot about me, so I can write things. It's not your name, it's not your face, it's this completely different thing where you can just have fun and be whoever you want to be or really be yourself.

Being able to be one's self through anonymity allows the individuals to more freely be themselves without the constraints of what others may or may not know about the person behind the avatar. While for some it is their shyness that causes them to create an alter-ego, researchers also believe it could be due to self-consciousness (Brunet and Schmidt 2008). "I'm a pretty shy person. Online I'm more comfortable. This whole experience has made me a different person, in a good way, I think," Nicole said.

Many of the women discussed the closeness they felt with their followers. Stephanie reported:

> I have a lot of personal connections with other Twilighters. Many of them I feel extremely close with. I feel I can tell them anything and there will be no judgment. I tell some of the girls things I can't tell my friends in real life.

While *Twilight* and its fandom are what brought them together, the friendships form in ways that connect them to one another. Silvia adds, "We don't need to hide our feelings on Twitter—we are all there for the same reason. We spend a lot of time there because we *enjoy* the company and conversations with each other." Since they do not hide how they feel, conversations freely flow among the users.

## LASTING FRIENDSHIPS

The fourth theme examines whether these friendships would remain if/when the fandom dies down due to the end of the saga books and films. The majority of the women feel certain these friendships will remain, primarily because they have evolved from being based on a fandom to deeper relationships with one another. "I think the *Twilight* fans will follow the actor they love, and I think the Twi-fandom will stay for a long time," Letty said. Additionally, these women express a devotion to the actors who have portrayed these literary characters. Alice said, "I don't believe the Twi-fandom will die down anytime soon. Like me, many of my Twitter friends are Rob fans who will continue to support him in his future endeavors."

Friendships, online and face-to-face, require a willingness to listen and act as a confidant (Hoagland 2013). With regard to friendship, Jennifer says, "*Twilight* was a common interest that brought us together, but out of the common interest we have forged some really great friendships that will last indefinitely." As these friendships developed from superficial to something deeper, the women began to share more of their personal lives with one another. Gina adds, "We talk about so much more than *Twilight*! We discuss our families, our jobs, what goes on during our days . . . pretty much anything that friends in 'real life' would talk about." With the friends discussing topics other than *Twilight*, it may stand to reason why these friendships may last beyond the saga's completion.

On the other hand, Christie shared that she believes some friendships will stay, while others will not.

> The people I'm taking beyond Twitter, which is a very small group, those are the ones that I think will last. So many people stay your friends for life. You may meet them in person, but now the world is different, this is just how people communicate now with texting and e-mail.

A key in determining whether or not these friendships will last beyond *Twilight* depends on how the users listen to one another. Crawford (2009) explains that "tuning in" shows others online your level of engagement with them.

In early April 2011, when word came through Twitter from several actors of the *Twilight* saga regarding the wrap party for the filming of the final movie in the series, emotions ran high for *Twilight* fans. Following is a Twitter conversation between two of the women:

> Gina: Just because they might be done filming doesn't mean we lose the friendships
> Jennifer: oh I know, and I'm so thankful that this fandom brought us together! *big hug* Twi- is a common interest that led us to each other . . . We're stuck with each other ;)

The barrier of distance does not affect those who use Twitter. Regardless of state, country, or time zone, one can communicate with anyone, anytime, in any place. Additionally, a few of those interviewed have made the effort to meet their followers face-to-face, while others are planning get-togethers in the future. These meetings are similar to those Carter (2005) describes regarding how users of the virtual community Cybercity moved from online to off. Living within an hour of one another, Nekol and Nicole did not meet face-to-face until they traveled to North Carolina to attend a get-together with a mutual Twitter friend. "I think the whole time we were there we hardly talked about *Twilight* at all," Nekol said. Nicole describes it as "one of the best experiences. It was like we all walked in and knew each other." The more time people spends with others online, the more comfortable they are with them, thus leaving them feeling as if they know the individual on a deeper level prior to meeting face-to-face (Amichai-Hamburger, Kingsbury, and Schneider 2013).

On her blog, Nicole discussed reasons she felt spending face-to-face time with women she met via Twitter was important.

> The first reason is *you get to be yourself.* Not the "self" that includes all the baggage and past history that your real life friends know about. The second reason face time is important is even more beautiful than the first. *It opens up your world.* We all come from different places. Our careers range from working with abused women to running our own IT companies to manhandling small snot-nosed children all day long. We represent just about every culture there is. We get to know each other from the *inside out.* (Harlow 2011)

A blogger for the *Seattle Post-Intelligencer* regularly meets with her Twitter friends. They meet at a local coffeehouse to "cultivate a deeper relationship with like-minded sources" (Farhi 2009, 29). Similarly, the women interviewed do the same. They meet on Twitter daily to discuss topics they have in common, not only *Twilight* but also family, work, and an array of other topics. For those that cannot travel the distances, they are cultivating their relationships in other offline activities, such as phone calls and text messaging.

## CONCLUSION

In this study, the female relationships developed through the use of Twitter were examined. The results indicate these women may have originally come to Twitter only to find other like-minded people to talk to regarding the fandom; however, the relationships turned into something more and for many turned into lasting friendships that go far beyond the fandom. These women have formed a network of friends with whom they feel comfortable discussing everything from the fandom to their children, jobs, and everyday ups and downs.

There are several implications to this research. First, social media is a place where one can go to find like-minded individuals. Whether someone is looking to talk to others about a particular sports team, music group, an area of expertise, or in the case of the focus of this paper, a series of movies or books, with many millions of registered users (Twitter 2013) there is bound to be another individual or group of people willing and wanting to discuss similar topics. Also, the boundaries of friendship of the past are changing. No longer do you have to meet a person face-to-face to consider him or her your friend; meeting online, in this case via Twitter, tears that wall down. Participants in this study said repeatedly how they consider their followers (or at least the majority of their followers) to be their friends, individuals with whom they feel comfortable discussing things other than what brought them to the social network site in the first place. While some connections may be more superficial than others, many women have developed deep and meaningful connections.

Second, more research needs to be carried out with regard to friendships developed in online forums such as Twitter. There are studies discussing online dating relationships (Ellison, Heino, and Gibbs 2006), while there are few discussing friendship alone (Utz 2000). Twitter is a relatively new form of social media, and its impact on the development of friendships should be further explored. As mentioned earlier, the information obtained thus far represents a small sample of Twitter users who are also fans of the *Twilight* saga. With future research, social status, ethnicity, and socioeconomic status are areas that could be investigated as well.

In conclusion, through the use of social media, one may be able to witness a new form of relationships among individuals. On Twitter, especially due to its limit of 140 characters per message, the banter between like-minded individuals is interesting to observe. "People will find ways to negotiate the terms of their engagement online, how and with whom they engage, and when to switch off and be unavailable, unhearing and unheard" (Crawford 2009, 533). The decision to follow or unfollow someone on Twitter is as simple as a one button click. Therefore, the list of individuals that appear in one's Twitter feed is entirely up to the individual.

The friendships formed via Twitter because of *Twilight* are important. "Friendship, in our culture, is a voluntary, informal, personal and private relationship" (Jerrome 1984, 696). Carter (2005) reminds that friendships formed online and face-to-face both require trust in those with whom one forms a relationship. Nicole believes these relationships formed online are just as valid as those face-to-face. She states, "These friendships may not be traditional, but they are real." For the women in this study, trust in one another was evident, as well as the development of the friendships into more than simply surface-deep.

As new technologies continue to be developed and used in society, the ways in which we not only communicate with one another but also form relationships will be ever changing. It is technologies such as Twitter that allow individuals to meet people like them, to share with others, as well as build friendships that can stand the test of time. In the case of *Twilight* and Twitter, these women have shown there is more to their relationships than a book and movie series about vampires; it is all about them and how they relate to one another.

# REFERENCES

Amichai-Hamburger, Yair, Mila Kingsbury, and Barry H. Schneider. 2013. "Friendship: An Old Concept with a New Meaning?" *Computers in Human Behavior* 29 (1): 33–39.

Arceneaux, Noah, and Amy Schmitz Weiss. 2010. "Seems Stupid until You Try It: Press Coverage of Twitter, 2006–9." *New Media and Society* 12 (8): 1262–79.

Aristotle. 2006. *Ethics*. Middlesex: Echo Library.

Bargh, John A., Katelyn Y. A. McKenna, and Grainne M. Fitzsimons. 2002. "Can You See the Real Me? Activation and Expression of the "True Self" on the Internet." *Journal of Social Issues* 58 (1): 33–48.

boyd, danah m., and Nicole B. Ellison. 2008. "Social Network Sites: Definition, History, and Scholarship." *Journal of Computer-Mediated Communication* 13 (1): 210–30.

Brake, Michael. 1985. *Comparative Youth Culture: The Sociology of Youth Cultures and Youth Subcultures in America, Britain, and Canada*. London: Routledge.

Brunet, Paul M., and Louis A. Schmidt. 2008. "Are Shy Adults Really Bolder Online? It Depends on the Context." *Cyberpsychology and Behavior* 11 (6): 707–9.

Cappella, Joseph N. 1985. "The Management of Conversations." In *Handbook of Interpersonal Communication*, ed. Mark L. Knapp and Gerald R. Miller, 393–438. Beverly Hills, CA: Sage.

Carter, Denise. 2005. "Living in Virtual Communities: An Ethnography of Human Relationships in Cyberspace." *Information, Communication and Society* 8 (2): 148–67.

Crawford, Kate. 2009. "Following You: Disciplines of Listening in Social Media." *Continuum: Journal of Media and Cultural Studies* 23 (4): 525–35.

Davisson, Amber, and Paul Booth. 2007. "Reconceptualizing Communication and Agency in Fan Activity: A Proposal for a Projected Interactivity Model for Fan Studies." *Texas Speech Communication Journal* 32 (1): 33–43.

Eid, Mahmoud, and Stephen J. A. Ward. 2009. "Editorial: Ethics, New Media, and Social Networks." *Global Media Journal* 2 (1): 1–4.

Ellison, Nicole B., Rebecca Heino, and Jennifer Gibbs. 2006. "Managing Impressions Online: Self-Presentation Processes in the Online Dating Environment." *Journal of Computer-Mediated Communication* 11:415–41.

Farhi, Paul. 2009. "The Twitter Explosion." *American Journalism Review* 31 (3): 26–31.

Garcia, Angela Cora, Alecea I. Standlee, Jennifer Bechkoff, and Yan Cui. 2009. "Ethnographic Approaches to the Internet and Computer-Mediated Communication." *Journal of Contemporary Ethnography* 38:52–83.

Harlow, Nicole. 2011. "Musings from Facetime with Twitter Girls," *TwiMusings* (blog), March 10.http://twimusings.blogspot.com/2011/04/face-time-with-twitter-girls.html.

Hebdige, Dick. 1979. *Subculture: The Meaning of Style*. New York: Methuen.

Hine, Christine. 2000. *Virtual Ethnography*. Thousand Oaks, CA: Sage.

Hoagland, Edward. 2013. "On Friendship: The Intimacies Shared with Our Closest Companions Keep Us Anchored, Vital, and Alive." *American Scholar* 82 (1): 32–43.

Jansen, Bernard J., Mimi Zhang, Kate Sobel, and Abdur Chowdury. 2009. "Twitter Power: Tweets as Electronic Word of Mouth." *Journal of the American Society for Information Science and Technology* 60 (11): 2169–88.

Jenkins, Henry, III. 1988. "*Star Trek* Rerun, Reread, Rewritten: Fan Writing as Textual Poaching." *Critical Studies in Mass Communication* 5 (2): 85–107.

Jerrome, Dorothy. 1984. "Good Company: The Sociological Implications of Friendship." *Sociological Review* 32 (4): 696–718.

Kozinets, Robert V. 2001. "Utopian Enterprise: Articulating the Meanings of *Star Trek's* Culture of Consumption." *Journal of Consumer Research* 28:67–88.

Krohn, Katherine E. 2010. *Stephenie Meyer: Dreaming of "Twilight."* Minneapolis: Twenty-First Century Books.

Lindlof, Thomas R. 1995. *Qualitative Communication Research Methods*. Thousand Oaks, CA: Sage.

Marwick, Alice E., and boyd, danah. 2010. "I Tweet Honestly, I Tweet Passionately: Twitter Users, Context Collapse, and the Imagined Audience. *New Media and Society* 13 (1): 114–33.

McCracken, Grant D. 1998. *Plenitude 2.0: Culture by Commotion.* Toronto: Periph.:Fluide.

Memmott, Carol. 2008. "Meyer Unfazed as Fame Dawns." *USA Today*, July 31. http://usatoday30.usatoday.com/life/books/news/2008-07-30-stephenie-meyer-main_N.htm?loc=interstitialskip.

Meyrowitz, Joshua. 1985. *No Sense of Place: The Impact of Electronic Media on Social Behavior.* Oxford: Oxford University Press.

Nguyen, Melanie, Yu Sun Bin, and Andrew Campbell. 2012. "Comparing Online and Offline Self-Disclosure: A Systematic Review." *Cyberpsychology, Behavior, and Social Networking* 15 (2): 103–11.

Parks, Malcolm R., and Kory Floyd. 1996. "Making Friends in Cyberspace." *Journal of Communication* 46 (1). http://onlinelibrary.wiley.com/doi/10.1111/j.1083-6101.1996.tb00176.x/full.

Phillips, David. 2008. "The Psychology of Social Media." *Journal of New Communications Research* 3 (1): 79–85.

Puente, Maria. 2009. "Women Also Mooning over the Teen-Vampire *Twilight*." *USA Today*, November 23. http://usatoday30.usatoday.com/life/movies/news/2009-11-23-twilightmoms23_ST_N.htm?csp=34.

Schouten, John W., and James H. McAlexander. 1995. "Subcultures of Consumption: An Ethnography of the New Bikers." *Journal of Consumer Research* 22:43–61.

Scodari, Christine, and Jenna L. Felder. 2000. "Creating a Pocket Universe: 'Shippers,' Fan Fiction, and *The X-Files* Online." *Communication Studies* 51 (3): 238–57.

Scott, David M. 2010. "Are You a Cat?" *EContent* 33 (8): 32.

Simpson, Mark. 2010. "Tech Etiquette Is Just Common Sense." *Common Ground Journal* 7 (2): 81–88.

Stassen, Wilma. 2010. "Your News in 140 Characters: Exploring the Role of Social Media in Journalism." *Global Media Journal: African Edition* 4 (1): 1–16.

Sunnafrank, Michael, and Artemio Ramirez Jr. 2004. "At First Sight: Persistent Relational Effects of Get-Acquainted Conversations." *Journal of Social and Personal Relationships* 21 (3): 361–79.

Thornton, Sarah. 1997. Introd. to *The Subcultures Reader*, ed. Ken Gelder and Sarah Thornton, 1–7. New York: Routledge.

Tonkin, Sarah. 2010. "Getting Hyper-Personal." *Global Media Journal: Australian Edition* 4 (4): 1–9.

Turkle, Sherry. 1995. *Life on the Screen: Identity in the Age of the Internet.* New York: Simon and Schuster.

Twitter. 2013. "About Twitter." http://twitter.com/about.

Underberg, Natalie M. 2006. "Virtual and Reciprocal Ethnography on the Internet: The East Mims Oral History Project Website." *Journal of American Folklore* 119 (473): 301–11.

Utz, Sonja. 2000. "Social Information Processing in MUDs: The Development of Friendships in Virtual Worlds." *Journal of Online Behavior* 1 (1).

## Chapter Six

# *Twilight* Anti-Fans

*"Real" Fans and "Real" Vampires*

## Victoria Godwin

Those who dislike the *Twilight* franchise can be just as passionate as its fans. Typing "hate *Twilight*" into a search engine reveals plenty of people who feel the need to share their dislike of the franchise. In an ongoing struggle for dominance, groups present their worldview or definition of reality as "common sense" and marginalize groups with alternative views—who simultaneously promote their own views and interests. This particular hegemonic struggle for meaning challenges the *Twilight* franchise's fans and texts as problematic, yet ultimately constructs "real" fans and "real" vampires in equally problematic ways. Other fandoms also have anti-fandoms, which scholars explore in a variety of articles (Gray 2003; Theodoropoulou 2007; Johnson 2007). Multiple websites, threads, and other primary sources reveal certain trends in anti-fans' reactions to *Twilight*. This chapter focuses upon relevant examples from anti-fans and also from film critics, reviewers, scholars, and other arbiters of societal tastes who recapitulate and thus validate anti-fans' reactions—usually in a more coherent and grammatical form.

Numerous studies of *Twilight* fans and the pleasures they derive from the books and films already exist. Of these, *Bitten by Twilight* is noteworthy for its inclusion of an examination of anti-fans and their "rhetoric of superiority" (Sheffield and Merlo 2010). Lisa Bode's survey of film reviews of *Twilight* likewise examines how negative reviews also invoke an imagined sense of superiority. Typically, "the more negative the review, the more derisive is the language used to describe the audience, and maintain distance between the taste of the reviewer and that of the audience." In negative reviews, film critics construct "the adolescent girl as an imagined 'other'" against whom they reaffirm "their own cultural superiority . . . their knowledge of vampire and horror film genres," which allows them to define good or bad films. Bode likewise notes that such negative reviews express fears of horror genres' pollution or "contamination" by feminine genres such as romance (2010, 710–11, 717). This chapter builds upon Bode's arguments using a fan studies approach to examine problematic aspects of such discourses. Rather than yet another examination of what *Twilight* fans get out of the franchise, this chapter examines the backlash against *Twilight*. This is a fandom defined not by liking *Twilight* but by *dis*-liking *Twilight*.

Anti-fans are "those who strongly dislike a given text or genre, considering it inane, stupid, morally bankrupt and/or aesthetic drivel" (Gray 2003, 70). This is an apt description of anti-fans' reactions to the *Twilight* franchise. Anti-fans' discourse frequently adopts a paternalistic tone, claiming defense of worthwhile masculinized genres against an overwhelmingly popular yet inferior feminine franchise. In horror genres, audiences (usually male) watch monsters and serial killers (usually male) punish victims (usually female) for real or imagined transgressions. Although exceptions exist, these perceived gender norms shape anti-fans' discourse.

Anti-fans' discourse constructing normative gender roles for *Twilight* fans and vampires contain many tensions. First, anti-fans position *Twilight* fans as hysterical, out-of-control female or feminized Others. This reinscribes problematic representations of fans as passive, obsessive, hysterical, feminized cultural dupes, linked to mass culture or popular culture instead of to "worthwhile" (masculine, elite) culture. Fans of "real" vampires critique *Twilight*'s sparkly vampires and their fans. These anti-fans set up binary oppositions that elevate horror genres above romance genres and masculinized horror fans above feminized *Twilight* fans. Instead of critiquing mainstream interpretations of fandom as pathological, anti-fans offer *Twilight* fans as scapegoats. "They" are the pathological ones. In comparison, "we" fans of "real" vampires seem more acceptable and respectable.

Second, anti-fans construct "real" vampires as violent, hypersexual, and in control. Anti-fans reference "classic" vampires such as Dracula as support for these claims. Vampires who exhibit romantic behaviors are not "real" vampires and thus not worthy of inclusion in horror genres perceived as masculine. Yet anti-fans' discourse also criticizes *Twilight*'s constructions of romance as abusive behaviors. Such discourse actually rehabilitates *Twilight*'s version of romance as monstrous forms of patriarchal control, similar to that of "real" vampires, which anti-fans so ardently defend as superior to *Twilight*'s version. Thus, anti-fans' discourse ultimately renders these same derided behaviors appropriate for inclusion in supposedly masculine horror genres. Anti-fans' critiques of *Twilight* consistently highlight Edward Cullen's own violent and hypersexual nature, thus blurring the same boundaries between horror and romance that they seek to police. Furthermore, idealizing violent and hypersexual interpretations of vampires perpetuates problematic aspects of patriarchal masculinity that justify violent and sexual assaults. Only "real" vampires' constant exertion of excessive self-control prevents violent and sexual assaults upon vulnerable female potential victims. However, anti-fans also highlight how Edward Cullen controls Bella Swan—yet again blurring boundaries in attempts to enforce them. Anti-fans' conflicted constructions of Edward as both abusive and controlling, yet not a "real" vampire, reveal tensions in their own normative constructions for horror genres.

## *TWILIGHT* FANS AS INFERIOR OTHER

Bode's extensive analysis of *Twilight* saga film reviews includes numerous negative examples (2010). Likewise, Jessica Sheffield and Elyse Merlo discuss anti-fans' sense of superiority (2010). Anti-fans' claims about Edward Cullen and his ilk appear in numerous online discussions, articles, and reviews. A content analysis of every such instance is beyond the scope of this chapter. I will focus instead on claims indicative of much of the criticism leveled against the *Twilight* franchise and its vampires. Even cursory examinations of online discussions of *Twilight* quickly reveal variations on common themes, as evident in posts such as "I miss inhuman bloodsuckers from beyond the grave" and claims that *Twilight* "ruined . . . the vampire genre . . . I like my vamps evil as hell." More restrained and reprintable reactions to *Twilight* include multiple variations on assertions that "*Twilight*'s version of vampires ARE NOT VAMPIRES" (Vampire Barbie 2009; "*Twilight* vs. Vampire Lovers" 2010). Anti-fans of *Twilight* tend to define themselves as fans of "real" vampires. Anti-fans feminize *Twilight* fans: masses of teen and tween girls, immature or irresponsible older female fans, and effeminate or homosexual male fans. Ultimately, such anti-fan discourse constructs vampires as under threat of contamination by *Twilight* and its Othered fans.

For example, in *Esquire*, only "denial" can account for a scene in which "after their first sultry kiss, Edward and Bella (in her underwear!) decide to hang out in her bed and talk." Apparently, the idea of men and women preferring to have a conversation doesn't resemble the version of "objective reality" this critic constructs, wherein "hormonal rage" would put Bella's bed to a much different use, and her underwear would be nowhere to be seen. This is a simplified "B-movie" version of sex, "without all the messiness of courtship, relationships, and sexual frustration" (VanAirsdale 2009). Meanwhile, *Slate* sees "America's young women receiving troubling misinformation about the male of the species from *Twilight*. These women are going to be shocked when the sensitive, emotionally available, poetry-writing boys of their dreams expect a bit more from a sleepover than dew-eyed gazes and chaste hugs." *Slate*'s critic admits that young men likewise receive faulty images of love and sex online but concludes that "[t]he bigger problem here is that we're breeding sexually incompatible human beings, and vampires are to blame" (Hendrix 2009). Unfortunately, blaming vampires overlooks or absolves media misrepresentations of sex. The problem is not only unrealistic female romantic expectations but also unrealistic male sexual expectations. Yet, it is *Twilight*'s female fans who are Othered. They are naive. It is the girls who will be shocked, not the boys. The subtext is more troubling. It is the boys' sexual expectations that will be met, not the girls' romantic ones.

Typical negative fan stereotypes critiqued within fan studies include "the obsessed individual and the hysterical crowd" (Jenson 1992, 9), as well as "a dupe," a passive receiver for "corporate propaganda and establishment ideology," and a "strange social outcast" (Gray 2003, 67). Such stereotypes commonly recur in representations of *Twilight* franchise's fans. What differentiates these negative representations is that they often originate with fans of other texts and genres—typically those who profess some affection for "real" vampires and horror genres.

Redirecting the same Othering typically applied to fans in general at fans of the *Twilight* franchise achieves similar goals. If "fans are characterized as deviant, they can be treated as disreputable, even dangerous 'others.' Fans, when insistently characterized as 'them,' can be distinguished from 'people like us'" and from fans of more "reputable" or "respectable" texts and genres (Jenson 1992, 9). In contrast to hysterical, obsessive *Twilight* fans, horror genres and their fans become "reputable" or "respectable." Deriding perceived opposing groups boosts identity and self-esteem. This is of particular importance considering fans' identities and self-esteem suffer regular assault from negative mainstream representations of fans in general as hysterical, lacking social skills, and so forth. Projecting such lacks onto an Other is one means of coping.

The *Twilight* franchise's immense popularity among females engages another tension between fandom and anti-fandom. By definition, fans are passionate about their fan objects. However, too much enthusiasm pathologizes fans in gendered ways. Both perceptions of "fundamentally irrational, excessively emotional, foolish and passive" behavior and "the prevalent image of the unattractive, acne-suffering, 30-year old virgin male computer nerd" feminize fans (Gray 2003, 67). Jonathan Gray clearly evokes mainstream representations of male *Star Trek* and *Star Wars* fans, as in the infamous *Saturday Night Live* skit wherein William Shatner urges his fans to "Get a life!" Such stereotypes still resonate even though Geek Chic supposedly celebrates fanboys. To prevent further feminization and pathologization, fans police the boundaries between "us" and "them," offering themselves as respectable alternatives to disreputable Others. Both mainstream and anti-fan accounts construct fangirls as out-of-control, hysterical, overly sexual, and deviant. Within fandom, there also are accusations of "fake" fan/geek girls only interested in attention or attractive celebrities. Excessive enthusiasm and enthusiasm for inferior or incorrect fan objects differentiate disreputable "them" from respectable "us": fangirls from fanboys.

Already marginalized, fans further marginalize Others in order to establish some small sense of dominance for their own fandom. Joli Jenson analyzes reasons for characterizing fandom in general as pathological and addresses dichotomies drawn between fandoms of the powerful and of those who are not privileged. Stigmatizing fandom "as a deviant activity" promotes "particular values—the rational over the emotional, the educated over the uneducated, the subdued over the passionate, the elite over the popular, the mainstream over the margin, the status quo over the alternative." Such conservative beliefs "privilege the attributes of the wealthy, educated and powerful" (Jenson 1992, 24–25). By stigmatizing predominantly female and young fans of *Twilight*, anti-fans engage in hegemonic discourse that privileges masculinity and patriarchy. In this instance, gender defines the powerful instead of wealth and education as in Jenson.

It is possible to extend Jenson's argument to address specific fandoms. For example, the "geek hierarchy" immortalized in various charts and other online memes (Sjöberg 2002) highlights the common practice of belittling certain fandoms in order to reinforce one's own fandoms' relatively privileged status as cooler, smarter, or more popular. It is as if fandom is a zero-sum game: for one fandom to be reputable, some other fandom has to be disreputable. Anti-fans' dismissal of *Twilight* fans functions as a protective measure. Distancing oneself from a fandom seen as even more hysterical and feminized than one's own establishes a measure of credibility and respectability for one's own fandom. Anti-fans position themselves as superior by constructing *Twilight* fans as inferior.

## POLICING AND BLURRING BOUNDARIES

From the point of view of fan studies, anti-fandom constitutes a response to something that "is perceived as harming a text as a whole," such as *Star Wars* fans' antipathy for the character Jar Jar Binks (Gray 2003, 73). In a similar fashion, anti-fans perceive the *Twilight* franchise as undermining vampires and horror genres. Anti-fans' dislikes are motivated by expectations—of genre, of what is worthwhile, and of what is inferior (Gray 2003, 73). For those unfamiliar with supernatural romance, horror genres seem to be vampires' natural and only home. Vampires' inclusion in *Twilight* thus engages certain expectations for other familiar horror tropes. Frustration of these expectations prompts anti-fans' ire.

It also prompts reactions such as those documented in Vivi Theodoropoulou's discussion of anti-fans. First, hatred of another fan's fan object occurs because it is, or is perceived to be, in competition with the anti-fan's own object of fandom (2007, 318). "Real" vampires are eclipsed by the enormous mainstream appeal of *Twilight*'s version. In defense of their own fan object, anti-fans deride vampires who sparkle in sunlight and don't drink human blood. They also construct *Twilight* fans as obsessive Twihards, undiscerning fans of aesthetic drivel ignorant of vampires' "real" characteristics and genres. Anti-fans position themselves as paternalistic arbiters of taste and culture, of what vampires should be.

Second, textual proximity also invites anti-fandom, as in *Star Wars* fans' antipathy towards *Star Trek* (Theodoropoulou 2007, 318). Such dichotomous constructions exclude the all-too-common phenomenon of individuals who are fans of both *Star Wars* and *Star Trek*. The *Twilight* franchise creates such textual proximity due to its usage of vampires, a common trope from horror genres, in novels and films positioned within romance genres. Vampire fans respond to this textual proximity with anti-fandom. Such policing of horror genres' boundaries to prevent contamination by sparkly vegetarian vampires and their fans excludes the possibility that individuals can be fans of both horror and romance. Ironically, even as anti-fans' discourse positions the *Twilight* franchise outside horror genres, it simultaneously emphasizes how several of its tropes fit comfortably within horror genres.

Many anti-fans and critics focus upon the abusive and controlling nature of Edward and Bella's relationship in the *Twilight* saga. Anti-fans call attention to how creepy it is that Edward watches Bella sleep in both the novel (Meyer 2005, 293–94) and the film. They compare Edward to a stalker on a regular basis. They likewise point out that *Twilight* fans casting this incident as romantic is even more disturbing, once again Othering *Twilight* fans. Consider Edward's murderous musings in a leaked first draft of *Midnight Sun*, which retells *Twilight* from Edward's point of view. When Edward first encounters Bella, her scent strips away his—and her—humanity: "I was a predator. She was my prey." Edward contemplates killing the beautiful stranger he finds so desirable and promises himself Bella "would not have time to scream or feel pain" because he "would not kill her cruelly" (Meyer 2008, 9–10). Anti-fans use such passages to construct *Twilight* fans as misguided, misinterpreting cruelty and violence as romance. Even if Edward considers a painless murder cruelty-free, the ominous nature of his fantasy undermines any idealized romantic image of this vampire's self-control. However, it also reinforces Edward's resemblance to "real" vampires, similarities which anti-fans studiously ignore. His predatory urges inspire plans for murder worthy of any "real" vampires in horror genres.

Anti-fans frequently comment on Edward bruising his new bride during their wedding night in both novel and film *Breaking Dawn*. Vampire expert Mary Findley observes that Bella "worries only about whether or not he enjoyed himself" (Harris 2009). Even more disturbing, Bella "tries to hide her bruises so Edward won't feel bad" (Seifert 2009, 24). In *National Review Online*, Gina R. Dalfonzo comments that Bella's assuring Edward that she found this encounter "wonderful and perfect" should terrify "any parent with a daughter" (2008). Instead of the idealized romance the tween target audience sees, Findley identifies "the mentality of a woman that will be battered, and . . . a potential batterer" and "the dangers of this relationship" (Harris 2009). Like many anti-fans, Christine Seifert discusses the "worrisome" reaction of *Twilight* fans who are more upset by the consummation of Edward and Bella's marriage than by "the disturbing nature of Bella and Edward's sexual relationship" (2009, 24), wherein Edward's violent loss of control during sexual activity damages his wife and breaks their headboard. Once again *Twilight* fans are Othered, as potentially confusing abuse for affection due to their fandom for these texts. A vampire's fantastic danger pales next to the all-too-real danger of abuse.

Anti-fans highlight how Edward's violent controlling nature offers even more unfortunate parallels with an abuser or batterer. Many anti-fans note the problematic nature of his relationship with Bella and its possible effects on *Twilight* fans. Anti-fans Other fans as unable to detect such messages for themselves. For example, one anti-fan decries the risks of "girls growing up looking forward to getting in relationships with obsessive guys that are older than them and isolate them from people that can give them a proper perspective on what's really going on" (Vampire Barbie 2009). Brian Gibson's film review characterizes Bella as helpless, extremely passive, and "obsessed with surrender and submission to a man constantly tempted to kill her" (2008). She hardly is a worthwhile role model for *Twilight*'s supposedly impressionable young female fans. In both examples, anti-fan and reviewer position themselves in paternalistic roles, able to discern dangers to which *Twilight* fans remain oblivious. This also positions the narrative as if it was an idealized representation, not a work of fiction.

Anti-fans frequently list plot points in ways that emphasize Edward's controlling behaviors as indicative of an abusive relationship. For example, although much is made of the fact that Edward does not drink human blood, he:

> behaves like a predator in nearly every other way possible. He spies on Bella while she sleeps, eavesdrops on her conversations, . . . forges her signature, tries to dictate her choice of friends, encourages her to deceive her father, disables her truck, has his family hold her at his house against her will, and enters her house when no one's there—all because, he explains, he wants her to be safe. He warns Bella how dangerous he is, but gets "furious" at anyone else who tries to warn or protect her. He even drags her to the prom against her expressed wishes. (Dalfonzo 2008)

For Dalfonzo, it is even more disturbing that readers (young and adult) fall in love with Edward. Readers describe him as "beautiful," "sweet," and "mysterious," and favorably redefine his manipulative behavior, since they adore how he "takes care of Bella" (2008). Such discourse Others *Twilight* fans, constructing them as unable to assess problematic aspects of their favorite books and films. Scholars, critics, and anti-fans of course are able to perform such higher reasoning for them. In other words, scholars, critics, and anti-fans construct themselves as arbiters of taste, culture, and meaning: areas in which *Twilight*'s fans supposedly are woefully deficient.

## EMASCULATION AND AGGRESSION

Anti-fans' discourses criticize *Twilight*'s vampire protagonist Edward Cullen both for his emasculation and for his violence and hypersexuality, citing his control as evidence for both. For example, a *National Post* critic dismisses Edward and his ilk as "cuddly" or "neutered," a "vegetarian" "rebel without the claws" who is "defanged," "toothless," or "losing his teeth" (Harris 2009). Such criticisms decry a supposed loss of vampires' frightening predatory nature. Indeed, the article's title is "All Lark, No Bite." In *Esquire*, vampires are no longer "superhuman studs" but "spayed and neutered" and "*emasculated*" (VanAirsdale 2009). Animalistic comparisons prevail in each article and in each contrasting construction of vampires. For anti-fans, *Twilight* neuters vampires into cuddly pets: defanged, declawed, and otherwise made safe for the Othered teen and tween girls who love the series and its protagonist. Edward is a nonthreatening fan object, a sexually safe teen crush. In contrast, anti-fans construct "real" vampires as predators and studs, conforming to narrow normative definitions of masculinity as violent and hypersexualized. Constructing predatory vampires as preferable to *Twilight*'s safe teen crush overlooks the implications of existing linkages of masculinity with similar predator metaphors.

For instance, the use of "neutered" to describe contemporary vampires gains significance when examined in light of traditional popular perceptions of the vampire as a virile figure. In the most famous version of the vampire, Dracula's vampirism can be read as a very specific construction of masculinity: animalistic, active, fertile, virile, dominating, and primitive instead of civilized (Arata 1990, 628, 639). Criticisms of *Twilight* often privilege this interpretation. Dracula, especially Bela Lugosi's portrayal of this character, is emblematic of what "real" vampires should be. For example, an "Edward and Bela" t-shirt features Bela Lugosi's iconic Dracula holding Edward Cullen's severed bloody head (OffWorld Designs 2009). Likewise, there are online exhortations amongst anti-fans of *Twilight* to join Team Dracula, as well as merchandise to proclaim one's loyalty. *Twilight* fans tend to identify themselves as Team Edward or Team Jacob, depending on which character they favor as a heteronormative romantic partner for Bella. Team Dracula dismisses the appeal of Edward, Jacob, or any other *Twilight* character, especially when compared to the dangerous allure of a "real" vampire such as Dracula. One of many anti-fan threads includes posts demanding the return of vampires who, like Dracula, "can seduce their female victims despite their vile appearance. . . . Bring back the vampires that KILL PEOPLE" (*"Twilight* vs. Vampire Lovers" 2010). A "real" vampire links sex and death. His seduction is heterosexual. He doesn't have to be beautiful. He is a killer whose conquests belong in masculinized horror genres, not in feminized romance genres.

Thus, *Twilight*'s anti-fans appropriate Dracula as both symbol and protector of "real" vampires. *Dracula* in all its iterations (character, book, films, and so forth) supposedly constructs "real" vampires as conforming to heterosexual norms and conventional gender codes, often to the point of hypermasculinity. However, two aspects to positioning of Dracula as the epitome of vampires warrant further examination. First, unlike Christopher Craft's seminal analysis (1984), it overlooks Dracula's own challenges to the same heterosexual norms and conventional gender codes that Edward Cullen supposedly undermines. Constructing Dracula as a hegemonic version of vampire masculinity oversimplifies the character's own inherent challenges to patriarchal gender norms. Second, it also romanticizes the "conquest and domination" Stephen D. Arata discusses (1990, 628), even as anti-fans criticize *Twilight* fans' framing of Edward's violent abusive behaviors as romantic. Whether vampires seduce or kill their prey, *Twilight*'s critics idealize violent, hypersexualized, predatory masculinity as desirable. Problematically, anti-fans' discourse duplicates hegemonic masculinity instead of deconstructing it. Yet rather than address the problematic nature of this interpretation, anti-fans and other critics continue to appropriate Dracula and similar undead as more "real" and authentic representations of vampires. They are emblematic of everything recent vampires supposedly lack.

That perception of lack is telling in itself. Many vampire experts decry a perceived loss of menace, often referring to a trait that does not exist, such as missing fangs or claws (Harris 2009). These are obvious phallic signifiers. *Twilight*'s anti-fans regularly emasculate vampires, ignoring the fangs and claws very visible on screen. Supposedly "defanged" vampires lack the means to attack their prey, whether their goal is to devour or to seduce. Anti-fans' word choices for vampire attacks simultaneously idealize and conceal more ominous behaviors: assault, murder, and rape. Unfortunately, many anti-fans fail to examine whether a sexually aggressive predator is a productive metaphor for modern masculinity. However, it is a dominant metaphor. Society presents men as "naturally aggressive and territorial. Men are predators, while women are naturally passive, reserved and vulnerable—open prey for male aggression" (Adair 1992, 56). Even while claiming to recognize the dangers of defining such dominating or predatory actions as romantic, anti-fans' problematically criticize *Twilight* itself or its fans, rather than predatory, aggressive, and abusive behaviors. Anti-fans' discourse legitimates and glorifies predatory aggression and violence. Edward Cullen's perceived lack prompts emasculating insults. Although anti-fans use such insults to position Edward outside categories of "real" vampires and horror genres, they ignore specific examples of violence and hypersexuality in the *Twilight* franchise in order to do so. Ironically, a second aspect of anti-fans' discourse employs these same behaviors to denigrate both Edward and *Twilight*'s fans, while also ignoring their examples' similarities to anti-fans' own definitions of "real" vampires and horror genres.

## SELF-CONTROL AND PATRIARCHAL CONTROL

Although framed as a romantic hero, Edward exhibits a range of controlling and abusive behaviors. He regularly spies on Bella, tells her what to do, bruises her, and even plans how to kill her. *Twilight*'s narrative constructs such actions as signs of Edward's self-control and love for Bella. Ultimately, both books and films act "to promote conservative gender roles that demand women's submission to dominant male partners, but also to idealize and romanticize abusive relationships" (Borgia 2011, 3). Scholarly defenses of *Twilight* and its fans stress that these aspects relate to larger social issues, and Stephenie Meyer simply represents them. Anti-fans readily seize upon such contradictions as evidence of *Twilight* fans' status as cultural dupes, passively consuming retrograde messages. Such constructions obviously disregard how *Twilight* fans interpret and use such material, processes already covered by numerous other scholars. Furthermore, anti-fans' own constructions of "real" vampires contain similarly problematic elements, which remain unexamined and unquestioned even while deployed to interrogate the *Twilight* franchise.

Anti-fans' discourse illustrates the ease with which issues of self-control transform into issues of patriarchal control. As Seifert explains:

> Edward has taken on the role of protector of Bella's human blood and chastity, both of which, ironically, are always in peril when Edward is nearby. Bella is not in control of her body, as abstinence proponents would argue; she is absolutely dependent on Edward's ability to protect her life, her virginity, and her humanity. She is the object of his virtue, the means of his ability to prove his self-control. In other words, Bella is a secondary player in the drama of Edward's abstinence. (Seifert 2009, 25)

Indeed, Edward controls Bella as much as, if not more than, he controls himself. Although "Meyer and her publisher have promoted the [*Twilight*] books as being all about choice," Dalfonzo comments upon the significance of the numerous times Bella says, "I never had a choice." Bella is "a girl who discovers her own worth and gets all she ever wanted, by giving up her identity and throwing away nearly everything in life that matters. That's scarier than any vampire" (2008). Such conclusions stand in stark contrast to anti-fans' claims that *Twilight*, abstinence, and civilized self-control "de-fanged" recent vampires.

When anti-fans yearn for frightening vampires, the desirability of preda-tory violence remains unexamined. For example, one typical online post characterizes "the trend toward the domestication of vampires" as "very distressing. Part of their attraction comes from their very danger, the fact that they COULD rip off your head, but don't necessarily choose to" (Vampire Barbie 2009). For detractors of the *Twilight* franchise, violence or the threat of violence factors into their constructions of vampires and of desirable mas-culinity. Such critiques do not acknowledge the carefully controlled and definite violence evident in the *Twilight* franchise's actual texts.

On a related note, television horror series *Supernatural* mocks *Twilight*'s version of vampires in its episode "Live Free or Twihard" (2010). Attractive vampire Robert (named for the actor who plays Edward Cullen) lures vam-pire romance fan Kristen (named for the actress who plays Bella Swan) with his sensitive online posts. After her conversion into a vampire, she lures young boys, thus maintaining a strict normative heterosexuality. Both teens ultimately serve a more conventional vampire, an overlord whose own nor-mative masculine behavior of violence and hypersexualized harem-building remains unquestioned. He has no romantic interest in these or any other of his recruits, regarding them all as minions to do his bidding, creating more and more vampires to make him more and more powerful. Any pleasure is taken, not shared, as he forcibly drains their blood. *Supernatural* not only criticizes but assimilates supposed threats to normative vampirism. As such, it is emblematic of anti-fans' discourse's ultimate outcome, which, albeit inadvertently, is to frame *Twilight*'s protagonist as violent and hypersexual as any "real" vampire.

As we have seen, violence is an inherent element of anti-fans' construc-tions of "real" vampires. Its presence overrides any problematic challenges to patriarchal gender norms, as in the discourses appropriating Dracula as the epitome of "real" vampires or as in *Supernatural*'s reframing and reposition-ing of *Twilight* within more traditional horror genres. Violence's perceived absence obscures any contrary evidence, as with the aforementioned fangs, claws, and other phallic signifiers. Exerting self-control over any potential for violence prompts similar mental gymnastics. Anti-fans' construction of Edward Cullen's vaunted self-control likewise encompasses both emasculation and hyper-masculine versions of violence and sexuality. Seifert credits the *Twilight* books for launching a teen romance genre she dubs "abstinence porn" (2009, 23) due to the protagonists' unconsummated tension. This genre continues unabated within the franchise's films. The film *Twilight* offers safe "surrogate sex scenes" (Edwards 2009, 31). It is not surprising that abstinence appears as a key factor in teen romance. Such self-control makes Edward a safe love object for teen and tween girls. He is not sexually threatening. He restrains both his sexual passion and his lust for blood, abstaining from both for fear of losing control. Better to do without, or with a very restricted amount, than to risk draining too much of Bella's blood or injuring her during sexual activity. Edward's self-control manifests as avoiding drinking Bella's blood, having sex with Bella, or even being too close to Bella. Seifert's response is typical of many anti-fans, portraying fans who interpret these actions "as evidence of his innocent 'crush' on her" as oblivious to Edward's scheming to get what he wants from Bella (2009, 24): both blood and intercourse.

Like Seifert, other anti-fans likewise point out the threat of violence and abuse inherent in passages such as the following excerpt from the novel *Twilight*:

> I have to mind my actions every moment that we're together so that I don't hurt you. I could kill you quite easily, Bella, simply by accident. . . . If for one second I wasn't paying enough attention, I could reach out, meaning to touch your face, and crush your skull by mistake. You don't realize how incredibly *breakable* you are. I can never, never afford to lose any kind of control when I'm with you. (Meyer 2005, 310)

This comment highlights the risk of physical harm to (human) females should (vampire) males lose control. In both books and films, Edward's acclaimed self-control is but another manifestation of normative patriarchal gender roles. It offers a continual threat of carefully restrained violence against female victims. Anti-fans critique that restraint as emasculating without interrogating patriarchal gender roles predicated upon violence. Yet when anti-fans critique Edward Cullen's potential for violence, they also fail to recognize that without that self-control, Edward's described actions would match or exceed the violence of any vampire in horror genres. Despite repeated criticism of emasculated, "defanged," vegetarian vampires, the *Twilight* franchise's detractors ultimately construct Edward as perpetuating normative constructions of vampires as violent and hypersexualized.

## CONCLUSION

Anti-fans' discourse creates false dichotomies between "real," violent, hypersexualized vampires and their fans, and the *Twilight* franchise's sparkly emasculated version of vampires and their fans. Unfortunately, it quickly becomes apparent that anti-fans' own discourse collapses each of these categories.

First, anti-fans' Othering of *Twilight* fans recapitulates mainstream negative representations of fandom in general as hysterical, passive, feminized, cultural dupes. Anti-fans justify this Othering as protection of both "real" vampires and horror genres from the threat of contamination by *Twilight* and its Othered adolescent female fans. Anti-fans and the scholars, critics, and reviewers who support their opinions of the *Twilight* franchise assume paternalistic roles, positioning their taste, culture, and interpretation as superior to *Twilight* fans' inferior versions. However, such scapegoating of *Twilight* fans functions as a means to distance one's own fandom from a fandom perceived as even more hysterical, passive, feminized, and duped. Such discursive strategies ultimately attempt to establish one's own fandom as more credible and respectable than the Other's exaggerated extremes.

Second, anti-fans emasculate Edward Cullen, ignoring evidence of the character's violence and hypersexuality, which would position him within anti-fans' own constructions of the categories of "real" vampires and horror genres. Furthermore, they fail to question patriarchal gender roles predicated upon violence when they idealize "real" vampires, such as Dracula, who exhibit such behaviors. This is ironic considering anti-fans also acknowledge Edward's violence and hypersexuality but only in order to construct *Twilight* fans as confusing these behaviors for romance and thus as accepting abusive patriarchal ideology without question.

Anti-fans thus position Edward Cullen's violence and hypersexuality as evidence of *Twilight* fans' status as cultural dupes. For example, in the *Twilight* franchise's novels and films, Edward behaves like an abusive partner. Anti-fans construct fans as accepting these behaviors as demonstrating his love for Bella. He takes care of her and watches over her. Women still appear as property in need of protection by a more powerful male. According to such ideology, males control females, often through violence or the threat of violence. Meanwhile anti-fans' supposed superior taste, culture, and interpretative skills renders them immune to such messages. They cannot be duped as easily as their Othered opposites. However, both of these contrasting approaches to violence and hypersexuality ultimately reinforce patriarchal ideology, rendering anti-fans' claims of immunity and superiority both problematic and dubious.

# REFERENCES

Adair, Margot. 1992. "Will the Real Men's Movement Please Stand Up?" In *Women Respond to the Men's Movement: A Feminist Collection*, ed. Kay Leigh Hagan, 55–66. San Francisco: HarperSanFrancisco.

Arata, Stephen D. 1990. "The Occidental Tourist: *Dracula* and the Anxiety of Reverse Colonization." *Victorian Studies* 33 (4): 621–45.

Bode, Lisa. 2010. "Transitional Tastes: Teen Girls and Genre in the Critical Reception of *Twilight*." *Continuum* 24 (5): 707–19.

Borgia, Danielle N. 2011. "*Twilight*: The Glamorization of Abuse, Codependency, and White Privilege." *Journal of Popular Culture*, early view (September 21): 1–21. doi: 10.1111/j.1540-5931.2011.00872.x.

Craft, Christopher. 1984. "'Kiss Me with Those Red Lips': Gender and Inversion in Bram Stoker's *Dracula*." *Representations* 8 (1): 107–33.

Dalfonzo, Gina R. 2008. "In Love with Death: The *Twilight* of American Fiction." *National Review Online*, August 22. Accessed October 23, 2009. http://article.nationalreview.com/print/?q=MTE4OTNmNzcxNDAzMTI3MTk5MWFkZTllNDQzZmZlNDA=.

Edwards, Kim. 2009. "Good Looks and Sex Symbols: The Power of the Gaze and the Displacement of the Erotic in *Twilight*." *Screen Education* 53:26–32.

Gibson, Brian. 2008. "*Twilight*." *Vue Weekly*, November 27. Accessed October 23, 2009. http://www.vueweekly.com/article.php?id=10385.

Gray, Jonathan. 2003. "New Audiences, New Textualities: Anti-Fans and Non-Fans." *International Journal of Cultural Studies* 6 (1): 64–81.

Harris, Misty. 2009. "All Lark, No Bite." *National Post*, August 23. Accessed August 23, 2009.http://www.nationalpost.com/arts/story.html?id=1900403.

Hendrix, Grady. 2009. "Vampires Suck: Actually, They Don't. And That's the Problem." *Slate*, July 28. Accessed August 4, 2009. http://www.slate.com/id/2223486/.

Jenson, Joli. 1992. "Fandom as Pathology: The Consequences of Characterization." In *The Adoring Audience: Fan Culture and Popular Media*, ed. Lisa A. Lewis, 9–29. London: Routledge.

Johnson, Derek. 2007. "Fan-Tagonism: Factions, Institutions, and Constitutive Hegemonies of Fandom." In *Fandom: Identities and Communities in a Mediated World*, ed. Jonathan Gray, Cornel Sandvoss, and C. Lee Carrington, 285–300. New York: New York University Press.

Meyer, Stephenie. 2005. *Twilight*. New York: Little, Brown.

———. 2008. *Midnight Sun: Edward's Story*, August 28. Accessed January 25, 2010.http://stepheniemeyer.com/pdf/midnightsun_chapter1.pdf.

OffWorld Designs. 2009. "Edward and Bela T-Shirt." Accessed October 21, 2012. http://www.offworlddesigns.com/p-519-zz-edward-bela-t-shirt.aspx.

Seifert, Christine. 2009. "Bite Me! (Or Don't)." *Bitch: Feminist Response to Pop Culture* 42:23–25.

Sheffield, Jessica, and Elyse Merlo. 2010. "Biting Back: *Twilight* Anti-Fandom and the Rhetoric of Superiority." In *Bitten by "Twilight": Youth Culture, Media, and the Vampire Franchise*, ed. Melissa A. Click, Jennifer Stevens Aubrey, and Elizabeth Behm-Morawitz, 207–24. New York: Peter Lang.

Sjöberg, Lore. 2002. "The Geek Hierarchy," The Brunching Shuttlecocks. Accessed July 21, 2012. http://www.brunching.com.

Theodoropoulou, Vivi. 2007. "The Anti-Fan within the Fan: Awe and Envy in Sport Fandom." In *Fandom: Identities and Communities in a Mediated World*, ed. Jonathan Gray, Cornel Sandvoss, and C. Lee Carrington, 285–300. New York: New York University Press.

"*Twilight* vs. Vampire Lovers (Who Hate *Twilight*)?" 2010. Yahoo! Answers. Accessed February 13, 2011. http://answers.yahoo.com/question/index?qid=20100917215442AAfrz2N.

Vampire Barbie. 2009. *Men with Dolls*. August 15. Accessed August 26, 2009. http://menwithdolls.yuku.com/topic/8447?page=1.

VanAirsdale, S. T. 2009. "Is Harry Potter Emasculating America?" *Esquire*, July 15. Accessed November 2, 2009. http://www.esquire.com/the-side/hollywood/harry-potter-half-blood-prince-sex-071509.

*III*

# Characters and Their Cultural Referents

*Chapter Seven*

# Renesmee as (R)omantic Child

*A Glimpse into Bella and Edward's Fairy Tale Cottage*

## Lisa Nevárez

Team Jacob. Team Edward. Robsten. It is easy to become blinded by the "romance" of the *Twilight* saga, penned by Stephenie Meyer. After all, there are love affairs and moments of real intimacy between not only Bella and Edward but also between the other Cullen couples. This is not to mention the tension between Jacob and Bella, which so marks the series, both in the novels and films. The culminating novel, *Breaking Dawn* (2008), as well as the two films (2011, 2012) of it, are, in many ways, heartbreakingly "romantic." The first film begins with a fairy tale wedding, complete with a wooded setting and a ring belonging, touchingly, to Edward's mother. The second film, *Breaking Dawn Part 2*, released in the United States on November 16, 2012, and directed by Bill Condon, concludes with the latest Cullen couple returning to their cottage in the woods, which is decorated with books and pictures and soft lighting: it is a space of intimacy and love. This is the place, in front of the fire, where Edward and Bella for the first time tenderly make love as fellow vampires. Certainly, the films also depict moments of sheer passion as set forth in the novel, such as the shot of the absolutely destroyed bed following the consummation of Bella and Edward's marriage. A broken bed frame and feathers from a down pillow form the evidence of a passionate evening or, as Hila Shachar argues, a form of rape (Shachar 2011, 158). And, of course, that night of "love," depending upon one's view, results in Bella's pregnancy with a "dhampir" (half-human, half-vampire) child, Renesmee.

The "romance" of the series has been discussed widely. A quick recap of recent scholarly articles reveals as much. Colette Murphy discourses upon the fairy tale aspects of the series and deems Edward "chivalric" as "[he] includes many of the traditional traits of the fairy tale hero to which we are historically accustomed" (Murphy 2011, 58, 60). Edward, then, may be cast as not only a "prince charming" but also, as Ananya Mukherjea (2011) argues, as another type of "romantic" lead. She argues that the *Twilight* series fulfills the goals of other similarly "mass marketed romance novels," insofar as it "does provide ample fantasy and wish fulfillment for the involved reader" (75). The novel can provide not only a fairy-tale-esque nostalgia but also can serve as an outlet for the reader, a way of escaping the doldrums of everyday life.

In contrast and addition to the "small r" as in "romantic," one can find real gestures in the *Twilight* series of "capital R," "Romantic," related to the literary, social, and cultural movement in the late eighteenth through early nineteenth centuries.[1] This coexists with the "romance" of the series and, one can argue, complements the "romantic" passion and love by providing a degree of tension. Further, the character of Renesmee, who is the product of "romantic" love and a testament to its power, in fact provides the viewer and reader with a glimpse of the Romantic child. This conflation of Romantic and romantic, linked by the figure of Renesmee, offers a compelling perspective on *Breaking Dawn* and Meyer's crafting of a "new" vampire child. Finally, the viewer response to the cinematic *Breaking Dawn Part 2* offers an intriguing insight into the debate surrounding Renesmee.

## (R)OMANTICISM AND *TWILIGHT*

To begin at the beginning, with the *Twilight* novels, critics have pointed out Meyer's literary influences, which include William Shakespeare's *Romeo and Juliet*, Jane Austen's *Pride and Prejudice*, Charlotte Brontë's *Jane Eyre*, and Emily Brontë's *Wuthering Heights*. Further, Meyer herself, who holds a BA in English from Brigham Young University, has said that these texts inform the series; as she states on her website, http://www.stepheniemeyer.com, under "The Story Behind *Twilight*," the name "Edward" is derived from Edward Ferrars from Austen's *Sense and Sensibility* and Edward Rochester from *Jane Eyre*. In fact, *Twilight* follows *Pride and Prejudice*; *New Moon*, *Romeo and Juliet*; and *Eclipse*, *Wuthering Heights*. As Sarah Wakefield argues in her essay comparing the *Twilight* series to *Wuthering Heights*, Edward can be seen as functioning as an Edgar Linton figure and Jacob as a Heathcliff figure (Wakefield 2011, 117).

Critics Kate Cochran (2010), Jessica Groper (2011), and Abigail Myers (2009) have compared Edward to the emblematic Byronic hero that, obviously, earned its appellation from Lord Byron, Romantic author.[2] The Byronic hero, which originated in *Childe Harold's Pilgrimage* and is particularly evident in *Manfred*, is a brooding man who meditates on mortality and summons intense emotions upon visiting certain locales. For example, when

Childe Harold pays his respects to the Colosseum in Rome, he reflects upon the noble suffering of the gladiators who combated there, in canto 4 of the poem.[3] This comparison segues to the later Victorian Byronic figures, such as the aforementioned Heathcliff, and even to *Twilight* as a Gothic novel, as discussed separately by Anne Morey (2012) and Kristine Moruzi (2012).

With the Byronic hero as the starting point for a conversation about Romanticism, one then becomes aware of other Romantic themes emerging in the *Twilight* saga. Given Meyer's evident grounding in the British literary tradition, a conversation about Romanticism includes works by William Blake ("The Chimney Sweeper" from *Songs of Innocence* in 1789 and from *Songs of Experience* in 1794) and William Wordsworth ("We Are Seven" from *Lyrical Ballads* in 1798), and unfolds with the themes of Nature, the sublime, and the child.

One of the noteworthy presences in the text, but more so in the cinematic versions, of the *Twilight* saga is the abovementioned Nature, which merits a capital "N." From the first *Twilight* film with the pivotal moment when the Cullen clan and Bella play baseball and James, Victoria, and Laurent discover them amid lightning, thunder, and blowing wind to the sparkling—literally—beauty of the couple Bella and Edward in his favorite meadow, Nature is a presence. Nature appears in the lush landscape of the Pacific Northwest. Going beyond the striking natural imagery, though, is a frisson of danger, the edge of something "else." A prime example can be seen in *Breaking Dawn Part 2*. When Bella is newly transformed and is out for her first hunt, she espies a rock climber, precariously making his way along a sheer rock wall. This is a revision from the novel, where Bella only scents a human but does not see her/him. As the film version depicts, here too Bella is able to control a thirst for human blood to focus on animal blood. Bella is in the throes of the passion arising from the hunt: "My one goal was to run far enough away that the scent behind me would be completely lost. Impossible to find, even if I changed my mind. . . . Once again, I was aware of being followed, but I was sane this time" (Meyer 2012, 418; Meyer's ellipses).

Even though she is wracked by powerful hunger/thirst pains due to her recent conversion to vampirism, Bella does not attack the climber, but there is the question: would she? The camera cuts repeatedly from the climber to the deer she is stalking and finally to the mountain lion she takes down. The climber is in danger of falling at any moment, and in fact, he loses traction while climbing. This scene in the film does much to underscore Bella's newfound physical strength and stalwart moral will, when she resists this tempting morsel of blood that literally dangles in front of her. The audience familiar with the novel realizes that Bella does not attack humans, yet this is still a thrilling moment, both seeing the climber falter and seeing Bella struggle before both are saved.

Much of this scene—and there are others—hearkens back to the sublime moments that so mark much of Romantic literature. In fact, the abovementioned scene is reminiscent of William Wordsworth's recollection of climbing the cliffs in *The Prelude* (1798–1799, book 1), in one of his "spots of time," or recollections of his youth:

> Oh, when I have hung
> Above the raven's nest, by knots of grass,
> Or half-inch fissures in the slipp'ry rock,
> But ill sustained, and almost, as it seemed,
> Suspended by the blast which blew amain,
> Shouldering the naked crag, oh at that time,
> While on the perilous ridge I hung alone,
> With what strange utterance did the loud dry wind
> Blow through my ears! The sky seemed not a sky
> Of earth, and with what motion moved the clouds!
> (Wordsworth 1979, lines 57–66)

This "edge" in Nature, literally climbing on the "edge" of a cliff, can translate to the sublime or a feeling of intense emotion when confronted by the power of Nature, such as looming mountains or a deep abyss.[4]

With this similar daring in Nature and the discussion surrounding the Byronic hero, one can only continue this quest for Romantic themes in the novel *Breaking Dawn* and in the film *Breaking Dawn Part 2*. And one emerges with startling clarity, when viewed through this lens: Renesmee. The Romantic child, the one who coexists with sublimity and the Byronic hero, is a charged figure, one who combines childhood innocence with an adult's knowledge. To illustrate this, one can turn to the unnamed girl from Wordsworth's "We Are Seven" and Blake's also unnamed chimney sweeps. Wordsworth and Blake present entirely different settings for their poems, which leads to their appropriateness for a comparison to Renesmee.

Blake's male chimney sweep from *Songs of Innocence*, who lisps as a child might, shares his life's story, with his mother's death, his father selling him into the chimney sweep profession, and the truly sad dream, as told via the narrator, of Tom Dacre, who is the "lamb" who is shorn: "There's little Tom Dacre, who cried when his head, / That curled like a lamb's back, was shaved: so I said, / 'Hush, Tom! never mind it, for when your head's bare, / You know that the soot cannot spoil your white hair'" (Blake 1997, lines 5–8). The sweep from *Songs of Experience* shares this awareness of a world beyond him, but tenfold. This sweep is interrogated by a nameless individual who inquires, "'Where are thy father and mother? Say!'—" (line 3). The boy's mysterious answer is that his mother and father: "'They are both gone up to the church to pray'" (line 4). These two boys, placed in urban settings, evince the prescient child, who is aware of the weight of the world. They are torn from families and Nature and placed in the city as poverty-stricken, urchin workers.

Wordsworth's girl from "We Are Seven" in *Lyrical Ballads* is similarly a figure of the narrator and reader's pity. Again, a nameless visitor asks a little girl where her family is, and while two are at sea and two are at Conway, a nearby city, she shares that two others have died. Here, a rural setting leads to a different type of interaction—this girl, after all, has not been indentured or handed over into the sweep life—but she similarly displays stalwart forthrightness. She says, quite directly, that two of her siblings are dead: Jane dies from illness, and John dies an unspecified death. However, the girl indicates that they are, in fact, still with her at least in spirit by her insistence on the title "we *are* seven" (my emphasis). The distinct settings hearken to the different styles of Blake and Wordsworth, but key among them is the celebration of the child as a figure of knowledge and adult wariness.

## RENESMEE AS A ROMANTIC CHILD

Transitioning from these two figures, one can see Renesmee as similarly balancing between the innocent child and the startlingly mature one, without even the mind of an infant. Even from the beginning of *Breaking Dawn Part 2*, when she appears as a cooing child (who has been digitally altered), and reaches out to touch Bella's face and transmit her "memory" of Bella's labor, she is already painfully grown up. And it continues: Renesmee is a hyperaware child, who is clearly in tune with the complexities of the world she inhabits. As Ashley Benning points out, Renesmee is "almost a peer to her aunts and uncles as she learns to communicate and understands more about her place in the strange world of immortals" (Benning 2011, 93–94). Even when entering Charlie Swan's home for Christmas in the film version, Renesmee exhibits subdued excitement and is more adult-like. Contributing to this may be the fact that the actress who plays Renesmee, Mackenzie Foy, was older than the fictional Renesmee.

Another example: Bella, Edward, and Jacob journey to Denali, to meet the vampire "cousins." As Bella explains the gravity of the situation, Renesmee looks at her with a calm demeanor and emerges from her car seat to confront the as-yet nonbelieving vampires. Those vampires, posed against a snowy landscape in beige, white, and natural-colored outfits, are almost camouflaged in the scenery. In contrast, Renesmee wears a more colorful outfit, leading to Natalie Wilson's observation that Renesmee and her wardrobe are a "consumer culture's dream female, needing new clothes constantly" (Wilson 2011, 188). In addition to her outfit, Renesemee with her rosy cheeks serves as a visual reminder that she is different, even as she demonstrates her hybrid nature by extending her hand to transmit her gift of sharing her memories and thoughts.

Renesmee's otherworldly talent and adult calm deem her an unknown factor; her immediate vampire family does not know what to make of her, and they extensively document and research her existence. She is, as Ashley Donnelly points out,

> a threat to others . . . by her very existence. Renesmee is the first character on the side of "good" in the series that has the potential to cross boundaries. She is half human, half vampire and proves to be, though endearing and loving, monstrous in her unabashed desire for blood. Though her family loves her, she is dangerous and unstable, and no one is completely convinced that she will not continue to be a liability. (Donnelly 2011, 190)

Donnelly continues by observing that "things are safer" when "boundaries are not crossed, reiterating the need for heteronormative, patriarchal control" (190). Renesmee is an unknown but, I would argue, more preternaturally aware along the lines of the Romantic child instead of a "liability," even though she does bring the wrath of the Volturi upon her family. Still, Donnelly's point is well taken: in a novel and series that emphasize heterosexual relationships and those among members of the same "kind" (e.g., vampire–vampire), Renesmee in her dual nature is a mystery as she literally does not fit.

Time and again in the novel and in the film, Renesmee and her otherworldly knowledge are juxtaposed against intense Nature imagery, such as in the Denali scene. In the novel, for instance, Meyer places her in a fading autumnal field setting during a pivotal moment, when Irina espies Renesmee chasing snowflakes, hunting, and playing with Jacob, who is in his wolf form. The film emphasizes Renesmee's vampiric half by depicting her floating in the air. Irina mistakes her, then, for a true—and forbidden—vampire child, not a hybrid as she is. The viewer's knowledge that Irina takes that knowledge somewhere ruptures this playful scene. As Bella immediately concludes, something is wrong, as she rushes to defend her child: "Running at full speed, it only took me two seconds to reach them . . . 'I'm overreacting,' I assured them quickly. 'It's okay. I think. Hold on'" (Meyer 2012, 538). As the viewer—and reader—are made aware, Irina informs the Volturi, and the action commences.

In contrast to the scene with Irina, from the Denali meeting onward, the rest of the film is set in a snowy landscape following Alice's prediction that when the snow begins to stick, the Cullens and their friends will face their nemesis. The battle scene in *Breaking Dawn Part 2*, replayed as a "what if" scenario, which differs radically from the events in the novel, depicts intense fighting and bloodshed, with heads being ripped off and much screaming and carnage. Renesmee, prior to the fighting, touches Aro's cheek, and there is a tense moment when she must summon her maturity and talent to combat this lethal male adult vampire.

Following the commencement of the battle and the awareness that things are turning into a blood(less) bath, Jacob, transformed into a wolf, flees the scene. Renesmee rides on his back, her backpack with cash and passports firmly attached.[5] They race through the hills, combating vampires along the way, and the snow-covered forest whips by. This snowy scene underscores the contrast between the life-affirming and half-human Renesmee, the glimpse of the future, clutching the wolf, in a frigid, barren setting. She is oddly in control, even as she rides on Jacob's back, as she is fully aware of the gravity of the situation and flees for her life. Her glances back at their pursuers are not ones of panic. While she is clearly alarmed and frightened, she remains focused on the task at hand: staying with Jacob.

Mackenzie Foy, as mentioned previously, plays this cinematic Renesmee, who, as alluded to earlier, is a lovely girl, with flowing auburn curls and pale cheeks touched with roses. Renesmee looks innocent but by remaining as static a character as she does—she seldom speaks and instead transmits her sentiments by touch—she does not act like a child, by any means. Her pale hand caresses a cheek as she shares her vision without language: she is beyond any reliance on words. The audience response to this film-version Romantic child has been largely positive, yet with a degree of debate. Some critics have decried the digital altering of Renesmee as a baby and later as a "teenager," and the *New York Times*' Manohla Dargis writes, "Not only does she [Renesmee] look as creepy as the baby Brad Pitt in *The Curious Case of Benjamin Button*, she's sprouting as fast as a magical beanstalk and, worse yet, has attracted the attention of the Volturi, a vampire coven in Italy with papal-like authority" (Dargis 2012). Nevertheless, Dargis gives the film a highly positive review, stating, "Despite the slow start Mr. Condon closes the series in fine, smooth style." Diane (no surname provided) on the site *Comic Hero News* more candidly observes, "Holy Crap CGI. Renesmee might be the creepiest baby/child I have ever seen done in a movie. *Toy Story* had a more realistic baby in it than this movie and that is an animated movie. Now the wolves and such looked decent, about the same level as before but hands down the baby just took a person right out of the movie it was that bad" (Diane 2012).

This sentiment is echoed in Giles Hardie's review from the site Stuff (New Zealand) in "Ten Things Wrong with *Twilight*":

> Stephenie Meyer is said to have feared the final book in the *Twilight* saga could never be made because digital technology would have to improve in order to portray the infant Renesmee as she intended. Well, she can rest easy, baby Nessy (and yes we'll get to that nickname) was a visual success—assuming the goal was to portray her as a freakish looking digital reject from Titan

AE. That baby is the first truly terrifying creature in these five films, looking neither human nor half-mortal, just like an early demonstration of what Peter Jackson was trying to avoid with Gollum. The moment where Bella met Renesmee was far more precious (MY precious) than maternal and almost explained why Bella had all the maternal instincts of a park bench. Then there was that end scene with the older Renesmee wandering with the Twilight trio on the beach. Somehow she looked digital there too. Perhaps that's what you get when two one dimensional characters breed. (Hardie 2012)

Hardie, Dargis, and Diane respond powerfully to the digitized Renesmee, underscoring the creepiness of her character. In this sense, Renesmee captures a horrified reaction, but that is not due to any scare tactics on her part; viewers resist the technological rendering of the character. Nevertheless, the digitizing of Renesmee may distract some viewers from fully embracing the character and can potentially complicate her cinematic presentation as a child of Nature.

Yet another component of the reception of the cinematic Renesmee lies in the casting of Mackenzie Foy as the young Renesmee. While the reaction to Foy's portrayal of Renesmee is mostly positive, the *Twilight* fan community, especially that at http://www.twilightsaga.wikia.com, is still engaging in debate about that casting.[6] Renesmee is a beloved character by the *Twilight* fan community and, for example, is celebrated through a fan-made slide show of the Swan-Cullen family (see http://www.twilightsaga.wikia.com). In addition, one can peruse various online fan fiction stories featuring Renesmee. These present extended scenarios and interior monologues of the character and create future story lines.[7]

The number of *Twilight* fan sites abound. Meyer's official website contains a listing of numbers of them: http://www.stepheniemeyer.com/ts_ fansites.html. The site http://www.twilightsaga.wikia.com is particularly accessible (it is not password-protected, as are some sites' discussion boards) and active. Under the thread "Renesmee Cullen" created on October 12, 2010, as of December 26, 2012 at 9:15 a.m. EST, there were 4,217 posts. They range from the above mentioned debate about casting and digitizing to other praise (or denigration, at times) for Renesmee/Foy. On November 26, 2011, "Vampirefairy4" in fact writes, perhaps with humor, "im soo naming my next american girl doll renesmee! team edward."

## VAMPIRE TRADITION, HYBRIDITY, AND THE FUTURE

Given this largely positive reaction, and the coupling of Renesmee with a Romantic tradition, one can only ponder what this new direction for vampires holds. Renesmee is strikingly different from other vampire children, such as the child vampires from Stephen King's *Salem's Lot* (1975), Claudia, from Anne Rice's *Interview with the Vampire* (1976), or even Eli from John Ajvide Lindqvist's *Let the Right One In* (2004). Each of the above vampires is a figure of horror: they drink blood and engage in violent acts against humans and, in some cases as with Claudia, against their fellow vampires. Renesmee is barely related to these other child vampires. She enjoys drinking human blood—as a fetus she thrived on it when transmitted through Bella's intake of donor blood—but can exist on human food and animal blood. Of course, she is a Cullen child and, by extension, is part of a family, and series, where vampires are not grotesque creatures hearkening back to Bram Stoker's *Dracula* (1897), who looks quite demon-like: "His eyebrows were very massive, almost meeting over the nose, and with bushy hair that seemed to curl in its own profusion. The mouth, so far as I could see it under the heavy moustache, was fixed and rather cruel-looking, with peculiarly sharp white teeth" (Stoker 1997, 23). The *Twilight* vampires, Renesmee in particular, nowhere near resemble their vampire ancestor.

Since the *Twilight* vampires do not look to the past, I read their outlook on the future as positive, with Renesmee and Nahuel, the half-human, half-vampire children. In this fusion of human-vampire, Meyer has indeed crafted a startlingly innovative creature, one who is not only a hybrid but also a biracial and multicultural character, as is Jacob. As Alexandra Hidalgo argues, "It is the hybrids, the mixed, multicultural beings, who in the end have the easiest time adapting" (Hidalgo 2012, 85). If Renesmee and Nahuel lack the viciousness of previous vampire children and are harbingers of a more multicultural world, they are yet not entirely human in their behavior nor in their biological makeup. Renesmee and Nahuel are slow to age and, it seems, will remain as teenagers for many, many years to come. In fact, as Lindsey Issow Averill points out, Renesmee is presumably unable to give birth and, in so doing, is in fact at odds with the female's "power" and is thus "subordinate" to the male's power (Averill 2011, 234). Even that, though, remains a mystery.

The future is an unknown, but Nahuel, literally, shrugs off that concern in his dialogue with Aro: "[Aro asks] And you reached maturity at what age?' 'About seven years after my birth, more or less, I was full grown.' 'You have not changed since then?' Nahuel shrugged. 'Not that I've noticed'" (Meyer 2012, 736). Renesmee and, to an extent, Nahuel, who makes a relatively brief appearance in the novel and even less in the film version, then fuse vampire nature with human traits. In *Breaking Dawn Part 2*, Nahuel only appears at the very conclusion of the film, and speaks very little, whereas in the novel, he supplies his more extensive personal and family history.

Focusing on Renesmee, this combination results in a child who looks like a child and can do childish things but who contains a very adult nature. It is unclear if her talent at transmitting her thoughts and memories directly results in her seeming more mature than her years, or if something peculiar about her hybridity has matured her. Or, for that matter, one can take a longer perspective on Renesmee and see her as a child who has experienced real trauma, not unlike the Romantic children of Blake and Wordsworth. Furthermore, generally speaking, an adult is cognizant of the complexity surrounding the welcoming of a new child. In this case with Renesmee, her complete understanding of this changed world, which is of course utterly different with a human child, is unnerving.

The gestation and birth of these children is another matter, however. Meyer's creation of a method by which a male vampire can impregnate a human female has raised some eyebrows; after all, in traditional vampire lore, the vampire cannot birth or create a child because s/he is dead. These fetuses are bloodthirsty, quite literally, and can do damage or kill their human mother. Bella, after all, dies during the improvised cesarean section birth of Renesmee; only Edward's venom, plunged into her heart via needle, "saves" Bella by virtue of turning her into a vampire. True, Renesmee has everything a little girl could wish for: loving parents, a devoted extended family, shelter, and food, and books, toys, and music surround her. Underneath all this, however, Renesmee has endured a significant amount of trauma. Her birth was a violent one, as she clawed her way from the womb, and the last memory she has of Bella, prior to meeting her after Bella's conversion, is of an emaciated woman, who is clearly suffering. As Rachel DuBois points out, the entire birth scene inflicts trauma upon Bella and the reader (DuBois 2012, 140). One can extend this line of thinking, though, to read Renesmee's memory of a dying Bella as signifying what would be a moment of trauma for any human, vampire, human-vampire: witnessing the death of the mother.

While she is well taken care of by the Cullens and Jacob, and even by Charlie, prior to Irina's sighting of her, Renesmee is aware of family tension resulting from that event. Her "aunt" and "uncle," Alice and Jasper, leave the family suddenly; we later learn this is for Renesmee's protection and to search for answers to the conundrum at hand. In the aforementioned Denali scene, Renesmee is brought in and used to prove what is happening, and provide a means of garnering vampire support or "witnesses." And as the novel draws to a close and midway through the film, Renesmee endures a true test as she comes face-to-face with the lethal Aro and shows him her skill. In the novel, the tension between the Cullens, and their supporters, and the Volturi rather quickly dissipates at the conclusion, whereas in the film, the events of the flashback show Renesmee seeing at least a portion of the carnage. And, she must escape on the back of a wolf, seeing her family slaughtered and slaughtering. In this sense, one can see a nod to a version of "Little Red Riding Hood" and a girl's relationship with a wolf. As argued by Angela Tenga, in fact, "Little Red Riding Hood" and its emphasis on the sexually naive young woman ties in to Bella (Tenga 2011, 108). I would push this analogy further; one can see, in her daughter, an even further tie to the wolf via Jacob's "imprinting" upon Renesmee.

Are we perhaps ready to embrace a new, updated version of a Romantic child? After all, she is tucked into her bed in a romantic cottage but even then lies down as an oddly grown up child. She stands in contrast to more obvious Romantic or "natural" children, namely Nahuel, who exists as an indigenous individual, complete with his native garb. This may be why she flies under the radar and these Romantic tendencies perhaps remain more subtle. As the fan responses attest, Renesmee forms the focus of much debate and discussion, and she, and Bella, who are locked in an embrace with Renesmee gazing up at her mother while Bella looks out at the reader, even grace the cover of the movie tie-in of the novel, published in September 2012 (Meyer 2012). "Romance" abounds in the series, but alongside it exists an entirely different kind of "Romantic" imagery. No matter which team one takes, be it Team Jacob, Team Edward, or, even, Rob versus Kristen, one need only to peek inside the fairy-tale cottage to see someone truly unnerving and who forms her own one-person "team": Renesmee.

## NOTES

1. There existed different permutations of Romanticism across the globe, ranging in date from the late eighteenth century to the end of the nineteenth century. The British tradition, which speaks more directly to Meyer's literary influences, begins (debatably) circa 1789 with the French Revolution and the publication of William Blake's *Songs of Innocence* or in 1798 with the publication of William Wordsworth and Samuel Taylor Coleridge's *Lyrical Ballads*. The above mentioned themes of Nature, the sublime, and the child, as well as an emphasis upon the individual and the imagination, marked the literary Romantic movement. The "big six" Romantic authors include: Wordsworth, Blake, and Coleridge, as well as Percy Bysshe Shelley, John Keats, and Lord Byron. One can add to this list Mary Wollstonecraft Shelley and Jane Austen, among others. British Romanticism drew to a close in 1832 with the passage of the First Reform Act, although the last major figure, Wordsworth, does not die until 1850.

2. Lord Byron (1788–1824) is renowned not only for his poetry, including *Childe Harold's Pilgrimage* (1812–1818), *Manfred* (1817), and *Don Juan* (1818–1824), but also his colorful life. Byron embarked upon numerous affairs and traveled extensively and interspersed these adventures with moments of intense sorrow and personal conflict. These range from his separation from his wife and daughter to his racking up of momentous debts. Byron's life culminated in his passion for the Greek movement for independence and resulted in his death from fever and (unnecessary) bloodletting in April 1824.

3. As numerous critics have observed, the Byronic hero particularly lends itself to the figure of the vampire. The first piece of short fiction on vampires in the English literary tradition, *The Vampyre*, was authored by Byron's personal physician, John Polidori. When *The Vampyre* first appeared in 1819 with an attribution to Lord Byron, the avid reading audience believed it to be a new piece by Byron, which he then emphatically denied. The figure of Lord Ruthven in *The Vampyre* is certainly a Byronic hero figure, one who emphasizes the "darkness" of this character type: he is, after all, the title "vampyre."

4. For classical, eighteenth-century discussions of the sublime and the beautiful, see Edmund Burke's *A Philosophical Enquiry into the Sublime and Beautiful* (1757), as well as Immanuel Kant's *Critique of Judgment* (1790). One can readily apply these theories to Wordsworth and works by other Romantic authors.

5. Natalie Wilson provides an interesting reading of the white privilege, as she reads it, in that backpack (p. 58); see her essay "Civilized Vampires versus Savage Werewolves" in *Bitten by "Twilight"* (ed. Melissa A. Click, Jennifer Stevens Aubrey, and Elizabeth Behm-Morawitz, New York: Peter Lang, 2010).

6. See, for instance, the discussion at the *Twilight* wiki site: http://twilightsaga.wikia.com/ wiki/User_blog:Vampirefairy4/Who_loves_renesmee%3F.

7. The FanFiction.net site contains quite a few Renesmee-based stories, including "Rising Sun" (http://www.fanfiction.net/s/5101600/1/Renesmee-Cullen-Rising-Sun) and "Clouded Moon" (http://www.fanfiction.net/s/5009063/1/Book-1-Renesmee-s-Life-Clouded-Moon).

# REFERENCES

Averill, Lindsey Issow. 2011. "Un-biting the Apple and Killing the Womb: Genesis, Gender, and Gynocide." *Theorizing "Twilight": Critical Essays on What's at Stake in a Post-Vampire World.* Ed. Maggie Parke and Natalie Wilson. Jefferson, NC: McFarland.

Benning, Ashley. 2011. "'How Old Are You?' Representations of Age in the *Saga.*" *Theorizing "Twilight": Critical Essays on What's at Stake in a Post-Vampire World.* Ed. Maggie Parke and Natalie Wilson. Jefferson, NC: McFarland.

Blake, William. 1997. *The Complete Poetry and Prose of William Blake.* Ed. David V. Erdman, Harold Bloom, and William Golding. New York: Anchor.

Cochran, Kate. 2010. "'An Old-Fashioned Gentleman'? Edward's Imaginary History." *"Twilight" and History.* Ed. Nancy R. Reagin. New Jersey: Wiley.

Dargis, Manohla. 2012. "Infusing the Bloodline with a Problem Child." *New York Times.* November 15. http://movies.nytimes.com/2012/11/16/movies/the-twilight-saga-breaking-dawn-part-2-ends-the-series.html?_r=0.

Diane. 2012. "Twilight: Breaking Dawn, Part 2 : Review." *Comic Hero News,* November 19. http://www.comicheronews.com/twilight-breaking-dawn-part-2-review/.

Donnelly, Ashley. 2011. "Denial and Salvation: *The Twilight Saga* and Heteronormative Patriarchy." *Theorizing "Twilight": Critical Essays on What's at Stake in a Post-Vampire World.* Ed. Maggie Parke and Natalie Wilson. Jefferson, NC: McFarland.

DuBois, Rachel. 2012. "Coming to a Violent End." *Genre, Reception, and Adaptation in the "Twilight" Series.* Ed. Anne Morey. Burlington, VT: Ashgate.

Groper, Jessica. 2011. "Rewriting the Byronic Hero." *Theorizing "Twilight": Critical Essays on What's at Stake in a Post-Vampire World.* Ed. Maggie Parke and Natalie Wilson. Jefferson, NC: McFarland.

Hardie, Giles. 2012. "Ten Things Wrong with *Twilight.*" *Stuff,* November 21, 2012. http://www.stuff.co.nz/entertainment/film/7978565/Ten-things-wrong-with-Twilight.

Hidalgo, Alexandra. 2012. "Bridges, Nodes, and Bare Life: Race in *The Twilight Saga.*" *Genre, Reception, and Adaptation in the "Twilight" Series.* Ed. Anne Morey. Burlington, VT: Ashgate.

Meyer, Stephenie. 2012. *Breaking Dawn.* New York: Little, Brown. (Orig. pub. 2008.)

Morey, Anne. 2012. "Famine for Food, Expectation for Content." *Genre, Reception, and Adaptation in the "Twilight" Series.* Ed. Anne Morey. Burlington, VT: Ashgate.

Moruzi, Kristine. 2012. "Postfeminist Fantasies." *Genre, Reception, and Adaptation in the "Twilight" Series.* Ed. Anne Morey. Burlington, VT: Ashgate.

Mukherjea, Ananya. 2011. "Team Bella: Fans Navigating Desire, Security, and Feminism." *Theorizing "Twilight": Critical Essays on What's at Stake in a Post-Vampire World.* Ed. Maggie Parke and Natalie Wilson. Jefferson, NC: McFarland.

Murphy, Colette. 2011. "Someday My *Vampire* Will Come? Society's (and the Media's) Lovesick Infatuation with Prince-Like Vampires." *Theorizing "Twilight": Critical Essays on What's at Stake in a Post-Vampire World.* Ed. Maggie Parke and Natalie Wilson. Jefferson, NC: McFarland.

Myers, Abigail E. 2009. "Edward Cullen and Bella Swan: Byronic and Feminist Heroes . . . Or Not." *"Twilight" and Philosophy.* Ed. Rebecca Housel and J. Jeremy Wisnewski. New Jersey: Wiley.

Shachar, Hila. 2011. "A Post-Feminist Romance: Love, Gender and Intertextuality in Stephenie Meyer's Saga." *Theorizing "Twilight": Critical Essays on What's at Stake in a Post-Vampire World.* Ed. Maggie Parke and Natalie Wilson. Jefferson, NC: McFarland.

Stoker, Bram. 1997. *Dracula.* Ed. Nina Auerbach and David J. Skal. New York: Norton.

Tenga, Angela. 2011. "Read Only as Directed: Psychology, Intertextuality, and Hyperrreality in the Series." *Theorizing "Twilight": Critical Essays on What's at Stake in a Post-Vampire World.* Ed. Maggie Parke and Natalie Wilson. Jefferson, NC: McFarland.

Wakefield, Sarah. 2011. "Torn between Two Lovers: *Twilight* Tames *Wuthering Heights.*" *Theorizing "Twilight": Critical Essays on What's at Stake in a Post-Vampire World.* Ed. Maggie Parke and Natalie Wilson. Jefferson, NC: McFarland.

Wilson, Natalie. 2011. *Seduced by "Twilight."* Jefferson, NC: McFarland.

Wordsworth, William. 1979. *The Prelude* (1799, 1805, 1850). Ed. M. H. Abrams, Stephen Gill, and Jonathan Wordsworth. New York: Norton.

Wordsworth, William, and Samuel Taylor Coleridge. 2007. *Lyrical Ballads.* New York: Penguin.

*Chapter Eight*

# Isabella Swan

*A Twenty-First-Century Victorian Heroine?*

## Gaïane Hanser

Many heroines of vampire romance are inscribed in third-wave feminism: they are smart and sexy yet able to fend for themselves; they are dangerous and independent enough to fight their own demons, both literally and figuratively, as illustrated by their relationships with supernatural creatures. They also refuse to be treated as sexual objects but embrace their sexuality. Clumsy, accident-prone Bella, however, differs from her contemporaries: she may be clever and self-reliant, but as a human in need for protection, she will never be a slayer. Her definition of herself, and, as a consequence, the image she offers her readers, is mainly shaped by her love for the male vampire hero, Edward Cullen. Our perception of her—weak or strong, dependant or self-reliant, antifeminist or feminist—can never be fully dissociated from the vampiric dimension of her story.

With the choice of Edward, born in 1901, as a love object, the novels bring echoes of the Victorian and Edwardian eras; the presence of vampire characters allows the inscription within the novels of traditional—at times, old-fashioned—values. According to Ananya Mukherjea (2011), this is one of the reasons for the lure of the modern vampire:

> Many of the vampire romances that have become so popular in the 21st century so far, especially the ones aimed at a young adult readership, present us with old-school gentleman-vampires who are, certainly, sensitive and evolved in some ways, but who also offer the security and stability of old-fashioned gentlemen that some readers may now crave without being able to clearly articulate that craving. . . . Such a yearning has to do with the contradictory and conflicted relationship that many women have to feminism and femininity. (11)

Without a doubt, "Edward is quite old fashioned this way," but the first person narration encourages readers to focus on Bella's reactions to the values he stands for. The figure of the vampire is a means for modern writers to explore the construction of femininity and the tensions between the expectations of twenty-first-century society and those conveyed by fairy tales or previous (mainly Victorian) literature or between social constructs and what women experience as individuals.

What makes the *Twilight* series stand out in contrast to other vampire novels is that Bella, although she drives a truck, uses the Internet, and works to save for college, is quite an old-fashioned heroine. As Stephenie Meyer (2007) says in *The Story behind the Writing of New Moon*: "We can't all be slayers," and Bella fends for herself in her own way. Yet Meyer's choices go deeper than simply creating a heroine without superpowers: she is the locus of most contradictions in the novels, especially as they concern the definition of femininity. Mariah Larsson and Ann Steiner (2011) signal the two contradictory readings her character allows:

> On the one hand, it is quite possible to read the novels as a story of traditional, anti-feminist values—puritan, conservative, and patriarchal, promoting abstinence and old-fashioned gendered roles. . . . On the other hand, a feminist reading of the novels is quite possible in which the focus would be on Bella's near exclusive role as narrator of the novels, and her determination and psychological strength. Neither reading does full justice to the composite character of modern popular culture. (17)

The coexistence of these two contradictory readings of Bella's personality illustrates the tensions between Meyer's desire to inscribe her in a twenty-first-century context and her own religious upbringing.

Bella hardly ever comments on her values, yet her behavior and the ways she relates her story bring to mind images that are reminiscent of traditional Edwardian and Victorian heroines. They are, however, adapted to fit her modern setting: at first sight, there is no doubt that she belongs in the twenty-first century. This chapter will focus on the tension and the partial meshing between these contradictory readings, and the way they question the construction of femininity, within the text as well as for the readers. It will first focus on Bella's relatability for twenty-first-century readers, before seeing how she is reminiscent of the Victorian ideal of the "Angel in the House." We will then study how, paradoxically, these Victorian virtues, so different from the slayer qualities of Bella's contemporary heroines, are at the very source of her empowerment. Finally, we will concentrate on the treatment of sexuality, as this is the most ambiguous aspect of her personality.

## BELLA: AN "EVERY GIRL" ANY FEMALE READER COULD RELATE TO

According to herself, the human Isabella Swan is "absolutely ordinary" (Meyer 2005, 184); this partly explains why female readers react so strongly to her. Stephenie Meyer describes her as an "every girl," and the way she is characterized gives little information about her likes and dislikes or her hobbies; she is mainly defined by her clumsiness, her interest in books, and, of course, her undying love for Edward. This neutrality makes her easy to relate to, especially as the first-person narration facilitates readers' identification.

Bella describes herself as "a freak," and comments that even her appearance differentiates her from other people:

> Physically, I'd never fit in anywhere. I *should* be tan, sporty, blond. . . . Facing my pallid reflection in the mirror, I was forced to admit that I was lying to myself. It wasn't just physically that I'd never fit in. (Meyer 2005, 9)

This passage conveys her feeling that she does not belong, but her being a brown-haired teenager with pale skin hardly seems to justify the use of the word "freak." Indeed, she comments on her first day of school: "They were two girls, one a porcelain-colored blonde, the other also pale, with light brown hair. At least my skin wouldn't be a standout here" (Meyer 2005, 13). Her later statements about herself are slightly qualified, and most readers may identify with her when she emphasizes her ordinariness. Her insistence on lack of beauty are echoic of Jane Eyre's evocations of her appearance:

> I ever wished to look as well as I could, and to please as much as my want of beauty would permit. I sometimes regretted that I was not handsomer. . . . I felt it a misfortune that I was so little, so pale, and had features so irregular and so marked. (Brontë 1847, 100)

Both heroines deplore their pale skin and lack of color, even before meeting the men whose eyes they want to please. Their beauty is later revealed by the eyes of the beholders; however, whereas Jane is described as plain by other characters, Bella's perception of herself seems to be misguided. Yet, even when she acknowledges the interest taken in her by boys in Forks, she attributes it to her recent arrival in town and her consequent novelty. She needs Edward's translation of the male gazes to understand their true meaning: "You don't see yourself very clearly, you know. . . . you didn't hear what every human male in this school was thinking on your first day" (Meyer 2005, 184). This can be read as a message of hope for all the women who relate to her: their lack of confidence in their appearance will be proven wrong when they find true love.

Bella's description of herself stands in contrast with those of other heroines of modern teenage vampire romance: in *The House of Night*, the human Zoey Redbird is marked with a sign that she has been chosen by the Goddess to become a vampire, so her appearance signals her as different (Cast and Cast 2009). In the *Vampire Diaries*, Elena Gilbert, even when she is still human, never doubts her looks:

> In that instant, Elena was aware that she was beautiful. It wasn't just the dress, or the way her hair was done. She was beautiful in herself: slender, imperial, a thing made of silk and inner fire. . . . She had never been so sure of her power. (Smith 1991, 70)

L. J. Smith's heroine remains confident, even when she faces the vampire she is attracted to, Stephan Salvador. On the contrary, Bella keeps measuring herself to the standards of perfection she attributes to the Cullens and especially Edward: "The contrast between the two of us was painful. He looked like a god. I looked very average, even for a human, almost shamefully plain" (Meyer 2006, 65). Her concerns only stop after she has been turned:

> My first reaction was unthinking pleasure. The alien creature in the glass was indisputably beautiful . . . . All the while I studied and reacted, her face was perfectly composed, a carving of a goddess, showing nothing of the turmoil rolling inside me. (Meyer 2008, 403)

Bella's new assessment of her physical appearance is reminiscent of Elena's (they are characterized by the same inner glowing) but also of her perception of Edward—she has reached the same divine perfection. It does, however, require some adjusting: she uses the third person, and her now marble-like face does not reflect her interiority. This could be perceived as her receiving the gift of seeing herself for the first time as others see her, but this reading is invalidated by the fact that she has a new vampiric appearance. This passage seems to convey how difficult it is for her to reconcile her new image and her sense of self; her new body contrasts with her constant insistence on her plainness, and only vampirism can breach the gap between imperfection and perfection.

When it comes to her personality or her physical appearance, Bella is literally defined by love. Whereas most teenage vampire romances are coming of age stories, where heroines must understand who they really are, Bella knows from the start that her identity and her future are shaped by Edward:

> About three things I was absolutely positive. First, Edward was a vampire. Second, there was part of him—and I didn't know how potent that part might be—that thirsted for my blood. And third, I was unconditionally and irrevocably in love with him. (Meyer 2005, 171)

All subsequent events stem from these three axioms, including her decision to become a vampire to remain forever in love with him. True love is her ultimate quest, and marriage is the last step before she is linked to the man she loves for all eternity. Even their wedding ceremony calls for readerly identification: "Our vows were the simple, traditional words that had been spoken a million times, though never by a couple quite like us" (Meyer 2008, 49). The importance of the love story in the saga explains its popularity: as the texts offers identification between the narrator and the readers, the latter are offered a space where they can escape from daily life troubles. Moreover, Bella's seminal decision to be with Edward forever offers another appeal to the readers. Tanya Erzen (2012) explains that women are weary to live in a society dominated by the logic of empowerment through choice, which she calls "an illusion of postfeminism," leading women to believe that they can decide to be or do anything, independently from their social or economical circumstances:

> I was struck by how many girls I encountered, both at *Twilight* events and in my survey, who admitted to being weary of making decisions. Exhausted by being in charge, they expressed a craving to have someone else—specifically a boy—do it. . . . Bella's life boils down to the question of how she can be with Edward forever. Although she is presented with choices, it is always clear that, in her case, love trumps everything else. (Erzen 2012, 12–13)

Bella questions her right to choose when she first understands that Edward is a vampire: "I didn't know if there ever was a choice, really" (Meyer 2005, 121). Even when she decides to become a vampire to live with him for eternity, he remains in charge when it comes to choosing who will turn her and when it will happen. Thanks to the various devices facilitating readerly identification, the readers are enabled to feel temporary relief in the identification with a heroine who is freed from making decisions.

## BETWEEN MODERN HEROINE AND VICTORIAN ANGEL IN THE HOUSE

Most of modern vampire romances heroines are cheeky, mouthy, and independent women: Buffy Summers (*Buffy the Vampire Slayer*), Elena Gilbert (*Vampire Diaries*), Sookie Stackhouse (*The Southern Vampire Mysteries*), Anita Blake (*Anita Blake: Vampire Hunter*) all share these characteristics. Bella, on the contrary, is shy and self-conscious to the extreme. On her first day at her new high school, she does her best not to be noticed: "I kept my faced pulled back into my hood as I walked to the sidewalk, crowded with teenagers. My plain black jacket didn't stand out, I noticed with relief" (Meyer 2005, 13). This first reads as mere teenager awkwardness; Zoey

Redbird, for instance, expresses the same fear upon her arrival at the House of Night. Bella's self-consciousness is made fun of by Edward when she prepares to meet the Cullens for the first time: "And you're worried, not because you're headed to meet a houseful of vampires, but because you think those vampires won't approve of you, correct?" (Meyer 2005, 280). Her fear of being inadequate is exacerbated by the Cullens' perfection, so much so that she forgets that, if the Cullens represent a threat to her, it is because they are vampires, not because they may judge her. This desire to remain discreet and proper makes her more akin to Victorian heroines than to her contemporaries; she resembles the Victorian ideal of the "Angel in the House" as it was defined by Coventry Patmore's poems, the perfect (and fictional) woman whose virtues every girl should strive to emulate. This ideal woman was:

> intensely sympathetic. She was immensely charming. She was utterly unselfish. She excelled in the difficult arts of family life. She sacrificed herself daily. . . . She was so constituted that she never had a mind or a wish of her own, but preferred to sympathize always with the minds and wishes of others. Above all—I need not say it—she was pure. (Virginia Woolf, *A Profession for Women*)

Many aspects of Bella's personality find an echo in this definition, and her unselfishness and proneness to sacrifice inscribe her in the lineage of the Angel in the House. This is reinforced by her strong inscription in a patriarchal context, emphasized by Natalie Wilson (2011):

> Not only does Bella comply to the patriarchal rules of her fictional world, but so too are readers encouraged to comply with the message her character arc offers—you can be strong, smart, and capable, but you still need to be nice, you still need to look good, and you still need to marry and procreate. (67)

This is never directly stated in the text; however, Bella's actions, as well as her narration, tend to confirm it.

When she is not with (or dreaming of) Edward, Bella spends a lot of time doing the chores in her father's house. She takes charge of the cooking upon her arrival, then becomes responsible for the laundry and the cleaning. She jokes about Charlie's ability to survive without her and explains that the way they live is almost akin to independence: "In a lot of ways, living with Charlie was like having my own place" (Meyer 2005, 45–46). Taking care of the house is a way for her to keep busy, to avoid spending too much time thinking about Edward. However, more disturbing elements come to qualify Bella's statements that she never resents the situation. When she comes back from Italy in *New Moon*, she explains to Charlie: "I accept complete responsibility for my actions. . . . I will also do all the chores and laundry and dishes until you think I've learned my lesson" (Meyer 2006, 543). Thus, she equates doing the chores with being punished for her breaking the rules, which is surprising as these are things she does on a normal basis.

She also gives another explanation for her taking care of the house, which is more consistent with other elements of her personality: making life easier for her father. She puts herself in charge to alleviate his worries and make him feel better. She thus becomes the Angel in the House, according to the model offered by Coventry Patmore to Victorian young women: she makes the house a home for her father. Once she has proven herself, however, and become a vampire, she never needs doing the chores again: there is no need to cook or do the washing-up, and the Cullens are so rich that they never wear the same clothes twice. The disappearance of daily life troubles is enabled by the supernatural dimension; life as a vampire comes as a reward for becoming the perfect Angel in the House. The disappearance of daily life troubles facilitates the readers' full implication in the romance, which may explain why the films' directors have decided to downplay this aspect. The screen adaptations offer less insight into Bella's mind; the absence of Bella's first person narration to explain her reasons for doing chores would make it more difficult for a modern audience to identify with her.

Apart from her ability to make a house a home, Bella has other characteristics of the ideal Victorian lady, although they are presented in an unexpected fashion. One of Bella's main characteristics is the fact that Edward is unable to listen to her thoughts, which she presents as another failing on her part. Even though she sees it as a shortcoming, she is at times glad that Edward can't read her mind. She is too bad a liar to mask her feelings, yet she attempts to hide them to protect the people she loves from danger or grief. In this, she is reminiscent of Edwardian and Victorian heroines who try to remain unreadable to retain their modesty, as well as to preserve their loved ones: Charlotte Brontë's Shirley Keeldar, for instance, thinks she has been bitten by a morbid dog but refuses to burden anyone with her fear: "If you must tremble, tremble in secret! Quail where no eyes can see you" (Brontë 1849, 369). Jane Austen's Jane Bennet downplays her heartbreak after Bingley's departure, and numerous heroines use their veils when they are not in control of their emotions enough. That is exactly what Bella is doing when she leaves Florida to make her mother happy or why she blames herself for not putting up a better show in *Eclipse*. Bella's control of her emotions and her desire to protect the people she loves gradually become her greatest strength, making this Victorian heroine surprisingly suited for this modern world. This might find an echo for the readers, especially considering the emphasis put by the media on the *Twilight*ers' screams or fits of giggles and their incapacity to refrain their show of emotions (Steiner 2011, 202).

## PARADOXICAL FORMS OF EMPOWERMENT

Most heroines in vampire romances, be they for teenagers or adults, gradually gain physical strength or supernatural powers. Zoey Redbird is able to summon and master the five elements. Her powers develop over the novels, which is paralleled with the growing patterns of blue tattoos on her body, visible for all to see. These increasing abilities help define who the heroines are and give them power: Zoey is the first fledgling in history who controls the five elements, Sookie Stackhouse masters her telepathic powers and plays an important part in vampire politics, Anita Blake becomes an incredible necromancer, and Elena Gilbert turns into an angel. Some of them are so strong that their abilities reverse the balance of power when they face vampires; they are not preys or victims anymore but have become threats. Sophie Dabat explains: "Vampires have been deposed by petticoated Van Helsings who are not content with hunting them down, but are now decided to seduce them as well"[1] (Dabat 2010, 9, my translation). Buffy is the Slayer, Anita Blake is the Executioner, and both describe themselves as bogeymen the monsters have nightmares about—their wooden stakes are more than enough to face vampire fangs, and both have vampire boyfriends.

Bella, on the contrary, is weak as long as she remains human: she has to be protected against possible rapists, James, Victoria, the Volturi, and even herself. Edward comments on how "breakable" she is, and mocks her for requiring constant supervision. Tammy Dietz explains how Bella integrates this perception and casts herself in the role of the damsel in distress: "In *New Moon*, as Bella begins to purposefully put herself in danger in order to draw her love interest to the rescue, the reader begins to realize that she has fallen for the myth; in essence, she orchestrates her own imprisonment" (Dietz 2011, 108).

However, she gradually becomes able to turn her weakness into strength, even before she is changed. Her empowerment takes more discreet, unexpected ways, closer to her personality. Her readiness to sacrifice herself for the happiness of those she loves becomes stronger, and is emphasized by the possibilities offered by the supernatural dimension of her world. After leaving Florida, she agrees to put herself in danger to save her mother from James and save Edward from suicide and the Volturi. In *Eclipse*, she finds a role model in the Quileute legend of the third wife and her sacrifice. This tale resonates with Bella's conception of love: the third wife's sacrifice does not only save her people, it helps her sons grow into wolves—that is, into men. She is the character in the Quileute legends Bella can most easily relate to. In the book, she uses capital letters to evoke "the Cold Woman" but not for "the third wife." This reinforces the fact that nobody remembers her name because the act is more important than the person in the eyes of the tribe; it may also make her closer to a stereotypical character, which Bella herself could impersonate. Indeed, when they are attacked by Victoria and her army, this is the role she chooses to play:

> [Edward and Seth] needed help. A distraction. Something to give them an edge. . . . Was I strong enough? Was I brave enough? . . . Would this buy Seth time enough to get back on his feet? Would he heal fast enough for my sacrifice to do him any good? I raked the point of the shard up my arm, yanking my thick sweater back to expose the skin, and then pressed the sharp tip to the crease at my elbow. (Meyer 2007, 550)

Bella clearly associates her sacrifice with strength: behaving as the third wife (a Quileute variation on the Angel in the House) would enable her to literally save her loved ones and allow them to destroy their enemies. This changes when she finally becomes a vampire: as a newborn, she is even stronger than the other members of the Cullen family; she has now become as lethal and threatening as the other supernatural creatures in her life. However, her newly gained strength is an object of banter, mainly when she arm wrestles with Emmet, then lets off steam:

> Fascinated by the undeniable proof that I was stronger than the strongest vampire I'd ever known, I placed my hand, fingers spread wide, against the rock. Then I dug my fingers slowly into the stone, crushing rather than digging; the consistency reminded me of hard cheese. . . . I started giggling. I didn't pay much attention to the chuckles behind me while I punched and kicked the rest of the boulder into fragments. (Meyer 2008, 521)

Everybody in this passage is laughing because Bella's exhilaration is contagious, yet as her strength is never used for anything other than crushing rocks, it is hard not to hear a slightly derisive note in this laughter now that she finally is able to fend for herself. Because she is a newborn, she has to be taught and trained when they plan to fight the Volturi, and her physical strength is dismissed as an inefficient weapon.

Her real power as a vampire lies, as it did when she was human, in her ability to control herself. After regretting her lack of extraordinary powers, Bella immediately realizes the potentiality of being able to rein her urges and her emotions. In choosing to become a vampire, she had already accepted the fact that she would deny her thirst forever; now she is relieved that the other denials will not have as strong a hold as she had feared. Her other power becomes manifest when Eleazar calls her "a shield"; her ability to hide her thoughts literally become a weapon she can use to protect not only herself but also the people she loves. When facing the Volturi, she is able to shield every single person she cares about, thus rendering their weapons useless. She is, in Edward's words, "the superhero of the day" (Meyer 2008, 747). Her shield, which she evokes in very concrete terms ("I pushed it, shaped it," "this new muscle," "impenetrable," "wide dome," "elastic armor"), becomes a manifestation of her strength of will; her mind quite literally becomes the weapon with which she will be able to defend her friends and family: the qualities of the Angel in the House have become a superpower.

## SEXUALITY: DESIRE, VIOLENCE, AND MOTHERHOOD

Another echo to Victorian novels is that the hero refuses to shed the heroine's first blood before they are married. Victorian heroines had to remain chaste and pure or risked becoming the Angel in the House's opposite, the Fallen Woman. However, *Twilight* diverges both from Victorian fiction and contemporary vampire romances, as it offers an apparent paradox in vampire fiction, in shifting the eroticism from the vampiric bite to abstinence. Christine Seifert (2008) explains:

> Abstinence has never been sexier than it is in Stephenie Meyer's young adult four-book *Twilight* series. . . .The *Twilight* series has created a surprising new sub-genre of teen romance: It's abstinence porn, sensational, erotic, and titillating. And in light of all the recent real-world attention on abstinence-only education, it's surprising how successful this new genre is. *Twilight* actually convinces us that self-denial is hot. Fan reaction suggests that in the beginning, Edward and Bella's chaste but sexually charged relationship was steamy precisely because it was unconsummated—kind of like *Cheers*, but with fangs.

Readers are touched by the eroticism of the first three novels, and all the more so as they know that Bella and Edward's relationship will last forever and be consecrated by marriage. In these passages, Bella is closer to her contemporary heroines than anywhere else in the series:

> The thrill of victory was a strange high; it made me feel powerful. Brave. My hands weren't unsteady now; I got through with the buttons of his shirt this time easily, and my fingers traced the perfect planes of his icy chest. . . . I pulled his mouth back to mine, and he seemed just as eager as I was. One of his hands cupped my face, his other arm was tight around my waist straining me closer to him. (Meyer 2007, 449)

What truly differentiates Bella from the Victorian Angel in the House is her acceptance of her own sexuality. She acknowledges its "power," and being desired makes her feel confident. In that, she closely resembles her contemporaries who, even when they are virgins (Buffy Summers, Sookie Stackhouse) or abstinent (Anita Blake) at the beginning of the sagas, gradually embrace their sexual drives. Here, as always, Edward stops her: preserving his virtue is his one chance, according to him, to save his soul, and ultimately, he abstains out of religious considerations and not because he might hurt her.

This is, however, exactly what happens on their honeymoon, although Bella tries to minimize this fact:

> Under the dusting of feathers, large purplish bruises were beginning to blossom across the pale skin of my arm. My eyes followed the trail they made up to my shoulder, and then across my ribs. I pulled my hand free to poke at the discoloration on my left forearm, watching it fade where I touched and then reappear. It throbbed a little. (Meyer 2008, 89)

She explains to Edward—and the readers—that the bruises resulting from intercourse with a vampire fade in comparison to the pleasure she experienced, but it is hard to take her words at face value. This passage is one in many that help map sexuality as a dangerous territory for women to explore: they are prey or potential victims, and men are presented as predators. In the course of the novels, Bella is literally hunted by Laurent and possible rapists in Seattle, and the idea of predation underlies the whole text. As Natalie Wilson explains, "The fact that Bella is represented as a pawn or a prize for various males—not only Edward and Jacob, but also Mike, James, Tyler, and Laurent—suggests she is indeed the hunted" (2011, 69). The same association of sexuality to a threat is present in the *House of Night* series for young adults (Cast and Cast 2009) as teenager Zoey Redbird offers her virginity to adult vampire Loren Blake, only to realize that he was using her, as well as through the legend of the Cherokee fallen angel Kalona, who forces himself on the women of the tribe and whose appeal is almost irresistible. Both novels can at times be read as cautionary tales, highlighting the necessity of finding the right partner.

However, in *Twilight*, the heroine's own sexuality is more ambiguous: Bella is not only threatened by masculine violence but also she seems to validate it when she approaches unknown men in Seattle because they remind her of her potential rapists, remains friends with Jacob after he tried to force himself on her (and after she broke her hand trying to impress upon him that this was not okay), or seduces Edward to convince him to have sex with her again after being covered in bruises the first time. Her reaction to her injuries reveals that she expects sexuality to be dangerous: "We knew this was going to be tricky. I thought that was assumed" (Meyer 2008, 91). She expresses her surprise at how pleasurable it was but never at the pain, which she claims she cannot even remember. To convince her husband, she embodies the temptress, using lingerie, blackmail (by agreeing to remain human longer), and tears in order to have her way; her first words when she wakes up after their second time are: "How much trouble am I in?" (Meyer 2008, 108), betraying her feeling of guilt. This hypersexualization of Bella is then not so much an acknowledgment of women's sex drive as it is a warning against its possible excess. Danielle Dick McGeough (2010) explains:

> Bella's inability to control her intense sexual urges implies that the adolescent female body lacks control at both the physical and rational level. . . . Rather than celebrate or embrace Bella's sexual desires, the novels treat her sexual longing as excessive. Because Bella is unable to control her desire, Edward must regulate her desires for her. (90)

Paradoxically, Bella's strong sensuousness serves to reinforce her inscription within the patriarchal order, where men are in charge of female sexuality, rather than assert her right to control her own body. Carrie Anne Platt's analysis of sexuality in the novels says:

> Although the *Twilight* series is progressive in its recognition of the reality of adolescent female sexuality, the sexual politics of the saga are decidedly conservative. Far from being sexually empowered, Bella is rendered a perpetual victim of her own uncontrollable desires. . . . The overall ideological message is clear: to be young, female, and sexual is to court danger, destruction, or even death. (Platt 2010, 80)

This tension between sexual impulses and restraint betrays a conflict between Bella's certainty that young girls may not want to be married at eighteen but may still experience sexual desires, and Meyer's own religious beliefs and their focus on purity. It finds, once again, a resolution through the motif of vampirism. Once Bella is turned into a vampire, sex becomes a topic for banter and not a source of fear anymore.

Bella and Edward's honeymoon lovemaking, however, enables the inscription of motherhood as a core topic for the final part of the series and as the rightful consequence of intercourse. Pregnancy is depicted in terms even more violent than sexuality, as Bella's hybrid, blood-drinking baby nearly kills her, and she has to relinquish her human self in order to become a mother. However, *Breaking Dawn* reads as an ode to the joys of motherhood as the heroine finally finds her place in the world when she becomes both a vampire and a mother. She and her child immediately recognize each other and bond, and her joy is enough to compensate the pain and suffering of her pregnancy, making everything right again. Bella's completion through motherhood is announced throughout the first novels. Merinne Whitton (2011) explains:

> At the periphery of the overarching plot of intermale struggle for dominance . . . the female characters in the saga create a feminine narrative in which motherhood is the only licit objective of womanhood. This theme returns with increasing frequency through *New Moon* and *Eclipse*, reaching its apotheosis in the final installment, *Breaking Dawn*, by which point the subtext

has become overt—that in the *Twilight* universe, mothering is what women are for, and that it is the only role in which they can find true fulfillment. (125)

The importance of motherhood is suggested by the tales of Esme and Rosalie and confirmed by the stories of Bella and Leah in the last novel. Merinne Whitton (2011) comments on the juxtaposition of their two voices:

> In the contrast between Bella and Leah, Meyer presents a parable, a veiled warning to a generation of modern young women (many of whom share such ambivalent attitudes to motherhood) of the threat to their ultimate fulfillment, to their very femininity, posed by delaying or denying their maternal destiny. Bella's happy ending is the reward Meyer promises from motherhood; the tragic figure of Leah represents the grim fate Bella has escaped. (129)

Leah never considers having children until it is too late, and her becoming a werewolf makes her menopausal at twenty; she has to live with the fact that she has become a "genetic dead end" (Meyer 2008, 317). On that point, the *Twilight* saga stands in sharp contrast with other novels, in which motherhood is never mentioned (*The House of Night*, *Vampire Diaries*), seen as an unlikely option (*Buffy the Vampire Slayer*), or rejected as a lifestyle (*Anita Blake: Vampire Hunter*). Bella becomes another person when she gives birth, as it is conflated with her turning into a vampire, and she presents it as an ideal life.

## CONCLUSION: BELLA AS A REFLECTION OF TODAY'S SEARCH FOR LOST BEARINGS

*Twilight* readers or viewers can easily identify with Bella, particularly when she is human. Even though she is not meant to be a model for readers to emulate, her actions and narration provide them with one that is easier to adopt than that offered by other twenty-first-century heroines. Not everyone can be a Slayer, but almost any girl could become an Angel. The references to this Victorian ideal find an echo in today's fascination for Victoriana and the multiplication of prequels or sequels to novels staging a Victorian heroine. Yet Bella, if she is not a Slayer, definitely lives in this century and claims this inscription when she first refuses to marry Edward immediately after high school.

The tensions between tradition and modernity may be due, especially when it comes to sexuality, to the differences between Bella's desires as a young woman who discovers love and Meyer's beliefs as an adult member of the Church of Jesus Christ of Latter-Day Saints. Bella, even though she conveys some of the author's values, is not presented as her spokesperson, no more than she is given as a role model to her female readers. These tensions also reflect many readers' feelings of confusion and loss of bearings when it comes to femininity and the need to reconcile their sense of self with society's contradictory messages about what women should do or be. The series calls the readers to question their own perception of femininity in a society that conflates the promotion of purity and the hypersexualization of the (female) body, love at first sight or mind-reading, the necessity to communicate and build a relationship, the necessity to diverge from traditional patriarchal role models, and the right to choose to adopt them.

Bella is indeed an "everygirl" and may bring readers the hope that they will eventually manage a balance between what is expected of them and their own desires, ultimately finding where they belong.

## NOTE

1. The original in French reads: "En effet, le vampire s'est vu détrôné par des Van Helsing en jupons qui, non contentes de le traquer, se sont aussi mis en tête de le séduire."

## REFERENCES

Brontë, Charlotte. 1847 [2001]. *Jane Eyre: A Norton Critical Edition*, ed. by Richard Dunn, 3rd edition. New York: W. W. Norton and Company.

Cast, P. C., and Kristin Cast. 2009. *Marked: A House of Night Novel*. London: Atom.

Dabat, Sophie. 2010. *Bit-Lit! L'Amour des Vampires*. Lyon, France: Les Moutons électriques.

Dietz, Tammy. 2011. "Wake Up, Bella! A Personal Essay on *Twilight*, Mormonism, Feminism, and Happiness." In *Bringing Light to "Twilight": Perspectives on the Pop Culture Phenomenon*, ed. Giselle Liza Anatol, 99–112. New York: Palgrave Macmillan.

Erzen, Tanya. 2012. *Fanpire: "The Twilight Saga" and the Women Who Love It*. Boston: Beacon.

Larsson, Mariah, and Ann Steiner, eds. 2011. *Interdisciplinary Approaches to "Twilight": Studies in Fiction, Media, and a Contemporary Cultural Experience*. Lund, Sweden: Nordic Academic Press.

McGeough, Danielle Dick. 2010. "*Twilight* and Transformation of Flesh: Reading the Body in Contemporary Youth Culture." In *Bitten by "Twilight": Youth Culture, Media, and the Vampire Franchise*, ed. Melissa A. Click, Jennifer Stevens Aubrey, and Elizabeth Behm-Morawitz, 87–102. New York: Peter Lang.

Meyer, Stephenie. 2005. *Twilight*. 2007 ed. London: Atom, 2005.

———. 2006. *New Moon*. 2009 ed. London: Atom.

———. 2007. *Eclipse*. New York: Little, Brown and Company.

———. 2007. "The Story behind the Writing of New Moon." The Official Website of Stephenie Meyer. Accessed June 15, 2013. http://www.stepheniemeyer.com/nm_thestory.html.

———. 2008. *Breaking Dawn*. New York: Little, Brown and Company.

Mukherjea, Ananya. 2011. "My Vampire Boyfriend: Postfeminism, 'Perfect' Masculinity, and the Contemporary Appeal of Paranormal Romance." *Studies in Popular Culture* 33, no. 2 (Spring): 11–20. http://pcasacas.org/SiPC/33.2/SPC_33.2.pdf.

Platt, Carrie Anne. 2010. "Cullen Family Values: Gender and Sexual Politics in the *Twilight* Series." In *Bitten by "Twilight": Youth Culture, Media, and the Vampire Franchise*, ed. Melissa A. Click, Jennifer Stevens Aubrey, and Elizabeth Behm-Morawitz, 71–86. New York: Peter Lang.

Seifert, Christine. 2008. "Bite Me! (Or Don't)." *Bitch Magazine*. Accessed June 10, 2013. http://bitchmagazine.org/article/bite-me-or-dont.

Smith, L. J. 1991. *The Awakening.* Vampire Diaries. London: Hodder Children's Books.

Steiner, Ann. 2011. "Gendered Readings: Bella's Books and Literary Consumer Culture." In *Interdisciplinary Approaches to "Twilight": Studies in Fiction, Media, and a Contemporary Cultural Experience*, ed. Mariah Larsson and Ann Steiner, 195–212. Lund, Sweden: Nordic Academic Press.

Whitton, Merinne. 2011. "'One Is Not Born a Vampire, but Becomes One': Motherhood and Masochism in *Twilight*." In *Bringing Light to "Twilight": Perspectives on the Pop Culture Phenomenon*, ed. Giselle Liza Anatol, 125–38. New York: Palgrave Macmillan.

Wilson, Natalie. 2011. *Seduced by "Twilight": The Allure and Contradictory Messages of the Popular Saga.* Jefferson, NC: MacFarland.

Woolf, Virginia. 1931 [2013]. "Professions for Women." In *The Death of the Moth and Other Essays*, by Virginia Woolf. University of Adelaide web edition. Last updated February 7, 2013. http://ebooks.adelaide.edu.au/w/woolf/virginia/w91d/chapter27.html.

# Chapter Nine

# "Doesn't He Own a Shirt?"

## *Rivalry and Masculine Embodiment in* Twilight

## Nicole Willms

Particularly in U.S. society, scholars have argued that not only women but now men are in a state of "body panic" (Dworkin and Wachs, 2009). They are struggling with, among other things, societal pressures to have a "fit" and muscular body, as men's bodies are increasingly on display in consumer culture (Bordo 1999; Edwards 1997; Gill, Henwood, and McLean 2000; Grogan 2008; Nixon 1996). In the *Twilight* book and film series, supernatural creatures—namely, vampires and shape-shifter wolves—possess nearly perfect physical forms, immense physical prowess, and some manner of prolonged youth or immortality. In addition to being powerful, the women are beautiful with thin physiques, and the men are handsome with bodies that range from chiseled to muscular. In this fantasy world, becoming supernatural bestows bodily forms and abilities that "just happen" to coincide with what is often idealized and commodified in gendered ways within contemporary Western culture.

However, in *Twilight*, alongside the confidence that comes with powerful and attractive bodies, there is also an undercurrent of anxiety, and it does not solely come from the protagonist, Bella Swan, who is a vulnerable human with an immense lack of physical coordination. Bella's love interests, Edward Cullen, the vampire, and Jacob Black, the shape-shifting wolf, are preoccupied in their struggle over her affections with their relative attractiveness and masculine worth, as well as with what their respective bodies can or cannot do. They seem, in short, to have a degree of anxiety about their masculinity. In the movies, this anxiety is more clearly directed at the young men's physical forms. Although Edward is incredibly strong in practice, it is Jacob's visible muscularity that draws attention. In *Eclipse*, Edward seems to be fraught with jealously over his rival, engaging in many demonstrations of masculine protectiveness toward Bella. The movie also highlights his anxiety over Jacob's muscular form and his propensity toward going shirtless, leading him to the rhetorical question, "Doesn't he own a shirt?"

Embedded within this juxtaposition of fantasy and anxiety are many messages about Western cultural dilemmas surrounding masculinity and its connections to social status. In truth, the two men have fairly equitable masculine powers. They can both rescue Bella from the evils and mishaps of the world through their superhuman strength and special powers. But who is the more attractive mate? Is it the muscular Jacob who works on cars and motorcycles and who is less than enamored with school? Or is it the svelte, toned Edward who plays the piano and holds several college degrees, as well as two medical degrees (Meyer 2011)? The *Twilight* books and films set up a rivalry between these two heroic supernatural characters, each vying for Bella's affections. As rivals, they are placed in constant comparison. Their personalities, physical forms, supernatural powers, and lifestyles are all carefully examined throughout the series as Bella weighs her options.

This chapter argues that through their literary and cinematic rivalry, Jacob and Edward become representations of the ideals, ambiguities, contradictions, and anxieties surrounding the embodiments and practices of masculinity in the Western world. When examined, these young men are particularly emblematic of masculine symbols related to their race and social class (Jensen 2010; Wilson 2010, 2011a). This chapter focuses on the way contemporary cultural anxieties over masculinity, idealized embodiment, and competing notions of hegemonic masculinity may make the rivalry between Edward and Jacob particularly salient with readers and viewers. As many fans weigh the options and decide on which young man *they* would choose, even breaking into different fan-factions of "Team Edward" and "Team Jacob," they may also be reconciling their own ambivalence about what makes a man masculine or attractive and how race and class influence our understandings of ideal manhood.

## BODY PANIC

According to Shari Dworkin and Faye Wachs (2009), body panic arises in the context of a consumer culture. This is evident in the advertisements that prey on people's insecurities and the connected industries that market diet regimens and products, fitness gyms, and beauty aids, from makeup to plastic surgery (Dworkin and Wachs 2009; Grogan 2008). Consumption around physical improvement is a key feature in Western (and perhaps in most affluent) societies, indicating that attention to *Twilight*'s treatment of "the body" is extremely relevant to its context. The books and films are themselves products of consumption that speak to both the fantasy of perfect bodies and the anxieties and ambiguities surrounding these embodiments.

Fit bodies not only represent a commitment to health but also become markers of identity and morality. In this milieu, the body is a visible sign of one's character and convictions. Low body fat and muscle tone are the marks of bodily control and maintenance, indicating that one is able to abstain from indulgences and commit oneself to a regimen of diet and exercise (Dworkin and Wachs 2009; Gill, Henwood, and McLean 1999). As Richard Dyer (1997) argues, "Building bodies is the most literal triumph of mind over matter" (153). When fit bodies are not only a sign of attractiveness but also of moral worth, any deficiencies in bodily form take on a heightened importance. Adding to this pressure, bodies have different values in the consumer market and are scrutinized through this lens in media and commercial contexts (Dworkin and Wachs 2009).

Although both men and women's bodies are commodified in ways that create a sense of "body panic," Dworkin and Wachs (2009) argue that the signs and practices aligned with fit bodies diverge between men and women. Men and women are praised for looking "fit," but for women, this generally means thin and toned; while for men, it more often involves appearing physically strong and powerful. We may be invited by the media to gaze at male bodies, yet much of what makes them attractive are displays of power and strength: muscularity, connections to masculine-coded physical activities such as sport, or markers that signify access to wealth and resources, such as expensive clothing or evidence of high-end grooming. Thus, even in being objectified, men (especially white, heterosexual men) hold on to their subjectivity. Therefore, the men's objectification is in part an appreciation of their active self, an expression of their relative power.

In *Twilight*, readers and viewers are invited to "consume" the romantic male leads' presentations of masculine embodiment. In the films, Edward is often captured strutting or looking conspicuously cool, his perfectly tousled hair paired with carefully tailored clothing. Jacob is shown in James Dean style poses in black leather on a motorcycle or, more characteristically, as half-clothed, revealing his muscular torso as he runs through the forest. However, both men retain varying degrees of subjectivity because of how powerful they are. They are attractive physically and positioned as objects of desire for fans, but they also actively protect and care for Bella. Adding to their subjectivity, author Stephenie Meyer even provides them a voice: Jacob narrates portions of the books and Edward has his own spin-off manuscript.

Through their perfectly fit bodies and displays of strength, Edward and Jacob embody status and implicit moral worth. Even though the *Twilight* books and movies make no explicit mention of either Edward or Jacob "building" their ideal bodies (i.e., through diet or exercise), their physical forms are repeatedly praised. The implication is that their bodies are natural components of their supernatural embodiment or transformation. Jacob and Edward are bestowed with the signifiers of moral and physical worth but without having put in the efforts associated with achieving such a goal in the real world. The perpetual youth and beauty of the two male characters thus provide an escapist fantasy with immense appeal. In the *Twilight* world, supernatural creatures can be beautiful and fit, and implicitly hard-working and self-disciplined, without actually needing to apply the time, resources, or moral fortitude that would normally be required. This offers quite a seductive package, one that the protagonist, Bella, is eager to take part in by becoming a vampire. Although perhaps primarily a romantically driven request, fans wearing t-shirts inviting Edward to bite them may also be asking to be part of this world.

Within the escapist fantasy, male and female embodiments of supernatural power fall within gender-appropriate forms. Male and female supernatural creatures may share similar levels of strength and access to magical powers, but their physical forms follow conventionally appropriate levels of muscularity for each gender. Scholars have found that men and women tend to desire and direct their bodies toward very gender-specific embodiments—women coveting toned muscles and thin physique and men wanting large muscles (Dworkin 2001; Grogan and Richards 2002). Shari L. Dworkin (2001) describes this as the "glass ceiling" on women's strength, an "upper limit on women's bodily strength and musculature" (337) that is influenced by ideologies surrounding women's fitness. These conventions are echoed in most mainstream fitness magazines that principally feature thin, toned women and large, muscular men (Dworkin and Wachs 2009). Even toys reflect a change in ideals: Harrison G. Pope Jr. et al. (1999) documents a change in male action figures, where bicep and torso size has increased quite dramatically since the 1960s.

Whereas the male vampires and shape-shifters are toned, if not overtly muscular, the lone female member of the wolf pack and the female vampires introduced throughout the films are slender, without much evidence of muscle tone. Overall, the women do not show any evidence of muscularity that would help explain their superpower strength—their displays of power are part of the supernatural magic. In the case of female vampires, their thinness is even highlighted through fashionable, tight-fitting clothes.

For these supernatural women, being thin and beautiful keeps most appearance-based anxieties at bay—or at least these characters are not developed to the point where readers/viewers would be privy to these insecurities. Yet, the physical perfection bestowed upon the male supernatural creatures do not render them immune to insecurities about their relative strength or physical forms. Although in their rivalry, Edward and Jacob seem more boastful than anxious about their brand of supernatural prowess, the bravado actually reveals an undercurrent of insecurity that each man's bodily abilities and appearance might not be enough to attract Bella. In setting up a romantic rivalry, the author puts these men in a position of direct comparison, so the ideals of masculinity become open for interpretation and subject to scrutiny.

## HEGEMONIC MASCULINITY

Just as body panic can be understood as connected to status symbols that intersect with many idealized notions of masculinity, there are other embodiments, temperaments, and practices in *Twilight* that are also meaningful signifiers of our contemporary culture. Each of the two male supernatural rivals embodies a competing version of what has been called "hegemonic masculinity" (Connell 1995). According to the theory of hegemonic masculinity, there is a set of practices associated with the ideal man that help prop up certain men as superior to women and other marginalized men (Coles 2009; Connell 1995; Connell and Messerschmidt 2005). The practices that arise at any given time or place as most reaffirming of male dominance are constantly renegotiated as they encounter pressure from agents of contestation. Thus, what is considered to be ideal masculine practice is in flux—it is always being challenged, reconceptualized, and understood by individuals in new and diverse ways (Coles 2009). Moreover, what is considered "ideal" about men changes over time and varies by context. In *Twilight*, what is revered about men in a supernatural context may not hold true outside of it. But even though cultural standards shift our desires and expectations, hegemonic practices of masculinity continue to support the premise that men have access to more resources, power, and privileges due to "natural" attributes or processes (Coles 2009; Connell 1995; Connell and Messerschmidt 2005).

Axes of power in our society help create a myriad of masculine practices and embodiments and also provide locations at the margins from which to contest the current dominant practices. Thus, race, ethnicity, social class, sexuality, physical ability, religion, and other socially meaningful categories create different sets of masculine practices and contribute to defining what types of masculinities are idealized versus marginalized (Connell and Messerschmidt 2005). Some men, who seem to be "below" the canon through lack of access to wealth or power, may compensate by exhibiting characteristics such as physical strength or by looking threatening or able to commit violence. However, it is likely that these masculine practices will be devalued as too aggressive or too violent, keeping these men within an inferior, marginalized status.

In *Twilight*, we can see competing versions of masculinity inscribed on Edward and Jacob, but the texts complicate the idea of a "winner" and demonstrate the fluid and highly contested nature of idealized masculine practice. Edward, the symbol of upper-class, white masculinity, predictably "wins" by being chosen by Bella as a life partner. Nevertheless, Jacob, the symbol of working-class, nonwhite masculinity, is portrayed in a manner that demonstrates his value as a man and as a mate. He is a contender in many ways. Bella becomes conflicted about her feelings for Jacob and later admits to loving him and seeing him as the more appropriate romantic partner, despite her devotion to Edward. Therefore, readers and viewers may recognize Edward's connections to more hegemonic, exalted forms of masculinity but also see that these masculine practices are not immune to contestations. They may reconcile this with their idealization of Edward, or they may align with Jacob if they prefer the more down-to-earth, underdog, marginalized forms of masculinity that his character represents.

The differences in masculine practices between the two men are in some ways subtle. Both embody typically valued aspects of masculinity, such as physical strength, dominance, leadership, and protectiveness. Both are unpredictably dangerous. Given these characteristics, it is not a surprise that critics and scholars describe them as either old-fashioned or postfeminist. Natalie Wilson (2011a) argues that Edward and Jacob exhibit traits of conservative, traditional masculinity. She interprets their softer sides, the moments when the men express concern for Bella or speak freely about their emotions, as a contradiction to this. Her argument is that our culture is so confused about masculinity that characters emerge possessing ostensibly oppositional traits—aggressive yet sensitive, controlling yet understanding. However, these paradoxical pairings have been identified as a key component of many common plot lines in the romance genre (Radway 1983). Even in real life, the pairing of masculinity with sensitivity and caring may not be as antithetical as Wilson postulates, since many have begun to recognize contemporary men's strategic engagements with a softer, more emotional form of masculinity. This may be a newer, idealized standard practiced by men in particular status positions (Hondagneu-Sotelo and Messner 1994; Wilkins 2009).

## "NEW MEN"

Both Edward and Jacob are in some ways what Pierrette Hondagneu-Sotelo and Michael A. Messner (1994) call "New Men." They are willing to share their feelings and express romantic sentiments, verbalize progressive views on women, and exhibit self-control. The "New Man" is a performance of masculinity that positions itself in contrast to other forms—especially the stereotypes connected to lower-class men and men of color who are rendered as lacking self-control, being disrespectful of women, or as too "macho" to share feelings (Hondagneu-Sotelo and Messner 1994; Wilkins 2004, 2009). Although both Edward and Jacob have a softer side, *Twilight* makes subtle distinctions so that readers and viewers receive multiple messages about which young man's practice of masculinity is exalted. They are both romantic and seek self-control, but they diverge most in their embodiment, maturity, and temperament, with clear connections to race and class.

Because *Twilight* is mainly a romantic series, it is not surprising that Edward and Jacob are fairly free in expressing their feelings and demonstrating their affections for Bella. Wilson (2011a) finds this an odd pairing with some of their other behaviors that border on abusive. For example, both men attempt to control Bella's movements and decision making, including following or watching her without her permission. Edward says he would rather die if left without Bella, and Jacob expresses a desire that Bella die if she chooses Edward over him. However, this strategic use of emotional openness, even paired with more traditional and domineering behavior, may be a key revision to a contemporary form of hegemonic masculinity. Placing controlling behavior or excusing gender-based double standards in the context of romantic sentiments may help men (especially "new" men) smooth the way to maintaining dominance in romantic relationships and beyond (Wilkins 2004, 2009).

Thus, the desire for more soft emotionality from men has seeped into popular culture, creating a space in which men's display of soft emotions is often celebrated as a sign of gender progress and/or as good for women. But while men's participation in intimacy talk may be desirable, it does not necessarily undo gendered power relations (Wilkins 2009, 362). Edward and Jacob are romantic, vulnerable, and emotional while still acting aggressive, controlling, and obsessive. However, Edward grows more mature and self-restrained as time goes on, positioning himself not only as emotionally available but also as stable. As Hondagneu-Sotelo and Messner (1994) argue, practices and images of white, middle- to upper-class masculinity can involve characteristics like sensitivity and stability that help men in these social categories define themselves against other, "less progressive" men, typically those of marginalized socioeconomic and racial/ethnic groups.

Stability and self-control are components of contemporary masculinity that the *Twilight* texts thoroughly explore through its main characters. Conventionally, heterosexual interest and sexual prowess are key ways to enact masculinity in Western culture, but Wilkins's study of Christian men who intend to remain celibate until marriage reveals that these men reframe their chaste behavior as masculine (2009). Unable to use sexual conquests as a way to perform heterosexual masculinity, many men in her study opted for narratives of restraint. They asserted that the ability to abstain from sexual behavior in the context of temptation was a sign of true masculinity. Edward most exemplifies this: he has renounced both taking human blood/life and engaging in sex before marriage. For him, as for most vampires in the modern Western tradition, sexual and romantic temptation and the craving for human blood are interconnected (Bailey 2011).

Although Edward has spent almost a century refining his self-control, he still has to work hard to control himself with Bella. She represents a strong temptation—she pursues him sexually, and her blood has an alluring scent. Yet, Edward is shown to have the maturity and self-restraint necessary to resist his inclinations towards blood/sex, as well as her sexual advances. Just as the men in Wilkins's study distinguish themselves through their restraint, in many ways believing that they are better or stronger than men who do not abstain from sex, Edward takes the position of the suitor more capable of maturity and self-control (Bacon 2011). This sets him apart from Jacob who, like many marginalized men, is stereotypically portrayed as more sexually and emotionally unrestrained (Hondagneu-Sotelo and Messner 1994; Wilkins 2004, 2009).

As a new shape-shifter, Jacob is just beginning to develop his self-restraint and often demonstrates a lack of control over his anger and other emotions. Losing control could mean that he would transition into a giant wolf and potentially harm someone in his path. In *New Moon*, we learn that one of the other members of the wolf pack lost control in this way and scarred the face of his romantic partner. Moreover, after Jacob's transition (making him closer, perhaps, to his animal side), he becomes more insistent about winning Bella's affections, even kissing her against her will. Jacob can be read as the immature, aggressive suitor—the symbolic connections to stereotypes about working-class men and Native American men cannot be ignored (Wilson 2010, 2011a, 2011b).

## CLOTHES (AND NO CLOTHES) MAKE THE MAN

Edward is symbolic of upper-class, white masculinity in other ways, too. He is all about refinement, from his love of classical music to his talent as a pianist. His clothing in the films is casual, yet stylish and carefully tailored. Edward is slim, toned. His family has vast resources and access to many of the finer things in life. Colette Murphy (2011) describes him as an example of the literary "prince-like" vampire. He is also associated with the term *metrosexual* in the United States, which is generally used to describe men who put time and attention into their appearance. He is immaculately groomed, and his haircut seems to be fresh out of a high-end salon. Kristen Barber (2008) argues that these attentions to one's appearance are related to white, upper-class masculinity, where men in high-powered occupations engage in high-end beauty practices to present an image of upper-class refinement, with ensuing connections to power and prestige.

Although the metrosexual is a contemporary Western concept, in South Korea, many women interpret Edward's character, especially in the novel, as a "pin-up boy," praised for his sensitivity and beautiful feminine features

(Han and Hwang 2012). This is also evident in the graphic novel version of the *Twilight* saga (Meyer and Kim 2010, 2011, 2013). Thus, in many contexts, there are fans who appear to be attracted to Edward's feminine side, which is connected to the "feminine" practices being utilized by men to indicate upper-class status.

Upper-class, white masculinity is often conveyed through adornments and bodily practices rather than through the body itself (Barber 2008; Dyer 1997). Notably, Dyer (1997) argues that in films, especially prior to the emergence of the body-builders-turned-actors of the 1980s, white men rarely appear naked or shirtless. Unless the man is clearly physically powerful, it strips the character of his markers of class and potentially inscribes him as vulnerable or inadequate. "Clothes are the bearers of prestige, notably of wealth, status and class," the author says (146). In the novels, Bella views Edward as possessing statuesque beauty (another marker referencing classical European standards). Yet, for the most part, Edward remains clothed—he is rarely described or depicted in anything but his high-style wardrobe.

When Edward does appear shirtless, his bodily form becomes a multifaceted source of vulnerability. In sunlight, his skin sparkles, giving away his status as different, as a "monster." In the first book and film, Edward expresses to Bella a deep insecurity about his ability to be accepted and loved by a human, in light of his vampirism. Could Bella really love him as a monster who has killed people, who is not truly alive and possibly has no soul? He challenges Bella on this by demonstrating his strength (carrying her to the tops of trees) and making himself vulnerable: opening his shirt in the sunlight, so she can see his chest sparkle. The first time we see him with full chest exposed is at the end of *New Moon*, at an immensely vulnerable moment when he is about to commit suicide by exposing his body to a crowd of onlookers, showing himself while violating a vampire code that carries a penalty of death. Although his disrobing reveals a chiseled torso, the focus is on his sacrifice and his pain rather than on his attractiveness.

Jacob, in contrast, is symbolic of nonwhite, working-class masculinity. He is Native American from the Quileute Nation (author Stephenie Meyer took inspiration from this Northwest Native American nation and its legends but fictionalized a great deal of their stories and experiences—see Jensen 2010). Jacob lives on the reservation and fixes automobiles and motorcycles as a hobby. His father likes to hang out with Bella's father to watch sports and drink beer in an act of stereotypical working-class male bonding. Although Jacob and the other Quileutes are complex characters that are often treated with respect and as worthy of friendship by the principal white characters, they are rendered in many stereotypical ways—as magical and as the "Noble Savage" (Jensen 2010; Wilson 2010, 2011a, 2011b). Brian Klopotek (2001) says:

> The noble savage, the good Indian, is a virtuous, dignified, stoic, hard-working man. . . . He believes in personal responsibility and loyalty, and he bravely answers calls to arms for noble causes. One with nature, he is free of the corruptions industrial society places on a man's character, yet he embraces the causes of "civilization" and white Americans. He is physically superb, animal-like in his athletic abilities. In many ways, he embodies the ideal traits white society ascribes to manliness. (252)

Jacob and many other Quileutes turn into wolves, which presents a connection to animalistic stereotypes. Jacob also plays a heroic role, helping to protect Bella and defend the area from villainous vampires, but often his missions involve supporting or protecting the white characters. Thus, the complexity and respect afforded him are diminished (Jensen 2010; Wilson 2010, 2011a, 2011b).

Although Bella never overtly mentions Jacob's class or race position, she does remark upon others' reactions to him, noting his physical presence as imposing:

> I noticed other faces . . . the faces of my classmates. I noticed how their eyes widened as they took in all six foot seven inches of Jacob's long body, mus-cled up the way no normal sixteen-and-a-half year old ever had been. I saw those eyes rake over his tight black t-shirt—short-sleeved, though the day was unseasonably cool—his ragged, grease-smeared jeans, and the glossy black bike he leaned against. Their eyes didn't linger on his face—something about his expression had them glancing quickly away. And I noticed the wide berth everyone gave him, the bubble of space that no one dared to encroach on. With a sense of astonishment, I realized Jacob looked dangerous to them. (*Eclipse*, 77)

So, although Bella is apparently blind to the fears that a large man of color might inspire, particularly when adorned with markers of lower social class (the motorcycle, the "ragged" jeans), she is able to see the reaction of others and at least superficially understand the meanings associated with his race and class position.

Jacob and his Quileute pack become almost clichés as they appear almost exclusively shirtless. The explanation is that their clothes are ripped to shreds during their transformation from human to wolf—the best that they can do is tie a pair of shorts around an ankle. In the books, Jacob starts out lanky, but once part of the wolf pack, he becomes incredibly tall and muscular. In the film, it is his muscularity that is featured, and this sex appeal is heavily exploited. This racializes Jacob and the Quileute tribe as less civilized than Edward and his vampire family (Wilson 2011a) and continues a trope in film where nonwhite men are sexually exotic (Dyer 1997).

Looking behind the scenes, Taylor Lautner, the actor who plays Jacob in the films, was allegedly trying to keep his role after the first movie (Cunningham 2012). The book makes clear that as his shape-shifter abilities develop, Jacob quickly matures physically and grows to a towering 6 feet 7 inches. Lautner is shorter than the character but promised to bulk up to represent Jacob's transformation. He did so and kept the role. The second film, *New Moon*, includes several moments where Bella comments on Jacob's new physical form. In the opening scene, she greets him by teasing him about his muscles: "You know, anabolic steroids are bad for you." Later, Jacob easily lifts two motorcycles out of the back of Bella's car, and she comments, "Jacob, you're like buff." During most of the second half of the movie, he appears shirtless.

Jacob's muscular physique is the focus of the next movie, *Eclipse*, as well. It is in this film where Edward's connections to hegemonic masculinity become contested. Whereas in the books it is Bella who asks Jacob to explain why he is so often missing clothing, in *Eclipse*, Edward asks Bella: "Doesn't he own a shirt?" Understanding Edward's discomfort and jealously, Jacob later quips at him: "Let's face it, I'm hotter than you." The films more firmly engage with contemporary anxieties about masculine embodiment. Ostensibly, Edward has all the advantages (wealth, status, etc.), but these lines in the movie suggest that he fears losing Bella and that Jacob's advantage is his sex appeal, most closely connected to his muscularity. Edward never discusses his own physicality, but he is not comfortable with Jacob being the "hotter" rival. Because many of Edward's attributes are related to status symbols, he has a vulnerability: the sexiness and physical superiority attributed to the nonwhite, exotic other (Dyer 1997). This conflict plays out more overtly in the movies, following the long history of film images that tend to stereotype and dehumanize men and women of color (Collins 1990).

## CONCLUSION

If in today's Western societies, we are living in a culture of "body panic" where our gendered, classed, and racialized embodiments are subject to scrutiny in ways that question not only our commitments to health but also our very moral fiber, then it is no wonder that fictional characters who seem to have access to a supernatural "free pass" are an attractive escapist fantasy. However, what is revealed in *Twilight* is that even in a state of perfection lies ambiguity and anxiety. Although many people fantasize about achieving a perfect body, what is considered "perfect" is constantly changing over time and setting, perpetually contested, and often influenced by race and class position. Thus, we are given a moving target, and even fictional, supernatural characters face insecurities. Some may never fully possess the "right" kind of body due to connections to marginalized statuses. Others may find that their hegemonic embodiments are vulnerable due to the transitory nature of their related status symbols.

Through their supernatural status and the physical gifts that come with it, Edward and Jacob are able to embody competing characteristics of idealized masculinity. However, the differences between their embodiments reveal the story of a rivalry that extends beyond their two characters. On the surface, it's a question of what makes the man. Is it the clothes or the six-pack abdominals? But below the surface, there is much more to the story. Edward represents upper-class, white masculinity. He is educated, refined, wealthy, sensitive, and caring. His dominance, strength, and power are undisputed but are not necessarily advertised through large muscles or an overtly strong personality. In contrast, Jacob represents working-class, nonwhite masculinity. He works with his hands, is not too interested in school, and is prone to outbursts of emotion. Once fully a shape-shifter, his body morphs into a mature, tall, muscular form. His strength is visible and on display, as he is rarely fully clothed. The race and class symbolism shines brightly underneath the sexy images sold to *Twilight* fans.

As if soothing the cultural anxieties about masculinity, the *Twilight* texts seem to be reassuring fans that white, upper-class masculinity will always win first prize, while allowing certain readers/viewers to explore and fantasize about (maybe even fetishize) the merits of alternative forms. Thus, through the books and films, readers/viewers can both celebrate and scrutinize aspects of masculine practices and embodiments that are valued in Western societies, with their respective connections to race and class symbols (and embedded racism).

In the end, the *Twilight* books and films sell readers and viewers both the fantasy as well as the ambiguities, giving them multiple ways to imagine and ponder their own conflicted views on contemporary masculinity—albeit in a context where the messages are limited and the playing field is not entirely level. *Twilight*, like any good story, becomes both imagined and real. Edward and Jacob may be fictional, but their stories and images are likely "true" to many fans' experiences precisely because they are representative of Western cultural anxieties about masculinity and its connections to race and class. Team Edward or Team Jacob? Perhaps we are still reconciling our choices and the implications they hold.

## NOTE

The author would like to acknowledge two generous colleagues who provided guidance and feedback while completing this chapter: Jeffrey Montez de Oca and C. Richard King.

# REFERENCES

Bacon, Simon. 2011. "Lost Boys: The Infernal Youth of the Cinematic Teenage Vampire." *THYMOS: Journal of Boyhood Studies* 5:152–62.

Bailey, Helen T. 2011. "Blood Ties: The Vampire Lover in the Popular Romance." *Journal of American Culture* 34:141–48.

Barber, Kristen. 2008. "The Well-Coiffed Man: Class, Race, and Heterosexual Masculinity in the Hair Salon." *Gender and Society* 22:455–76.

Basso, Matthew, Laura McCall, and Dee Garceau, eds. 2001. *Across the Great Divide: Cultures of Manhood in the American West*. New York: Routledge.

Bordo, Susan. 1999. *The Male Body: A New Look at Men in Public and Private*. New York: Parrar, Straus, and Giroux.

Clarke, Amy M., Marijane Osborn, Donald E. Palumbo, and C. W. Sullivan III, eds. 2010. *The "Twilight" Mystique: Critical Essays on the Novels and Films*. Jefferson, NC: McFarland.

Coles, Tony. 2009. "Negotiating the Field of Masculinity: The Productions and Reproduction of Multiple Dominant Masculinities." *Men and Masculinities* 12:30–44.

Collins, Patricia H. 1990. *Black Feminist Thought: Knowledge, Consciousness, and the Politics of Empowerment*. New York: Routledge.

Connell, R. W. 1995. *Masculinities*. Berkeley: University of California Press.

Connell, Robert W., and James W. Messerschmidt. 2005. "Hegemonic Masculinity: Rethinking the Concept." *Gender and Society* 19:829–59.

Cunningham, Mark D. 2012. "Traveling in the Same Boat: Adapting Stephenie Meyer's *Twilight*, *New Moon*, and *Eclipse* to Film." In *Genre, Reception, and Adaptation in the "Twilight" Series*, ed. Anne Morey, 199–214. Burlington, VT: Ashgate.

Dworkin, Shari L. 2001. "'Holding Back': Negotiating a Glass Ceiling on Women's Muscular Strength." *Sociological Perspectives* 44:333–50.

Dworkin, Shari, and Faye Wachs. 2009. *Body Panic: Gender, Health, and the Selling of Fitness*. New York: NYC Press.

Dyer, Richard. 1997. *White: Essays on Race and Culture*. New York: Routledge.

Edwards, Tim. 1997. *Men in the Mirror: Men's Fashion, Masculinity and Consumer Society*. London: Cassell.

Gill, Rosalind, Karen Henwood, and Carl McLean. 2000. "The Tyranny of the 'Six-Pack': Men Talk about Idealised Images of the Male Body in Popular Culture." In *Culture in Psychology*, ed. Corinne Squire. London: Routledge.

Grogan, Susan. 2008. *Body Image: Understanding Body Dissatisfaction in Men, Women, and Children*. New York: Routledge.

Grogan, Susan, and Helen Richards. 2002. "Body Image: Focus Groups with Boys and Men." *Men and Masculinities* 4:219–32.

Han, Hye Chung, and Chan Hee Hwang. 2012. "Adaptation and Reception: The Case of *The Twilight Saga* in Korea." In *Genre, Reception, and Adaptation in the "Twilight" Series*, ed. Anne Morey. Burlington, VT: Ashgate.

Hondagneu-Sotelo, Pierrette, and Michael A. Messner. 1994. "Gender Displays and Men's Power: The 'New Man' and the Mexican Immigrant Man." In *Theorizing Masculinities*, ed. Harry Brod and Michael Kaufman, 200–218. Thousand Oaks, CA: Sage.

Jensen, Kristian. 2010. "Noble Werewolves or Native Shape-Shifters?" In *The "Twilight" Mystique: Critical Essays on the Novels and Films*, ed. Amy M. Clarke, Marijane Osborn, Donald E. Palumbo, and C. W. Sullivan III, 92–106. Jefferson, NC: McFarland.

Klopotek, Brian. 2001. "'I Guess Your Warrior Look Doesn't Work Every Time': Challenging Indian Masculinity in the Cinema." In *Across the Great Divide: Cultures of Manhood in the American West*, ed. Matthew Basso, Laura McCall, and Dee Garceau, 251–74. New York: Routledge.

Meyer, Stephenie. 2007. *Eclipse*. New York: Little, Brown and Company.

———. 2011. *The Twilight Saga: The Official Illustrated Guide*. New York: Little, Brown.

Meyer, Stephenie, and Young Kim. 2010. *Twilight: The Graphic Novel*, vol. 1. New York: Yen.

———. 2011. *Twilight: The Graphic Novel*, vol. 2. New York: Yen.

————. 2013. *New Moon: The Graphic Novel*, vol. 1. New York: Yen.

Morey, Anne, ed. 2012. *Genre, Reception, and Adaptation in the "Twilight" Series*. Burlington, VT: Ashgate.

Murphy, Colette. 2011. "Someday My Vampire Will Come? Society's (and the Media's) Lovesick Infatuation with Price-Like Vampires." In *Theorizing "Twilight": Critical Essays on What's at Stake in a Post-Vampire World*, ed. Maggie Parke and Natalie Wilson, 56–69. Jefferson, NC: McFarland.

Nixon, Sean. 1996. *Hard Looks: Masculinities, Spectatorship and Contemporary Consumption*. London: University College.

Pope, Harrison G., Jr., Roberto Olivardia, Amanda Gruber, and John Borowiecki. 1999. "Evolving Ideals of Male Body Image as Seen through Action Toys." *International Journal of Eating Disorders* 26:65–72.

Radway, Janice A. 1983. "Women Read the Romance: The Interaction of Text and Context." *Feminist Studies* 9:53–78.

Squire, Corinne, ed. 2000. *Culture in Psychology*. London: Routledge.

Wilkins, Amy C. 2004. "Puerto Rican Wannabes: Sexual Spectacle and the Marking of Race, Class, and Gender Boundaries." *Gender and Society* 18:103–21.

————. 2009. "Masculinity Dilemmas: Sexuality and Intimacy Talk among Christians and Goths." *Signs: Journal of Women in Culture and Society* 34:343–68.

Wilson, Natalie. 2010. "Civilized Vampires versus Savage Werewolves: Race and Ethnicity in the *Twilight* Series." In *Bitten by "Twilight": Youth Culture, Media, and the Vampire Franchise*, ed. Melissa A. Click, Jennifer Stevens Aubrey, and Elizabeth Behm-Morawitz, 55–70. New York: Peter Lang.

————. 2011a. *Seduced by "Twilight": The Allure and Contradictory Messages of the Popular Saga*. Jefferson, NC: McFarland.

————. 2011b. "It's a Wolf Thing: The Quileute Werewolf/Shape-Shifter Hybrid as Noble Savage." In *Theorizing "Twilight": Critical Essays on What's at Stake in a Post-Vampire World*, ed. Maggie Parke, and Natalie Wilson, 194–208. Jefferson, NC: McFarland.

*IV*

# Issues of Gender, Sex, Class, and Race in *Twilight*

# Chapter Ten

# Chastity, Power, and Delayed Gratification

*The Lure of Sex in the* Twilight *saga*

Brynn Buskirk

Vampires have been featured in legends and folklore for ages, and people have continuously been infatuated with them. Bram Stoker's *Dracula*, written in 1898, defined the vampire trope in literature, which is still prominent in worldwide literature and film today (Barrows 2010, 69; Bruner 2009). Vampire books, movies, and TV shows have been global commercial successes, especially recently. The *Twilight* saga's international popularity is often attributed to several age-old successful plot devices: the star-crossed lovers conundrum, issues related to choice, the idea of the "other," and numerous motifs used time and again in both literary and popular fiction (Granger 2010; Bruner 2009; Gravett 2010). But something different happens in the *Twilight* books and films that makes them more significant worldwide. Both Stephenie Meyer, author of the novels, and the directors for the films successfully use all of these plot devices and then up the ante by adding sexual tension to the equation (Grossman 2008; Bruner 2009). This keeps readers/viewers craving more, creating the *Twilight* frenzy that's taken the world by storm.

Delayed sexual gratification is the driving force behind the *Twilight* novels and films. Meyer develops the plight of the uncommon human girl and the self-loathing, romantic vampire boy, both wanting something they cannot have. This is painfully stretched out for three books and films before readers/ viewers finally receive the satisfaction of Bella and Edward consummating their relationship. As the plotline develops, factors in Bella's and Edward's chastity, power play, and sexual urges serve to catapult the *Twilight* saga

155

from basic teen romance series into something much more powerful for female readers/viewers. This chapter asserts the importance of the Edward Cullen Effect and illustrates how Meyer uses the unique characterizations of both Edward and Bella to resonate chiefly with female readers/viewers. Through close evaluation of the texts and films, we will see how they function together to delay gratification and entice the audience. Therefore, to understand the sexual dynamic between Bella and Edward, we must first look at each individual character.

## THE EDWARD CULLEN EFFECT: WHY WE LOVE HIM

When the saga premiered, Edward Cullen was set apart from many other vampires featured in literary works and film. A breath of fresh air for the tired vampire trope, Edward suppresses both his sexual and violent physical urges to partake in a romantic relationship with a human. This restraint, compounded by his vampirism, makes him truly irresistible to both Bella Swan and *Twilight*'s female readers/viewers—seducing them with what I call the "Edward Cullen Effect." Edward is not after sex, as so many teenage boys and men are, nor is he after blood, like most other vampires. Edward is looking for true love. Movie blogger Steven D. Greydanus (2010) calls him, "a romantic addict, dangerously seductive, proudly resentful, drawing Bella in with those most irresistible words: *Stay away from me for your own good.*" As he captivates Bella, he also enraptures fans. His ability to abstain—yet entice—makes him an actual embodiment of forbidden fruit, creating a hypersexual response in female readers/viewers. Greydanus asks, "Does Edward somehow offer women something that real men have lost or forgotten?" The unique marrying of old-fashioned traits—chivalry and chastity—with the vampyric traits of beauty, immortality, danger, and power makes Edward incomparable to any existing male and beyond desirable to millions of *Twilight*'s female readers.

Edward as forbidden fruit has led to a cult-like following of his character and of Robert Pattinson, the actor who plays him in the film franchise. Pattinson, who was virtually unknown before portraying Edward in the films, was named one of the "Sexiest Men Alive" in 2008 and 2009 by *People* magazine (*People* 2008; *People* 2009). *Forbes* also listed Edward Cullen as the fifth most powerful vampire, and *Entertainment Weekly* named him "one of the greatest characters of the last 20 years . . . a literary influence and love of girls and women everywhere for a long time to come" (Streib 2009; Lynne 2010). Edward's fan base spans the globe, and he is known for his unique fusion of characteristics of abstinence and chivalry with vampyric immortality and beauty.

In order to tug at female heartstrings, Meyer sets Edward up as a self-hating, conflicted vampire. This lost-boy characteristic has been used before in vampire fiction. Joan Grassbough Forry explores this dynamic, specifically citing Louis in *Interview with the Vampire* and some portrayals of Dracula as illustrating these traits. She says, "Sophisticated male vampires usually play the role of vampire protagonist in vampire films and television. In this role, the male vampire is usually a character struggling for self-definition. Having retained some semblance of humanity, he tries to navigate between the loneliness and boredom of immortality and the ethics of killing humans" (Forry 2006, 246–47). These male vampires express emotions and see beauty in everyday worldly objects, but they feel troubled by the world around them. This characterization describes Edward perfectly. Like Louis, Edward has a conscience, is troubled by his actions, considers himself monstrous, and drinks the blood of animals. However, in *Interview with the Vampire*, the reader/viewer sees Louis relent to vampiric monstrosity when he bites and feeds on a young child (Rice 1991). In this respect, Edward is different from common protagonist vampires in his control around humans. While, in the past, Edward has killed humans, he is depicted as a vigilante hero because he killed humans who were dangerous to society and committed crimes. Edward thinks he is going to hell because he has killed people and believes his soul is damned. He calls himself a "deplorable" creature (Meyer 2005, 278); he is portrayed and accepted, however, as the hero and underdog because of all he must endure to be with Bella. Though many vampires, such as Count Dracula and Lestat, have no problem indulging in their instinctual desires and guilty pleasures, Edward abstains (Stoker 1993; Rice 1991). He oozes overt sexuality but is able to suppress his urges to feed on and sexually defile the humans surrounding him. As far as vampires go, Edward does not appear monstrous, only conflicted. The readers/viewers like him immediately because of his "otherness" and internal struggles.

Edward is presented as non-monstrous in both the books and the films. In the saga's transition to film, Meyer was guaranteed the first film would hold true to her original depictions of the characters (Sperling 2008). In contrast to the common vampire trope, Edward does not wear dark capes and does not sleep in a coffin (Meyer 2005, 329). He is not damaged by sunlight. In fact, it makes his skin sparkle (Meyer 2005, 260). The differences don't stop there. Unlike Count Dracula's overtly sexualized dwelling, a castle filled with phallic and vaginal walls and corridors (Stoker 1993, 23–24), Edward's domestic setting is not at all sexually dominating. Even Bella says the open, airy three-story house it is not what she expected (Meyer 2005, 321). Edward's bedroom at the top of the steps is full of light and windows, a stark contrast to Dracula's room found at the end of a dark corridor (Meyer 2007, 438). It seems, although he is a vampire, Meyer takes care to present everything about Edward as safe for Bella.

Perhaps even more telling of Edward's non-monstrous nature is the elemental suppression of his vampyric need to drink human blood, although he does have the urge to feed on Bella. He tells her, "It's not only your company I crave! Never forget that. Never forget I am more dangerous to you than I am to anyone else" (Meyer 2005, 265). In *Midnight Sun* (Meyer 2008b), the reader sees how powerful and fixating his craving is. The audience sees, though, that despite his thirst, Edward is not as dangerous as he thinks himself to be. He tells Bella, "Don't be afraid. I promise . . . I *swear* not to hurt you . . . I *can* control myself" (Meyer 2005, 265). Toward the end of *Twilight*, Bella is bitten by a villain vampire and begins to change into one herself. Edward sucks the venom out of her bite, but still stops before killing her, a feat impossible for most vampires. As she narrates the scene, Bella describes Edward as doubting at first but then determined to save her and, later, triumphant at beating his urge to drink her dry (Meyer 2005, 455–56). Undoubtedly, Edward loves Bella's company more than the taste of her blood. Readers/viewers see Edward continually defy the odds for the girl he loves, a trait seen as both heroic and romantic by many women.

Additionally, Edward is the old-fashioned hometown boy you can take home to meet your parents, and that is exactly what Bella does. Before their first date, he tells her father, "She'll be safe with me, I promise, sir" (Meyer 2005, 359). Edward's respect for Bella's father, and other adults, shows his old-fashioned values and morals. Since Edward is actually much older than his seventeen-year-old body suggests, it is clear that chivalry, a trait lacking today, is important to him. His acts of chivalry, from opening doors for Bella to holding her throughout the night while she sleeps, are often viewed by feminists as demeaning (Dietz 2011; Seifert 2008), but to many female fans, they simply illustrate the concern Edward has for Bella's well-being. He is invested in their relationship, something not common for teenage boys (or grown men) of the twenty-first century.

Both monster and heartthrob, Edward's seductive danger is especially true for *Twilight*'s readers/viewers. J. L. McMahon illustrates Edward's allure to female fans when she writes, "Unlike other works that emphasize the desperate solitude and moral corruption of vampires, *Twilight* romanticizes them. . . . Because they arouse and exacerbate our appetite for inhumanity, the humanistic vampires of *Twilight* are more deeply seductive, and ultimately more dangerous, than the vicious variety" (McMahon 2009, 206). Edward is the forbidden fruit—the bad boy—but at the same time, Bella, and readers/viewers alike, succumb to the Edward Cullen Effect. His restraint and unabashed romantic qualities, coupled with his vampiric qualities, make him the perfect combination of romance and danger.

## BELLA THE EMPOWERED: WHY WE WANT TO BE HER

Edward's seductive appeal is catalyzed by the uniqueness of the female heroine in the saga. Bella, the narrator for almost the entire saga, provides the reader/viewer a voyeuristic view into her thoughts and desires. Through her point of view, Bella objectifies Edward throughout *Twilight*, which further intensifies the Edward Cullen Effect. Bella is commonly examined in two ways—as a teenage girl with low self-confidence emotionally abused by her controlling boyfriend or as an "every girl" with no distinctive characteristics (Bruner 2009; Dietz 2011). She is not typically seen this way by *Twilight*'s fans, however. Even if audiences don't love Bella, they like her enough to align themselves with her.

John Granger (2010) explores the interesting alignment female readers have with Bella, naming her modesty and sense of humor as traits that make her likable. He also notes she is characterized as a sort of orphan who needs to take care of herself, similar to other likeable characters, such as Oliver Twist and Harry Potter (26–27). Bella is also special because she attracts the handsome, charming Edward who has been waiting a hundred years for his soul mate. Fans live vicariously through Bella to partake in her unusual relationship with the vampire. Additionally, because female fans read the books and watch the movies to experience Edward, they ultimately do not want anything bad to happen to Bella. If Edward harmed her, it would destroy his heroic character. To enjoy the saga, fans must experience and appreciate Bella's narration.

Meyer positions Bella as different; indeed, she seems vampiric from the beginning. She is an outsider who has recently moved from the desert to the lush, green landscape of Forks, Washington. When Bella sees the Cullens for the first time, she immediately identifies with them, noting their similar appearance and saying they were "the palest of all of the students living in this sunless town. Paler than me, the albino" (Meyer 2005, 18). Bella associates herself with the Cullens, in short, because they share "otherness."

Bella's power and independence are then illustrated through her keen awareness and ability to appropriately look at things, people, and events throughout the saga. I relate Bella's ability to look at Edward without being harmed to Rhona J. Berenstein's genius assessment in *Attack of the Leading Ladies: Gender, Sexuality, and Spectatorship in Classic Horror Film* (1996). Berenstein explains that the "male gaze" dominated 1930s' horror films, such as *Dracula* and *King Kong*. The dynamic of the gaze worked in four ways: (1) the audience for classic horror was predominately comprised of sadistic male spectators; (2) any females in attendance did not watch and instead cowered in fear; (3) the plotlines of these classic films were created for this specific audience; the woman (victim) could not look at the monster (male) without being harmed or killed; and (4) the classic horror plots focus on monstrous desire (Berenstein 1996, 2). The male gaze reinforced the social belief that women were the ones to be looked at, not the ones looking. Berenstein argues against these earlier studies of female exploitation and actually empowers the female gaze in classic horror films, saying, "Instead of aligning the heroine's gaze solely with masochism and passivity, I argue that beneath its vapid veneer rest intimations of power, desire, and monstrosity" (Berenstein 1996, 30). She assigns both agency and power to a woman looking at the monster even if there are consequences.

Meyer, like Berenstein, turns the notion of the woman as the object of the gaze on its head and makes Edward—not Bella—the spectacle. Bella is rewarded for looking, which provides her knowledge and enables her to realize that the Cullens are different. Bella is masculinized in the saga, as her eyes are always exposed as she looks and chooses. She is never harmed or punished for her ability to look. Before Edward and Bella officially meet, they often "meet gazes" in class or across the crowded cafeteria. Edward seems to challenge Bella with his gaze, but she doesn't back down. She says, "Edward was staring at me curiously, that same, familiar edge of frustration even more distinct now in his black eyes. I stared back, surprised, expecting him to look quickly away. But instead he continued to gaze with probing intensity into my eyes. There was no question of me looking away." The teacher calls on Edward, and he is forced to avert his eyes from Bella's to answer the question (Meyer 2005, 73). This scene sets Bella above Edward as the most powerful player in their newly forming dynamic. Edward comments on Bella's "penetrating gaze" (Meyer 2008b, 32). He is the phallic, male vampire equipped with piercing teeth and penis, but she is the one penetrating him. He is on the receiving end of her aggressive gaze. She looks, and she is neither ashamed nor scared. According to Berenstein's formula, it is Bella who holds the powerful characteristics of the monster, which supports Bella's control of Edward and her strength as a female character. Additionally, the sexual symbolism is overt as she looks, foreshadowing Bella's actions as sexual actor. Bella's and Edward's eyes are also the subject of close-ups throughout the films. *Breaking Dawn Part 1* ends with Bella's transformation, and the closing shot shows her opening her eyes as a vampire. Her irises glow red, and she has a new way of seeing the world. She looks directly at the camera and the future, undoubting and unafraid. Bella's power is exacerbated by her vampiric state. Scholars have noted this frequently, stating that vampiric Bella "is more herself than ever before" (Jones 2009, 150). She is the strongest of the Cullen vampires and able to protect herself and anyone of her choosing with her superpower of projecting a shield that stops harm. Her ability to act behind this shield, impervious to the influence of others, shows Bella's powerful authority.

Integrally connected to Bella's ability to look is the objectification of Edward in the saga. Edward is continually portrayed through Bella's gaze—a complete change from earlier vampire texts—as Meyer is using the male, not the female, to incite desire. Marc E. Shaw (2009) writes, "Meyer focuses on the carnal instead of the spiritual with her array of lengthy descriptions of Edward's looks. Because almost all of the *Twilight Series* is told from Bella's point of view, and because Meyer fixates on Edward, *Twilight* returns the gaze that is usually reserved for men looking at women" (235). Edward is described from Bella's viewpoint as being beautiful—so beautiful that Bella compares him several times to the Greek god of rebirth, Adonis (Meyer 2005, 299, 317). Edward-as-spectacle is hard to miss as he sparkles in sunlight and has abdominal muscles and a chest made of cool, hard marble. Female readers/viewers experience Edward through Bella's eyes, giving them the ability to look and be in control.

For the audience, Bella's power over Edward is more clearly depicted as the saga progresses. In one of the most frequently quoted scenes, Edward searches for a fitting analogy to explain the control Bella has over him. First he compares her to chocolate ice cream and then to hundred-year-old cognac, but he finds that neither provides a strong enough description of enticement. He finally tells Bella, "You are exactly my brand of heroin" (Meyer 2005, 267–68). Heroin, a drug that entrances and hypnotizes, is an interesting choice, for it explains how Edward is helpless and Bella, the "heroin," is in control. This is also a play on words: Bella is heroin *and* heroine. As both, she entices Edward physically with her drug-like command, but she also acts heroic and keeps him "good" by loving him. The idea of being hypnotic to men also evokes a longing in female readers/viewers who likewise hunger to be desired, which is perhaps why this scene is a favorite for many fans.

While Bella is female, she has dominant, classically male characteristics, such as the ability to look, control, and act assertively. Carol Siegel calls Bella's unique identity "the combination of toughness and femininity, self-assertion and voluptuous yielding" (Siegel 2007, 58). Bella is a different type of female from the classically feminist heroines of vampire literature and film, such as Mina (and her "man's brain") from *Dracula* and Buffy (Deffenbacher and Zagoria-Moffet 2011). Though self-conscious, her charisma and power always enable her to get what she wants: she learns that Edward is a vampire, she convinces Edward to have sex with her when she is still human, she carries a child to full term even though others urge her to abort it, and she ultimately becomes a vampire, something she has wanted since falling in love with Edward. As a human, Bella conveys power in her control of Edward as she chooses her future for herself. Female readers/viewers see her mature from gawky teenager to fulfilled grown woman and mother and attribute her success to both her power and the decisions she made along the way.

## BUILDING UP TO SEX IN *TWILIGHT*: WHY IT IS WORTH THE WAIT

Bella's role as powerful—acting and wanting Edward—is intensified by references Meyer makes to Eden throughout the saga, as she writes Edward and Bella to parallel Adam and Eve. She begins *Twilight* with a quote from Genesis, and the jacket cover of the novel shows pale hands offering a perfect, red, unbitten apple. The entire first book and film are ripe with the forbidden-fruit analogy, which Meyer incorporates consciously as she sets the stage for the star-crossed lovers. The metaphor works in multiple ways because the forbidden fruit can represent Bella for Edward, Edward for Bella, their love, their relationship, or sex, among others. Because the metaphor is multifaceted, it is hard for even a young, teenage reader to miss.

One cannot ignore the references to the creation story, but the interpretation of Bella as Eve often affords her more criticism than merit (Granger 2010; Shaw 2009). In *The Women's Bible Commentary*, Susan Niditch (1998) provides a refreshing reading of Eve, one not bogged down by the stigma of Eve as the Fallen Woman. In Niditch's reading of Genesis, she sees Eve as a seeker of knowledge who knowingly eats from the tree of good and evil because she yearns for a meaningful existence in the world. She calls Eve the "bringer of culture" because Eve, not Adam, is the "conscious actor choosing knowledge" (17). Niditch describes Adam as passive in the Garden of Eden, only eating the fruit after Eve hands it to him. Mormon theology, Meyer's faith tradition, presents Eve in a similar light, calling her "wise" in eating the apple and causing "The Fall." Experiencing and resisting sin is part of a Mormon's path to divinity. Without "The Fall," there is no sin and no divine path (Toscano 2010, 24).

Using Niditch's interpretation, Bella is a likely Eve. In *Midnight Sun*, with Edward narrating, Bella "picks up an apple and twist[s] it in her hands." She looks at Edward and says, "I'm curious. What would you do if someone dared you to eat food?" (Meyer 2008b, 234). Edward describes how, without looking, he picks up the closest item and bites into it, knowing he will have to throw it up later. This scene parallels the reading of Genesis that Niditch provides. Edward, like Adam, eats just because Bella, like Eve, challenges him. Both Bella and Eve tempt the men, and both men imbibe despite the implications. The women are powerful, and by acting on the requests of these women, the men prove passive.

Forbidden fruit is also figuratively symbolic for the insatiable sexual yearning Bella and Edward experience throughout the saga. Romantically linked, the two are unable to act on their sexual desires due to their circumstances. Edward tells Bella that sexual intercourse is not possible because of their different states of being. In *Twilight*, after he and Bella share their first kiss, he explains to her, "It's just that you are so soft, so fragile. I have to mind my actions every moment we're together so that I don't hurt you" (Meyer 2005, 310). Edward explains why sexual relations are risky; however, the readers/viewers question his reasoning. We know his strength is always a potential issue, yet Edward maintains absolute self-control in Bella's presence. Then, in *Eclipse*, Edward tells Bella another reason why he has not initiated sex: he wishes to wait until marriage to consummate their relationship. Like Edward's chivalry, his traditional belief in abstaining from premarital sex is another old-fashioned ideal not often manifested in society today. Even more surprising is the fact that Edward has been a vampire since 1917 and is still a virgin, and proud of it. Vampires in most any other work are sexually promiscuous, so for Edward to be chaste is representative of his strong morals. Bella finds all the rules regarding chastity to be old-fashioned, but Edward is traditional, and even as a vampire, he manages to control his sexual urges and respect Bella's virginity. He tells her, regarding both of their virginities, "This is the one area where I am just as spotless as you are" (Meyer 2007, 454).

Though Edward's virginity is unusual and enticing for female audiences, the sexual dynamic between the main characters is unique and gripping. Meyer distorts the usual boy/girl sexual relationship common today. Both Bella and Edward are aware of the reversal; Edward comments on how unusual it is that the boy is playing "hard to get" and the girl is pursuing the sexual relationship. When Bella no longer wants to wait for sex, he says, "Do you get the feeling that everything is backward? Traditionally, shouldn't you be arguing my side, and I yours?" (Meyer 2007, 451). This scene is an example of why teen girls (and grown women) fall head-over-heels for Edward. Bella wants something she can't have, which makes her, and the audience, want it so much more. Additionally, teenage girls, who have so much pressure from Western culture to be objects of sexual desire may find it refreshing to see a seventeen-year-old boy interested in a romantic relationship that places sex to the side. Bella has assumed the more dominant role of sexual actor, and Edward is submissive and acted upon. Sarah Seltzer, freelancer for the *Huffington Post*, explores this dynamic:

> Now that's a real fantasy: a world where young women are free to describe their desires openly, and launch themselves at men without shame, while said boyfriends are the sexual gatekeepers. *Twilight*'s sexual flowchart is the inversion of abstinence-only / purity ball culture, where girls are told that they must guard themselves against rabid boys, and they must reign [*sic*] in both their own and their suitors' impulses. (Seltzer 2008)

Seltzer is accurate in that Bella is the sexual aggressor and Edward is mostly sexually passive. Bella is the initiator, seeking what she wants. At points where Bella doubts Edward's desire for her, Edward tells her, "I may not be human, but I am a man," and "I have human instincts—they may be buried deep, but they're there" (Meyer 2005, 311). Readers/viewers see that when the two kiss passionately Edward, at times, allows himself to get carried away, but he has the self-restraint to stop and not disregard his values. During their most passionate make-out scene in *Eclipse*, Bella narrates:

> His mouth was not gentle; there was a brand-new edge of conflict and desperation in the way his lips moved. I locked my arms around his neck, and, to my suddenly overheated skin, his body felt colder than ever. I trembled but it was not from the chill. He didn't stop kissing me. I was the one who had to break away, gasping for air. Even then his lips did not leave my skin, they just moved to my throat. The thrill of victory is a strange high; it made me feel powerful. Brave . . . I pulled his mouth back to mine, and he seemed just as eager as I was. (Meyer 2007, 450)

In this scene, Edward nearly succumbs to his sexual desires. It is evident that when Edward is vulnerable, he is able to be a passionate, sultry lover in bed. But, ultimately, he murmurs in her ear, "Bella, would you please stop trying to take your clothes off?" Adding, "not tonight" (Meyer 2007, 450). Meyer brings the reader/viewer into Bella's and Edward's sexual awakening and then abruptly shuts it down right before takeoff.

Not only is the prolonged sexual gratification thrilling for the audience but also is the inherent danger of the situation for Bella. The reader/viewer is left to wonder what would happen if they did have sex. Would Edward kill Bella? Would he be too tempted and bite her first? When this make-out scene is shown in the *Eclipse* film, the lyrics to the music playing in the background assert "life on earth is ending, life on earth is changing," showcasing the limbo Bella's life is in. With a simple bite, her life would be over, and she would be changing into a vampire, adding an element of suspense to the already growing sexual tension. Forry (2006) examines the sexuality of the vampire bite, saying:

> The promise of a vampire's sexuality lies in the vampire's method, seducing victims so they become willing participants. The bite is often represented as highly pleasurable for both vampire and the victim . . . during the bite, both vampire and victim appear as if they are in the throes of orgasm. (242)

Edward has Bella in the position of willing participant. He hovers near her neck, but the absolute *lack* of what Forry describes is what makes Edward so irresistible. Edward does not bite or have sex. While vampires act promiscuously, Edward struggles internally to repress his sexual urges to remain a virgin. Edward has all of the qualities humans find attractive in vampires: immortality, strength, beauty, and passion, but he does not rape his victims or drink their blood. This makes him less monstrous and more heroic.

Edward and Bella finally consummate their relationship after they are married, in what is now an infamous sex scene. Bella preps herself in the bathroom but shuns the typical sexualized female trope by neglecting to wear the lingerie packed for her by sister-in-law Alice. She walks determinedly out onto the beach and then toward both Edward in the water and what she describes as "the white light" (Meyer 2008a, 84). It reads almost as a near-death experience. Bella's description ends by saying Edward pulls her deeper into the water. The book leaves the rest to the imagination, but the film shows several short glimpses into the encounter. Bella laughs, not in a nervous sense, but confidently, as she lies under Edward in a large, soft bed. She assures him, "It's okay" when he inadvertently breaks the bedframe (*Breaking Dawn Part 1* 2011). In the morning after, Edward is shaken and upset that Bella was bruised due to his strength in the encounter, but Bella is happy and calls the soreness "not an unpleasant feeling" (Meyer 2008a, 88). The readers/viewers see Bella admitting her sexual pleasure and not shying away from the fact that she enjoyed the pain that occurred with it. For both the female character and audience, Meyer again sensuously mixes the monstrous with the alluring.

Fans waited with bated breath for the *Breaking Dawn Part 1* film, and the sex scene was heavily played up in the trailers. The movie earned the franchise's most money—$291 million—on its worldwide opening weekend and become the highest grossing film of the saga (Subers 2011). Because the sexual act was heavily anticipated since the first book, the scene is a victory for the readers/viewers, who feel—in a voyeuristic sense—like they lost their virginities with Edward, too.

## SEX AND VAMPIRES: THE MORNING AFTER

Sex proves to be the turning point in the saga; Bella gets everything she has wanted since the beginning, save becoming an actual vampire. But then she gets that, too. With sex come adult decisions and responsibilities, namely pregnancy, childbirth, and parenting. They do not come without their rewards; Bella becomes a mother (something she never knew she wanted but enjoys once it happens) and a vampire (something she has wanted since she met Edward). Once a vampire, Bella also experiences the promise of a "forever" that mortal readers can never have. Bella will "forever" have Edward, sexual fulfillment, and power. The film *Breaking Dawn Part 2* illustrates all three of these "forevers" during their sexual encounter once Bella is a vampire. She takes the dominant role as sexual actor atop of Edward, while a fire burns in the background. She is sexual, powerful, and has Edward, all in the same moment and for eternity.

The chastity and enticement of Edward, the empowerment of the female narrator, and the promise of forever are reasons why the series has resonated so well with female audiences. Though the books were written without the mention of any sexually anatomical terms or lewd language, and the films lack nudity and leave much up to the imagination, the central theme of the saga is sex and desire. The books have been removed from Mormon bookstore shelves, banned from school libraries, and questioned by parent groups for this reason (Puente 2010). Lev Grossman (2010) writes in *Time*, "That's the power of the *Twilight* books: they're squeaky, geeky clean on the surface, but right below it, they are absolutely, deliciously filthy."

Vampire books and movies continue to hit the market in whiplash fashion, riding the wake of *Twilight*'s success, all trying to capture what was already done magically by Meyer. She developed a new breed of vampire that effectively spurred a new genre of vampire texts and films and introduced a sexually powerful female who is ultimately unashamed of her sexual assertiveness. Worldwide, both teenagers and grown women experienced the erotica of delayed sexual gratification and the "first time" through these two fascinating characters, who are rewarded with eternal happiness. Bella's and Edward's unique characteristics, relationship, and power play develop the Edward Cullen Effect, which is further exacerbated by the female audience's ability to "gaze" upon the male spectacle. The perfect arrangement of these qualities creates a distinctive and captivating experience for readers and viewers, who become thirsty for more, feeding the worldwide *Twilight* phenomenon.

## REFERENCES

Barrows, Adam. 2010. "Heidegger the Vampire Slayer: The Undead and Fundamental Ontology." In *Zombies, Vampires, and Philosophy: New Life for the Undead*, ed. Richard Greene and K. Silem Mohammad. Chicago: Carus.

Berenstein, Rhona J. 1996. *Attack of the Leading Ladies: Gender, Sexuality, and Spectatorship in Classic Horror Film*. New York: Columbia University Press.

Bruner, Kurt. 2009. *The "Twilight" Phenomenon: Forbidden Fruit or Thirst-Quenching Fantasy?* Shippensburg, PA: Destiny Image.

Deffenbacher, Kristina, and Mikayla Zagoria-Moffet. 2011. "Textual Vampirism in *The Twilight Saga*: Drawing Feminist Life from *Jane Eyre* and Teen Fantasy Fiction." In *Bringing Light to "Twilight": Perspectives on the Pop Culture Phenomenon*, ed. Giselle Liza Anatol, 31–42. New York: Palgrave Macmillan.

Dietz, Tammy. 2011. "Wake Up, Bella! A Personal Essay on *Twilight*, Mormonism, Feminism, and Happiness." In *Bringing Light to "Twilight": Perspectives on the Pop Culture Phenomenon*, ed. Giselle Liza Anatol, 99–112. New York: Palgrave Macmillan.

Forry, Joan Grassbough. 2006. "'Powerful, Beautiful, and without Regret': Femininity, Masculinity, and the Vampire Aesthetic." In *Zombies, Vampires, and Philosophy: New Life for the Undead*, ed. Richard Greene and K. Silem Mohammad, 237–48. Chicago: Carus.

Granger, John. 2010. *Spotlight: A Close-up Look at the Artistry and Meaning of Stephenie Meyer's "Twilight Saga."* Allentown, PA: Zossima.

Gravett, Sandra L. 2010. *From "Twilight" to "Breaking Dawn": Religious Themes in "The Twilight Saga."* St. Louis: Chalice.

Greydanus, Steven D. 2010. *"Twilight* Appeal: The Cult of Edward Cullen and Vampire Love in Stephenie Meyer's Novels and the New Film." *Decent Films Guide.* Accessed May 24, 2013. http://www.decentfilms.com/articles/twilight.

Grossman, Lev. 2008 "Stephenie Meyer: A New J. K. Rowling?" *Time Magazine*, April 24. Accessed May 26, 2013. http://www.time.com/time/magazine/article/0,9171,1734838-1,00. html.

Jones, Beth Felker. 2009. *Touched by a Vampire: Discovering the Hidden Messages in "The Twilight Saga."* Colorado Springs, CO: Multnomah Books.

Lynne, Amanda. 2010. "Robert Pattinson's Edward Cullen named one of the greatest characters of the last 20 years." Gather.com. Accessed 2013-05-16. http://entertainment.gather. com/viewArticle.action?%20articleId=%20281474978263287.

McMahon, J. L., 2009. "Twilight of an Idol: Our Fatal Attraction to Vampires." In *"Twilight" and Philosophy: Vampires, Vegetarians, and the Pursuit of Immortality*, ed. Rebecca Housel and J. Jeremy Wisnewski, 193–208. Hoboken, NJ: Wiley.

Meyer, Stephenie. 2005. *Twilight*. New York: Little, Brown.

———. 2007. *Eclipse*. New York: Little, Brown.

———. 2008a. *Breaking Dawn*. New York: Little, Brown.

———. 2008b. *Midnight Sun*. Unpublished draft. Accessed February 6, 2012. http://www. stepheniemeyer.com/pdf/midnightsun_partial_draft4.pdf.

Niditch, Susan. 1998. "Genesis." In *The Women's Bible Commentary*, ed. Carol A. Newson and Sharon H. Ringe, 13–29. Louisville KY: Westminster John Knox.

*People*. 2008. "2008's Sexiest Man Alive." Accessed 5-16-2013. http://www.people.com/ people/package/%20gallery/%200,,20237714_20241212_20545173,00.html#20545173.

*People*. 2009. "2009's Sexiest Man Alive." Accessed 5-16-2013. http://www.people.com/ people/package/gallery/0,,20315920_20320457,00.html#20705504.

Puente, Maria. 2010. "Adults Fret That *Eclipse* Lacks Good Role Models for Teens." *USA Today*, July 7. Accessed May 23, 2013. http://usatoday30.usatoday.com/life/movies/news/ 2010-07-07-eclipse07_CV_N.htm?csp=usat.me.

Rice, Anne. 1991. *Interview with the Vampire*. New York: Ballantine Books.

Seifert, Christine. 2008. "Bite Me (or Don't)." *Bitch Magazine* 42 (Winter). http:// bitchmagazine.org/article/bite-me-or-dont.

Seltzer, Sarah. 2008. *"Twilight*: Sexual Longing in an Abstinence Only World." *Huffington Post*, August 9. Accessed February 11, 2012. http://www.huffingtonpost.com/sarah-seltzer/ twilight-sexual-longing-i_b_117927.html.

Shaw, Marc E. 2009. "For the Strength of Bella: Meyer, Vampires, and Mormonism." In *"Twilight" and Philosophy: Vampires, Vegetarians, and the Pursuit of Immortality*, ed. Rebecca Housel, J. Jeremy Wisnewski, and William Irwin, 227–36. Hoboken, NJ: Wiley.

Siegel, Carol. 2007. "Female Heterosexual Sadism: The Final Feminist Taboo in *Buffy the Vampire Slayer* and the *Anita Blake Vampire Hunter* Series." In *Third Wave Feminism and Television: Jane Puts Jane It in a Box*, ed. Merri Lisa Johnson. London: IB Taurus.

Sperling, Nicole. 2008. *"Twilight*: Inside the First Stephenie Meyer Movie." *Entertainment Weekly*, July 16. http://www.ew.com/ew/article/0,,20211840,00.html.

Stoker, Bram. 1993. *Dracula*. New York: Penguin Classics.

Streib, Lauren. 2009. "Hollywood's 10 Most Powerful Vampires." *Forbes*. Accessed 2013-05-16. http://www.forbes.com/2009/08/03/true-blood-vampires-business-entertainment-vampires_slide_6.html.

Subers, Ray. 2011. "Around-the-World Roundup: *Breaking Dawn* Lights Up Overseas." *Box Office Mojo*, November 22. Accessed May 25, 2013. http://www.boxofficemojo.com/news/ ?id=3313.

Toscano, Margaret M. 2010. "Mormon Morality and Immortality in Stephenie Meyer's *Twilight* Series." In *Bitten by "Twilight": Youth Culture, Media, and the Vampire Franchise*, ed. Melissa A. Click, Jennifer Stevens Aubrey, and Elizabeth Behm-Morawitz, 21–36. New York: Peter Lang.

*Chapter Eleven*

# Alice, Bella, and Economics

*Financial Security and Class Mobility in* Twilight

Paul A. Lucas

Two reasons that can help explain *Twilight*'s worldwide appeal are found in portrayals of class mobility and financial security. These characteristics are emphasized by portrayals of an attractive potential mate—juxtaposed against an atypical gender portrayal of that mate's sister, insofar as the sister has financial and material independence. The *Twilight* series presents an optimistic view of social-class mobility, and, thanks to Alice Cullen, that optimistic view is also fully immune to almost any form of economic decline.

Today's economy is weak, and many individuals find themselves on tighter budgets and struggling to make ends meet. In a time of clear class-related anxiety, fueled in large part by the economic fall beginning in 2008, audiences can look to *Twilight* as an indicator of one's ability to move outside of social class—more importantly, to enjoy full financial security in a context where there virtually is none. Removed from the current economic context, *Twilight* shows the way one's life can be in light of a more materialistic existence, which, within reason, is a desirable lifestyle when individuals otherwise are feeling pressures from budget constraints. In this chapter, then, three major representations in *Twilight* will be addressed: 1) the way *Twilight* appeals to fans by showing a "better" world with the possibility of increased social status and financial security in a time of economic uncertainty, 2) the way that Alice is representative of a caregiver and provider, and 3) how these elements are indicative of a fan base and culture that is willing to accept *Twilight* for its value and optimistic portrayals.

Class-mobility representations have been discussed in previous *Twilight* literature (Buttsworth 2010; Wilson 2010). For example, issues of race are at times intertwined into explaining Bella's interest in Edward. Natalie Wilson

(2010) characterizes the issue of race and class as indicative of "real-world white privilege" (56), with Edward at the forefront. Sara Buttsworth (2010) even comments on *Twilight*'s similarity to "tales of upward mobility" (51). While these takes on *Twilight* are relevant, the purpose of this particular study is to examine the way in which *Twilight*'s portrayals of class and materialism are more positive and may actually be indicative of a culture that is looking for artifacts that suggest the possibility of both class mobility and the chance to escape current economic constraints.

Specifically, this work will focus on the way that *Twilight* allows fans a fantasy experience where they can envision themselves in a wealthy, financially secure existence. Given the reality of a tough economy, fans are likely open to such existence, especially since Alice Cullen makes it almost worry-free. With an eye toward understanding Bella's transition to a materialistic lifestyle, this work will also look at Alice as the source of that lifestyle, which is important considering that she backs up her materialism with her unique ability to see the future—and foresee stock market trends.

## BELLA: A CASE FOR CLASS MOBILITY

Bella is obviously not financially well-off when audiences first meet her; even at the start of the *Twilight* series, her class status is made clear. Before Bella encounters or seriously considers her place with Edward and the Cullens, she faces the necessity of acquiring a vehicle—enter the role of the iconic pickup truck. Despite the fact that Bella is appreciative of her father, Charlie, taking the initiative to get a car for her, she does express concern about the pickup's quality, even expressing worry about needing to pay for vehicle troubles and general maintenance (Meyer 2005, 7). Later in the first book, Bella notices the truck's gas-guzzling tendency, which is a potential problem for her, financially (Meyer 2005, 80). In the first *Twilight* film, Bella expresses much more appreciation for the gifted truck as compared with the first book, but that is likely linked to the fact that Jacob plays a bigger role in giving the truck to her.

Bella's financial situation is also conveyed later in the series. In *New Moon*, Bella thinks about what little money she had growing up, especially in light of her father making a modest income as the chief of police; furthermore, Bella's personal finances are fully dependent on a part-time job she holds at a small neighborhood store (Meyer 2006, 13). In no way is Bella's financial standing hidden. While she is not poor, she does come from a modest-income family with a modest lifestyle, which greatly differs from Edward's wealth.

Bella also has awareness of her own financial standing as compared with others. Audiences familiar with *Twilight* know she has her fair share of resistance to a materialistic lifestyle. In many ways, Bella enjoys her truck. At the same time, however, Bella is self-conscious of it when she compares it with vehicles other people own. Bella expresses relief that many other students in Forks drive vehicles like hers, thinking about how her previous experience at a school saw other students driving "new Mercedes or Porsches" (Meyer 2005, 14).

In Forks, Bella reflects that "the nicest car here was a shiny Volvo, and it stood out" (Meyer 2005, 14). Although audiences eventually discover that the Cullens own fancier vehicles, such as a Mercedes, a Porsche, and a Jeep, Edward's Volvo, and how nice it looks, is the primary vehicle of Bella's focus. This is due to the Volvo being the first Cullen vehicle she comes into contact with, so it serves as a window into Edward's wealth and status early. Bella is inclined to remember many details about Edward, but in an early instance, she refers to him as a "stupid, shiny Volvo owner" (Meyer 2005, 83), connecting him with the car she had seen. Though Bella would have readers believe she rejects materialism, she is aware of her financial standing, using vehicles as a point of social comparison.

A lack of material and financial success can bring on this kind of self-consciousness (Sennett 1998, 119). Social comparison often stems from looking at consumer products and how "some persons have them and others do not" (Leiss, Kline, and Jhally 1990, 298). In the books, it is clear that Bella feels these kinds of pains and pressures, at least in terms of noticing what other people have and what she does not. Her awareness of what other people drive would suggest less satisfaction in her standing than what she otherwise would lead readers to believe. Though Bella is outwardly comfortable and happy with her position, audiences are privy to her less-confident thought processes.

Cars are generally thought to be among the strongest indicators of financial standing and are used throughout the series to convey an image of the Cullens' wealth; it therefore makes sense that Bella puts so much energy into thinking about her truck. Mihaly Csikszentmihalyi and Eugene Rochberg-Halton (1981) use cars as a leading example of status indicators, since nice cars are often likened to a "person" with "distinctive" or "superior qualities" (29). Bella is interesting to consider in this regard. While she does seem to appreciate what she has, valuing things in life over material wealth—such as love and family, for example—she recognizes representative symbols of the material success of others, particularly the Cullens' choices for vehicles. The fact that Bella is ultimately willing to buy into and accept the wealthier, materialistic lifestyle of the Cullens, including their purchasing a car for her, indicates that she is open to a different and higher social status.

Consumers can determine the worth of the Cullens' vehicles because of the identities they have by association. The vehicles also become characteristics of worth and signs of achievement because consumers are taught, through marketing, branding practices, and social interaction, that these are the cars they should desire. Bella is not immune to this way of thinking. Beyond just financial security, the need to be secure enough to consume and to have nice things is a central motivator toward materialism and status, even for Bella. Consumer-filled lifestyles are not without potential problems, but "capitalism faces the problem of 'realization,' of making sure that the huge numbers of goods produced beyond [a] minimal level are consumed" (Leiss, Kline, and Jhally 1990, 20). Consumption is a way to deal with the surplus characteristic of a healthy economy (Baran and Sweezy 1966, 79), and *Twilight* emphasizes this.

## OF LOVE AND LIFESTYLE: *TWILIGHT* AND MATERIAL CULTURE

The *Twilight* books and films are full of Bella's assessments of how unbelievably attractive the Cullens are. At its core, *Twilight* is a love story; however, Bella's willingness to accept Edward as a husband is also indicative of her willingness to accept all that he is. Bella introduces herself into a wealthy situation by becoming both a Cullen and a vampire. In some ways, Bella is willing to enter this life change, considering she is the one constantly pushing Edward into changing her from human to vampire. Bella's full understanding of entering the world of the Cullens is indicative of her willingness, maybe even her desire, to enter the world of wealth and materialism, even though she does not openly acknowledge this.

When Bella first tries to make sense of her perceptions of and feelings for the Cullens at school, she reflects that they wear nice, expensive-looking clothing—and the style and quality of the Cullens' clothing becomes more prominent as the series progresses. To that end, Bella thinks to herself "it seemed excessive for them to have both looks and money" (Meyer 2005, 32). Bella envisions the Cullens as ideal; she sees the family as beautiful beyond comparison. Along with that feeling, Bella has a grasp of the money the family has, accepting Edward as belonging to this wealthy context.

In *Breaking Dawn*, Bella fulfills her goal of becoming a vampire. Once that happens, she is fully a member of the Cullen family and can be with Edward forever. For Bella, the act of turning into a vampire is one of "transformation, purpose, and meaning" (Jones 2009, 145). In this way, the *Twilight* series reads as a story that potentially romanticizes the consumerist and capitalist lifestyle. Bella "has no such qualms in accepting the benefits of the Cullens' wealth after marriage" (Buttsworth 2010, 66), and movement toward this end is an ongoing process throughout the series.

## The Connection to Youth

Bella's desire to attain immortality is fueled in part by "her horror at growing older" (Jones 2009, 146). Bella takes issue with her own aging, as she glamorizes the idea of becoming a vampire and negatively envisions herself older. In the beginning of *New Moon*, for example, Bella worries about wrinkles, and even protests against attempts to draw attention to her birthday (Meyer 2006, 7–8). Concerns about growing older can be strongly linked to consumer behavior.

One defining feature of materialistic living is the way product identity is transmitted to the consumer. Benjamin Barber (2007) characterizes such identities as "substitute identities" (167), which become cultural markers for consumers. An aspect of both marketing and consumption today, applicable to Bella, hinges on "the celebration of youth" (Barber 2007, 16), where products become linked to youth culture and feeling young. The inevitability of aging is not appealing for many people who feel and see themselves getting older. Edward, in all his materialistic glory, is not only the love of Bella's life, but also represents a better future in general, since he can actually grant Bella a way to prevent these pains of aging—which material and consumer culture promise, as well. Thus, Bella can make a decision about how best to etch out the identity she is looking for.

For audiences who might envision a quality of life that includes an ability to be more materialistic, these two aspects depict a way such a life change might work. As a series that "validates the message that youth culture is desirable and can be obtained" where "the products one buys demonstrates one's worth" (Wilson 2011, 188), *Twilight* presents audiences with a better life described through consumer roles. The representation makes sense since many individuals like being consumers and want to take part in the consumer process. Although James B. Twitchell's (1999; 2002) work has been questioned, he argues that consumers are excited to consume. He believes that consumer drive necessitates discrimination in purchases, so consumers can select goods based on their own individual inclinations (Twitchell 1999, 38).

The difference in the series for Bella, as opposed to a typical consumer, is that she has a true outlet for youth. Her husband is a vampire, and so, eventually, is Bella herself. She will forever remain the age she is, and so her transformation is a little more concrete than what products can realistically provide. Still, many products are marketed in such a way they "grant a boon: eternal life, youth, prowess, togetherness, unfulfilled dreams" (Gossage 1967, 367). Materialism, marketing, and consumption, wrought with brand promises that products will give a better quality of life, are in large part symbolized in the life Bella is entering into as a Cullen.

## The Consumer Search

It is important to understand these quality of life promises in *Twilight*, before criticizing Bella as a woman who seeks out wealth and material life simply by marrying into it. While marketing and consumption have their fair share of evils, they are characteristics of capitalism that are not going away. The analysis of materialism and its depictions in pop culture is therefore very relevant. As George Soros (1998) notes, "how people ought to live their lives" is an example of a "question" that "ought not to be answered on the basis of market values. Yet this is happening" (43). Much like Bella, part of what drives consumers is their desire to get "bearings and make sense of [their] lives in a time when the meaning of it all is not obvious" (Morris 1997, 7). The generation of meaning through the market as an aspect of consumer life is essential in recognizing Bella's search for meaning in *Twilight* and how embracing material culture is part of how she discovers such meaning.

Bella finds in the Cullens a wealthy and materialistic lifestyle that aids her in making sense of herself—a characteristic further exaggerated by Bella's inability to function as well as a human as she can as a vampire. From Bella's perspective, she was "born to be a vampire" (Meyer 2008, 524). As an elegantly dressed, newborn vampire, Bella says, "I found my true place in the world" (Meyer, 2008 524), and materialism is part of that world. Though a consumer mentality potentially allows marketing practitioners to prey upon consumer weakness, the fact remains that consumers "need ideas as much as [they] need food, air, or water" (Morris 1997, 25). Consumers want to find meaning, and certainly the marketplace can help them find it; similarly, Bella is looking for meaning in her transformation.

Some disagree with consumer and material culture, as well as with its overpowering role in contemporary life, but there is no denying that most people seek a better life quality. Barber (2007) describes the way in which capitalism and consumerism go hand in hand, explaining that "good-willed but self-seeking individuals" have the ability to "produce a radically commercial culture which many of those same individuals despise and for which no one is directly responsible" (129). Self-realization and success are often thought to be linked to making more money and having nice things, which fosters material culture. From a negative stance, materialism can function as a form of pressure, compelling consumers to buy goods in line with their status, even leading to financial trouble; the current state of the economy can make money and material living more difficult to attain and manage.

In that regard, people may, by nature, drive materialism, even if they have difficulty achieving what they want. Csikszentmihalyi and Rochberg-Halton (1981) emphasize how "the ultimate 'goal' of other animals is to live," whereas "the ultimate goal of humankind is conditioned by additional evolutionary purposes as well, which determine us to live well" (232). Humans are not generally satisfied with daily survival, at least not in the way animals might be. For example, eating the necessary number of calories will sustain life; why, though, eat a hamburger if you can have steak? Animalistic levels of survival are not sufficient for human understandings of life, since even "basic needs," such as "food, warmth, security, and so on," turn into "addictive habits rather than necessities" (Csikszentmihalyi and Rochberg-Halton 1981, 229). Even basic needs can be met at a minimal level or can potentially be met at an extravagant level.

But most people are not geared to stop consuming; they are geared to continue it. As Albert O. Hirschman (1982) states, "Humans, in contrast to animals, are never satisfied" (11). In *Twilight*, Bella has a few apparent reasons for desiring change; she envisions a better life with Edward, and therefore wants it and is driven by it. Bella is someone who marries up, but that is as a result of envisioning a better life with Edward for a variety of reasons—one of which would include her self-seeking nature. Considering that Bella's upward mobility is apparently fueled by love, *Twilight* is very much in tune with other rags-to-riches narratives.

Still, criticism of Bella is likely warranted. Buttsworth (2010) claims that for Bella, "it is the right marriage that elevates one out of the dark cabin in the woods to the sunlit castle on the hill" (50). The argument is difficult to disagree with, given Bella's seeming dependence on Edward and other male characters. What appears to be overlooked, though, is that a secondary female character, Alice, is at the heart of materialism and wealth in the Cullen family, and she is also a caregiver. She is the one all Cullens, including Edward, rely on for their incredible financial prosperity and is also the one coveted by the Volturi.

Are there reasons to look at Bella as a dependent female character who only achieves wealth as a result of marriage? Probably. Are there reasons to take issue with Bella's selection of Edward over Jacob, even relating the selection to issues of race and culture? Probably again. Still, Bella appears to have her priorities straight, choosing Edward over Jacob out of love (or so it seems) and not necessarily for the additional material acquisition. This is where one more aspect of material culture and the communicated meanings of *Twilight* come into play: the important feeling of financial security. Even for individuals who have problems with Bella, and who do not largely give in to consumer desires, the need for financial security is one that makes sense.

## FINANCIAL SECURITY AND THE ROLE OF ALICE CULLEN

Bella's friend Jacob is not a character who would be interpreted as providing financial security, but it is not fully accurate to proclaim Edward as the key to financial security, either. Enter the role of the most important character in this regard: Alice Cullen. While it is complicated to look at Bella as being dependent on a man, since Edward is not financially independent and not even technically human, there is an even more prevalent dilemma, seeing how the finances of the Cullen family are linked to a woman: Alice. She is truly a fascinating character, possessing the rare vampire ability to see visions of the future, which serves numerous purposes—including financial gain.

## Alice as a Commodity

Considering how valuable her gift is, it follows that Alice is seen as a precious commodity throughout the films and books. On a variety of occasions, the Cullens use Alice's abilities to help them determine impending problems and attacks—most notably in relation to Victoria and the Volturi. The Volturi are accordingly interested in having Alice join them. Aro takes issue with Alice's valuation on the limits of her powers, proclaiming that her ability is unlike anything he has ever seen before (Meyer 2006, 468). In the bonus scene at the end of the *Breaking Dawn Part 1* film, Aro makes reference to how much he covets Alice by claiming the Cullens have something he wants, and we see how much he wants her in *Breaking Dawn Part 2*, when he lights up when Alice enters the battlefield.

Even Jane, a member of the Volturi who often appears virtually without emotion, reacts to Alice. In *The Short Second Life of Bree Tanner*, Bree supposes that Jane hates Alice even more than Bella (Meyer 2010, 177). Though implicit, this negative feeling is likely a result of jealousy, of seeing how much the Volturi want Alice and how everyone seems to value her. But there is no evidence the Volturi would want Alice for financial benefit, which demonstrates the diversity of application for Alice's gift.

The Cullens, though, recognize Alice's power as linked to financial prowess, even though other members of the Cullen family would be able to provide income. Carlisle, the father figure, is a doctor, so his occupation would be indicative of both success and financial stability. In *New Moon*, Bella makes sense of the money the Cullens have as "something that accumulated when you had unlimited time on your hands" (Meyer 2006, 13). Yet despite different ways the Cullens might have for making money, Alice's ability is still the most useful. There is no question that other family members could thrive on their own. The key distinction between Alice and the other characters, however, is that she is largely the reason for the family's impervious material and financial state. It would be very difficult for Alice to feel adverse effects from economic downturns.

Living multiple lifetimes would help to explain how wealth might be attained, but overwhelming financial success for the Cullens hinges on "a sister who had an uncanny ability to predict trends in the stock market" (Meyer 2006, 13). Among other purposes, Alice's visions can be utilized to foresee economic and stock market developments—and the Cullen family uses this to their advantage. Alice is consequently very important, in material terms, as the limits on her power do not appear to limit her ability to predict economic trends. Her powers show possible visions of the future, which can change at times. Alice explains this by saying "some things are more certain than others . . . like the weather. People are harder. I only see the course they're on while they're on it" (Meyer 2005, 435). Prediction of economic trends and the stock market would likely be a little more concrete for Alice as compared with life progressions, seeing as how people can change their fates as they make decisions.

Alice is therefore able to play an important role in capitalism and to influence the well-being of her family by successfully determining which companies she and her family should have a stake in at specific times. Edward might well be utilizing the Cullens' money for Bella's benefit, but he is only able to do so because of Alice being the strongest source of that money. By relying on the wealth of the family, Bella is actually relying on another woman much more than she is on Edward.

## The Materialistic Member of the Family

Potentially, Edward could be self-sufficient. Having lived so long, he is highly educated and savvy—audiences see Edward's ease in passing high-school courses, and he frequently displays his intellectual prowess. Edward is also offered admission to Dartmouth College, since he comments that Bella's Dartmouth letter is one of "acceptance" because "it looks exactly like mine" (Meyer 2007, 225). The unfinished manuscript of *Midnight Sun* states that he actually has two graduate degrees. Throughout the series, however, Edward has less drive toward a material lifestyle than Alice, so Alice is really the family member interested in vast wealth.

An advantage of seeing material representations in the *Twilight* films is that audiences can visually assess how rich the family is—the full extent of Alice's financial gain is on display. The Cullens' house, clothes, cars—Edward's Volvo appears consistently throughout the films—and even island are on display. In *Breaking Dawn Part 2*, we see the car Edward supplied Bella with to replace her more modest pickup truck. In *New Moon*, when Alice steals a car to get to Edward faster, she makes sure to get the nicest looking and fastest car she can find, and she even tells Edward she eventually wants one for herself (Meyer 2006, 493).

To that end, Edward embraces—or at least, does not completely reject—his materialistic and secure lifestyle, and so, ultimately, does Bella, but Alice is the epitome of materialism and wealth. In light of the dependence on a man that most critics accuse Bella of, Alice is extremely independent. And she is not only one of the most accepting members of the Cullen family when it comes to Bella, but also she is the most liked by Charlie—and one of the most popular among fans. She represents strong independence, stability, and financial success; she is an ideal. As a character, Alice is assessed as "able to accept Bella . . . in spite of the wariness coming from other members of the Cullen family" (Loiacono and Loiacono 2010, 127). In several instances in the *Twilight* series, Alice shows her fondness for Bella. In fact, in the first *Twilight* film, Alice more readily accepts Bella than Edward does; she is willing to have Bella in the family before Edward has effectively managed his bloodlust. Though Alice expresses the likelihood that she would kill Bella in the attempt, she is the one who seems the most in favor of Bella becoming a vampire—by actually suggesting she should bite Bella and initiate the change.

Alice also plays key roles in Bella's transition to a more materialistic lifestyle. She is constantly thrusting outfits, gifts, and other luxuries on Bella throughout the series, with mixed reactions from both Bella and Edward. In *Breaking Dawn Part 1*, Alice unsurprisingly takes charge of the over-the-top, luxurious wedding between Bella and Edward, and she even chooses Bella's designer dress. She even states in the film that Bella would need to get more ·into fashion, since the two are now officially related.

In the final book, *Breaking Dawn*, audiences are treated to Alice's greatest feat of materialism. Edward informs Jacob that, when it comes to the whole Cullen family, "Alice rarely allows us to wear the same thing twice" (Meyer 2008, 273). A quick online search shows that fans have reacted to this line—not to mention the line's inclusion in the *Twilight* saga Wiki entry for Alice. Though this is just said in passing, it portrays Alice as extremely invested in fashion. The Cullens are all very stylish; the fact that their expensive clothes are only worn once before being sent off to charity—which is also indicated in the book (Meyer 2008, 273)—is so materialistic it is difficult to fathom. Again, Alice is at the forefront of the materialism, and she is also the one responsible for the family's financial health. The implications for fans and audiences are numerous, as Alice is an embodiment of capitalism itself.

Other portrayals in *Twilight* may not convey as much affinity for materialistic lifestyles, but this example is striking. Today's consumer is thought to be "ever avid for new things, discarding old if perfectly serviceable goods" (Sennett 2006, 5). As different technologies, innovations, trends, and ideals emerge, consumers look to the next products to buy, feeling incomplete with the current ones. Materialistic living has been characterized as having more than what is required (Twitchell 2002, 1), and Alice has well beyond what is essential. Her affinity for clothing is seemingly boundless, and her overwhelming desire to grant constant new looks for her family members is also evidenced in the way she sets up, and fully stocks, a huge walk-in closet for Bella in *Breaking Dawn*. Despite the fact that the Cullens are trying to blend in with the people living in Forks, Alice's love of fashion obviously trumps that concern.

Having more than needed and being able to make purchases when desired is an earmark of financial well-being. Since the Cullens are vampires, they would not need to worry much about an extensive wardrobe—their bodies do not age or change, so they would not outgrow their clothing. The Cullens would have an easy time utilizing clothing for functional purposes only, yet in order to keep up with fashion, this would not do. The material lifestyle embraced by them is no better represented than when audiences discover that they don't wear outfits a second time, which is sustained and encouraged by Alice.

## CONCLUSION

The *Twilight* series, in its portrayal of consumer culture, shows audiences how materialism and financial well-being are desirable traits. Bella, in choosing to marry Edward, gives audiences an outlook on class mobility, where Bella marries into a wealthy family—even though she does so out of love. Bella undergoes a clear transformation in the series, seeking meaning and a life that she feels she was destined for. Though there is appeal for any audience, people finding themselves in the midst of a damaged and declining economy are likely to be very receptive of these portrayals, especially considering how "real" financial security is difficult to achieve.

A portion of Bella's search for meaning is found in her ultimate acceptance of the materialistic life provided by the Cullen family. At the same time, however, Bella's reliance is difficult to pinpoint as being on a man. What is ultimately communicated to readers is a strong woman at the backbone of the Cullen family—so much so that Alice's planning and timely appearance make all the difference in the final confrontation with the Volturi. Alice's abilities greatly assist the family in terms of financial security and materialistic living, both characteristics consumers strive for. And they are all but immune to economic instability. Since Alice can predict the future, including economic trends, the financial security that the family enjoys is almost impossible to achieve in real life.

However, these portrayals may not be as bad as some critics conclude. After all, this is a fantasy world, with vampires and werewolves, fancy cars, and designer clothes. Bella marries out of love, not money, and Alice is by far the most materialistic character—an interesting aspect considering that she is very well liked and well received by those outside the Cullen family and even by fans. Values are still in place for wealth achievement, since

Bella has good motives for marriage and change, and Alice reaps the rewards of her own supernatural abilities.

## REFERENCES

Baran, Paul A., and Paul M. Sweezy. 1966. *Monopoly Capital: An Essay on the American Economic and Social Order*. New York: Modern Reader Paperbacks.

Barber, Benjamin. 2007. *Consumed: How Markets Corrupt Children, Infantilize Adults, and Swallow Citizens Whole*. New York: Norton.

Buttsworth, Sara. 2010. "Cinderbella: *Twilight*, Fairy Tales, and the Twenty-First-Century American Dream." In *"Twilight" and History*, ed. Nancy R. Reagan, 47–69. Hoboken, NJ: Wiley.

Csikszentmihalyi, Mihaly, and Eugene Rochberg-Halton. 1981. *The Meaning of Things: Domestic Symbols and the Self*. New York: Cambridge University Press.

Gossage, Howard Luck. 1967. "The Gilded Bough: Magic and Advertising." In *The Human Dialogue: Perspectives on Communication*, ed. Floyd W. Matson and Ashley Montagu. 363–70. New York: Free Press.

Hirschman, Albert O. 1982. *Shifting Involvements: Private Interest and Public Action*. Princeton, NJ: Princeton University Press.

Jones, Beth Felker. 2009. *Touched by a Vampire*. Colorado Springs, CO: Multnomah Books.

Leiss, William, Stephen Kline, and Sut Jhally. 1990. *Social Communication in Advertising: Persons, Products, and Images of Well-Being*. 2nd ed. Scarborough, Ontario: Nelson Canada.

Loiacono, Grace, and Laura Loiacono. 2010. "Better Than 'Cured'? Alice and the Asylum." In *"Twilight" and History*, ed. Nancy R. Reagan, 127–44. Hoboken, NJ: Wiley.

Meyer, Stephenie. 2005. *Twilight*. New York: Little, Brown.

———. 2006. *New Moon*. New York: Little, Brown.

———. 2007. *Eclipse*. New York: Little, Brown.

———. 2008. *Breaking Dawn*. New York: Little, Brown.

———. 2010. *The Short Second Life of Bree Tanner*. New York: Little, Brown.

Morris, Tom. 1997. *If Aristotle Ran General Motors: The New Soul of Business*. New York: Henry Holt.

Sennett, Richard. 1998. *The Corrosion of Character: The Personal Consequences of Work in the New Capitalism*. New York: Norton.

———. 2006. *The Culture of the New Capitalism*. New Haven, CT: Yale University Press.

Soros, George. 1998. *The Crisis of Global Capitalism: Open Society Endangered*. New York: Public Affairs.

Twitchell, James B. 1999. *Lead Us into Temptation: The Triumph of American Materialism*. New York: Columbia University Press.

———. 2002. *Living it Up: Our Love Affair with Luxury*. New York: Columbia University Press.

Wilson, Natalie. 2010. "Civilized Vampires versus Savage Werewolves: Race and Ethnicity in the *Twilight* Series." In *Bitten by "Twilight": Youth Culture, Media, and the Vampire Franchise*, ed. Melissa A. Click, Jennifer Stevens Aubrey, and Elizabeth Behm-Morawitz, 55–70. New York: Peter Lang.

———. 2011. *Seduced by "Twilight": The Allure and Contradictory Messages of the Popular Saga*. Jefferson, NC: McFarland.

## Chapter Twelve

# "I Know What You Are"

## A Philosophical Look at Race, Identity, and Mixed-Blood in the Twilight Universe

## Michelle Bernard

". . . I've done something wrong, Dad, but I'm not going to put up with your prejudices."
—Bella Swan (Meyer 2007, 54)

Stephenie Meyer's *Twilight* saga takes on the subject of stereotypes in today's media-saturated society by cleverly showcasing them in the world of vampires, werewolves, and the everyday citizens of tiny Forks, Washington. Bella, who is at the epicenter of it all, is the one that challenges the "norms" that are thrown at her. She is "Switzerland" as she calls it, which does serve her purpose for a while. But even she realizes that things need to change in the long run. Her relationship with Edward, with Jacob, with Charlie—they all start one way and end another. Did Bella's willingness to disregard the "otherness" of Edward and the Cullens lead her to the enlightened thinking that all are created equal (vampire, werewolf, and human)? Is this type of thought what is needed in today's multicultural society? In this chapter, I propose that this is exactly what our world needs—for people to realize that stereotypes and prejudices are outdated and in desperate need of change.

"Otherness" is a philosophical theme that originates from queries about the nature of identity. A person's definition of the "other" is part of what defines or even constitutes the self (in both psychological and philosophical sense) and other phenomena and cultural units. It has been used in social science to understand the processes by which societies and groups exclude "others" whom they want to subordinate or who do not fit into their society. When considering the "otherness" factor of race in popular culture and its continued flourishing, we need to look back at its beginnings in religion in the Middle Ages (Gunn 1979, 96, 114). Medieval Christianity was part of the foundation of the feudal estates of nobles, clerics, and peasants, each occupying their God-given place. The concept of "otherness" is also integral to the comprehending of a person, as people construct roles for themselves in relation to an "other" as part of a process of reaction that is not necessarily related to stigmatization or condemnation. Othering is imperative to national identities (especially as they are represented in pop culture and mass media), where practices of admittance and segregation can form and sustain boundaries and national character. Othering helps to distinguish between home and away, the uncertain or certain. It often involves the demonization and dehumanization of groups, which further justify attempts to civilize and exploit these "inferior" others.

The idea of the other was first philosophically conceived by Emmanuel Levinas and later made popular by Edward Said in his well-known book *Orientalism* (1979). Despite originally being a philosophical concept, "othering" has political, economical, social, and psychological implications. Wherein lies the identity of someone? Is the difference between "same" and "other" a matter of essence or existence? Stephenie Meyer cleverly examines the identities of her characters through glasses not quite rose colored but definitely intriguing. She shows that we must begin the process of asking questions about stereotyping in the world, beyond our immediate experience. Thanks to *Twilight*, there is a new interest in the Quileute Nation and in Native American culture in general. In a world with little cultural coherence, all meanings are now in play and up for grabs, and this terrible freedom represents our greatest hope and despair, all in one. Looking deep enough, *Twilight* offers ideas on how to overcome stereotyping and race differences and how to "agree to disagree" as the old saying goes. All the characters confront their own stereotypes, and they have to learn to overcome them or deal with the serious lessons coming their way.

## THE RIGHT TYPE OF MONSTER: RACE, STEREOTYPING, AND PREJUDICE

Popular culture can aid to break down stereotypes; however, the problem is that for the message to reach mass audiences, it has to be so watered down so it doesn't get to critical questions. I propose that a key component of the change in pop culture's depictions of race is its creative participation in it. Society can take up the texts and products that are given in pop culture and refashion them so as to make them reflect the truth behind their meanings. The *Twilight* saga does that. The fact that we all stereotype in twenty-first-century society only proves that each generation continues to perpetuate stereotypical misconceptions—like "pimp," "gansta," "mongrel," "leech," "dog." When society can get past the "homeboys" and "rez politics," then emancipation from racial stereotyping and cultural misconceptions can begin to take place. I'm tired of hearing, for example, that blacks are loud and lazy, American Indians are drunks and live in teepees, Hispanics sell fruit and smell, Asians are hyper-intelligent and can't drive decently, and Jews are penny pinchers and control the media. Ridiculous! As a person of mixed background, I may be loquacious, but I'm not loud, I don't drink, and I live in a colonial house in the Highlands of Maine.

So why examine race, identity, and mixed-blood in the *Twilight* universe? Why do Jacob, the pack, and the Quileute people dislike and distrust the Cullens (those "leeches and blood suckers") so much? Why do Edward, Rosalie, and most other vampires describe Jacob and the pack as "dogs, mutts, and mongrels?" Is it just because they are "natural enemies" as Jacob tells Bella, or is it because that's the way things have always been? Is it historical, or is it convenience? It's all of these and also the anxiety of the unknown. It is easier to believe what society and pop culture express as a negative image.

The complacency of race and identity stereotyping can be felt in every part of the United States, from migrant workers in California to the blueberry fields of northeastern Maine. Racial and ethnic inclusiveness has grown to be more important, as society has become increasingly diverse. Why? Because we feel we have to protect our heritage. Jacob has problems with Bella liking Edward not just because he's in love with her but also because Jacob is receiving all his "racial" knowledge about Edward and the Cullens from secondhand ideas. He really hasn't gotten to know them because he's going off of the information they gave him; just as Edward is basing his biases on years of racially charged situations with the Quileute Nation. None of them has bothered to see the individual person—just the race. In the words of one of Stephenie Meyer's favorite authors, Charlotte Brontë (2005), "Prejudices, it is well known, are most difficult to eradicate from the heart whose soil has never been loosened or fertilized by education; they grow firm there as weeds among stones" (346). It isn't until Bella enters the picture and be-friends them both that Edward and Jacob, and their two races, are forced to confront the stereotyping that has permeated their "relationship" for centu-ries.

Philosopher John Stuart Mill (Mill and Bentham 1987) believed that the goal of good knowledge is the reform of society. This reform, in this case including popular depictions of race and identity, comes when people set aside prejudgments and start accepting each other as equals. Mill (cited by Sher in Mill 2002) believed that,

> Utility, or the Greatest Happiness Principle, holds that actions are right in proportion as they tend to promote happiness, wrong as they tend to produce the reverse of happiness. By happiness is intended to produce pleasure, and the absence of pain; by unhappiness, pain and the privation of pleasure. These supplementary explanations do not affect the theory of life on which this theory of morality is grounded—namely, that pleasure, and freedom from pain, are the only things desirable as ends; and that all desirable things (which are numerous in the utilitarian as in any other scheme) are desirable either for the pleasure inherent in themselves, or as means to the promotion of pleasure and the prevention of pain. (II 2; cf.II 1)

To put it in nonphilosophical speech, liberty, or the freedom from the oppressive (in our case, stereotyping) is the most important pleasure that minorities (vampire, werewolf, and human alike) have. We ought to act in such a way that the consequences of our actions produce the greatest overall amount of good. Everyone is entitled to live life free from the oppressive effects of racial and cultural stereotyping. The complacency of these and other stereotypes can be explained further by referring to Friedrich Nietzsche's *Beyond Good and Evil* (1989). He explains,

> There are moralities which are intended to justify their authors before others; other moralities are intended to calm him and make him content with himself; with others he wants to crucify and humiliate himself; with others he wants to wreak vengeance, with others hide himself, with others transfigure himself and set himself on high; this morality serves to make its author forget, that to make him or something about him forgotten; many moralists would like to exercise power and their creative moods on mankind; others, Immanuel Kant perhaps among them, give to understand with their morality: "what is worthy of respect in me is that I know how to obey—and things ought to be no different with you!"—in short, moralities too are only a sign language of the emotions. (187)

Nietzsche asserts that we actually register perception far less than we think we do. We may think ourselves enlightened (or having a well-informed outlook, as some of our favorite characters do), but we are not. For instance, when we see a tree, we don't see the detail of every branch and leaf but only glance at the rough shape of the whole and, from that, construct all the similar details. Likewise, when we read a book, we only take in a few words and then fit those words into what we already think we know. In this sense, Nietzsche suggests we are all inventors, artists, and liars: our so-called knowledge is our own make-believe. By allowing popular stereotypes, fictional or not, to be regurgitated in this way, we as a society are allowing this "knowledge," to perpetuate.

By looking beyond stereotypical beliefs and refocusing on positive aspects of cultural identities, society takes the first steps in reclaiming its humanity, just as the Cullens and the Quileutes do. Only after coming together are they able to defend the birth of Renesmee, a mixed-race child. She manages to unite the families even more than Bella herself did.

What is wrong with racial stereotypes or prejudices, precisely? The most readily available account is that they are wrong because everyone deserves basic moral respect, and this is incompatible with any form of stereotyping or prejudice. This argument is a popular one today, but its roots are very old, lying in the moral philosophy of Enlightenment scholar Immanuel Kant (2009). He believed that all rational beings are entitled to basic moral equality because they are rational and have a will of their own. He expressed this idea in a form he called the "categorical imperative": "One should always act so as to treat humanity, whether in one's own person or in that of another, as an end in itself and never as a mere means."

What Kant means is that every rational being has a will of his or her own, and therefore, the innate freedom to choose his or her own acts as well as his or her larger commitment in life. It is wrong to deprive persons of that freedom by forcing them to serve not their own interests but the interests of someone else. Based on what Kant is saying, the Cullens have every right to live their lives in Forks without having to endure attacks of narrow-mindedness. Charlie tells Bella in *Twilight* that he has no use for "people who talk," referring to the people gossiping about the Cullens.

Carlisle and company are completely rational, have will of their own, and have chosen to adopt a lifestyle that not only benefits themselves but also the community. There are obvious conflicts between Edward and Jacob, but they are just the extensions of a much larger problem: Do you continue to fault someone because of the sins of their past? Do you continue to hold a grudge or a prejudice toward them because of who or what they are? According to Kant, you don't. You go beyond; you evolve; you become more that what your past says you're supposed to be. And it is because of Bella's selfishness (if we can use that word) that all parties are forced to take a good look at themselves and their surroundings. Am I saying that Jacob and the Quileute Nation are primarily at fault here? No, of course not. No more than I'm trying to lay the fault primarily at the feet of Edward and the Cullens. The relationship of all parties involved could be boiled down to the idea of "separate, but equal." Some might even consider the treaty itself to be a farce. It never forced the parties in question to deal with each other as equals, it only ceased hostilities. They never bothered to identify whether the other party was a sentient being or not—just an enemy to be avoided.

The civil-rights activist Clarence Mitchell once said, "The minute you decide to judge someone solely on their race, and not on their growth or accomplishments, you open the door to discrimination" (cited in Bean 2009). Different times call for different measures, however. Because of Bella's personal implementation of her being "Switzerland," Edward and Jacob are forced to come to an understanding. Members of the Cullen and Quileute family are forced to make changes, think rationally, take the new knowledge that is presented to them, and make a difference.

Finally, what *is* race? *Webster's* defines it as "a group of persons related by common descent or heredity; an arbitrary classification of modern humans, sometimes, especially formerly, based on any or a combination of various physical characteristics, as skin color, facial form, or eye shape, and now frequently based on such genetic markers as blood groups." Sounds about right. But race can be so much more. Race is a paradox. It appears everywhere in popular culture, while the profound ways in which it factors into the "distribution of sadness," as Carlos Velez-Ibanez (1996) calls it, remain hidden from view.

In *Twilight*, we are thrown into a racial war that has been raging for a long time, and it's through these texts that we are forced to look at ourselves and our lives. Do you have problems with someone who is different from you? Do I? I'd like to think I don't, being multiracial myself. But would that be an honest statement? How many of us judge people by what they're wearing, by the color of their skin, by where and how they live? It can be telling to say, "What was she thinking when she stepped out of the house wearing that?!" or "Vampires don't count as people," or "You wouldn't feel the need to go risk your life to go comfort a dog" (Meyer 2007, 33). I hear the critics: "Oh, you're one of those *Twilight* people." And say it with me: "It's a *Twilight* thing, you wouldn't understand." No one likes to be judged—Charlie, Jacob, Edward, Sam, and the rest of our beloved cast of uncommon heroes and misfits are mirrors for us to look at. We should read the *Twilight* texts and take from them a profound lesson of tolerance. The characters have to learn to get along, whether they want to or not. Bella instigates this change by declaring that she will not take sides. Why? Because she loves them all. She sees the good and the bad attributes that people possess. We know whom she chooses to be with. However, despite everything, they're all still special to her.

## A STRONG WOMAN: ON FEMINISM AND "BEING SWITZERLAND"

Bella's refusal to choose a side could be attributed to the Egalitarian liberal feminist way of thinking. This school of thought conceives that freedom is personal autonomy or the freedom of the will—living a life of one's own choosing or being the coauthor of the conditions under which one lives. As the feminist Susan B. Anthony (1860) once wrote:

> Cautious, careful people always casting about to preserve their reputation or social standards never can bring about reform. Those who are really in earnest are willing to be anything or nothing in the world's estimation, and publicly

and privately, in season and out, avow their sympathies with despised ideas and their advocates, and bear the consequences.

She refuses to identify them as separate and different; to her, they both have the same number of eyes, arms, and legs. They both know how to show joy and sorrow, and they both know how to aggravate the snot out of her. Stephenie Meyer showcases this in *Eclipse* when she uses Robert Frost's poem entitled "Fire and Ice" for the book's epigraph. The author shows us through words just how difficult a choice this has become for Bella. So why was this particular poem chosen to preface the story? The obvious answer is in the title. The vampires of the book are cold, and the werewolves are abnormally hot, so we are presented with two opposing forces that could easily be represented by fire and ice. It's not an easy choice that is presented to Bella. To be with Edward, she must eventually die and become a vampire herself. To be with Jacob, she faces a temper that could kill her or the possibility of Jacob's imprinting on another woman and forgetting her entirely. Her life and possibly her heart are in danger with both men. Bella's story draws parallels to the possible inspiration for the Frost poem, as for so many other works: Dante's *Inferno*, an imaginary chronicle of Dante's journey through the nine circles of hell to ultimately reach heaven. Bella must use her feminist principles to trudge through the perils of her hellish experiences to ultimately reach her heaven.

In the poem "Fire and Ice" (Frost, Poirier, and Richardson 1995), Frost links "fire" with desire. Jacob desires Bella and makes no secret of that fact, not even to Edward. He can't let go of Bella, any more than she can let go of him. In fact, they are linked emotionally and physically, since she depends on both the Cullen vampire clan and Jacob's Quileute tribe of shape-shifting wolves to keep her safe from the threat of Victoria. Bella is the catalyst that draws together the explosive forces of fire and ice and holds them uncomfortably close in a shared goal, forcing natural enemies to cooperate and build bonds and to fight against their own kind in the name of protecting those they love. Frost's comparison of fire and ice and how the world will end is an appropriate backdrop for the story of *Eclipse*. The great philosophical tension of the story is not only how they must fight for Bella but also how they must go against their natural inclinations and prejudices in the process.

Why do they both want her to identify the other as the enemy? Because both are the antithesis of their upbringing and their surroundings. Vampires and werewolves are mortal enemies because, according to Quileute legend, a vampire or "cold one" had killed people of the tribe in the past. Feeling threatened, they resorted to shape-shifting into wolves in order to protect their people. They only changed into wolves if the "cold ones" came into the area. But despite the fact that they were now something more than just human, they were still in fact human. Even medieval Christian philosopher

St. Augustine states that even though the ability to change or metamorphose into a wolf is considered an abomination, the man still retains his human reason in his lupine form (Lecouteux 1992). Therefore, he still has a soul. Most vampires, on the other hand, believe they don't have a soul. Edward believes this because of the evil he's done in his life, the lives he has taken. Vampires live off of blood, the life force of a human. Some consider that tantamount to being a cannibal. So, we have creatures who, according to mythology, despite their transformation, retain their soul and others who lose their soul because they take from others' bodies. Thus, both Edward and Jacob feel that Bella would be better off not associating with the other kind. Yet Bella rebuffs this line of thinking and makes her intentions well known. She reverts to her feminist principles, chooses to do her own thing, and expects them to understand why she does so. She does not look at their "race" as much as who she believes them to truly be.

## VAMPIRE HYBRIDS: RENESMEE AND MULTICULTURALISM

As the story continues through all four books, we see that the families are learning—slowly but surely. They are learning to coexist and accept each other's differences, to look past the external diversity and to focus on the true nature of a person. The noted sociologist and philosopher Robert Bellah (2006) states that "we have to treat other as part of who we are, rather than as a 'them' with whom we are in constant competition." And noted scientist, humanist, and occasional philosopher Albert Einstein (1954) states,

> Our world is in great trouble due to human behaviour founded on old myths and customs. We must not conceal from ourselves that no improvement in the present depressing situation is possible without a severe struggle; for the handful of those who are really determined to do something is minute in comparison with the mass of the lukewarm and the misguided. . . . Humanity is going to need a substantially new way of thinking if it is to survive!

All the characters in *Twilight* are forced to grasp this new way of thinking. These lessons aren't readily accepted. It's not until the families and their closest friends are forced to face Bella and Edward's marriage, and the birth of their daughter Renesmee, that the lessons become real. Often, lessons aren't realized until "you yourself" are confronted with the truth of them.

Renesmee is a unique and beautiful aspect to the *Twilight* saga. Meyer chose to showcase the real identity behind being someone of mixed lineage and what better way to bring out the best in people than in defending the rights of a child. Most of what popular culture shows us about being multiracial is the division of family, the hurt it causes the individual. We see this when we first find out in *Breaking Dawn* that Bella is pregnant. The family is drawn into factions about the fetus/baby. Everyone immediately makes assumptions as to what is best, not realizing that this child might bring good things. How many times have we heard people talking about the difficulties they faced growing up in two different worlds? Do I identify myself as being one race, or do I identify with the other? Will society allow me to identify myself as being just "me"? Or will they pigeonhole me based on what they think I should be?

Both the Cullens and the Quileutes become united in defending the life and therefore the rights of Renesmee—because they love her but also because Renesmee has the right to be Renesmee. Does that make her any better or any less of a person? The Volturi, on the other hand, do not see Renesmee; they only perceive a threat to their lives and how they live them. They cannot see past their own prejudices to realize that she is a gift, a blessing that should be loved, enjoyed, and celebrated. Instead, they see her as an abomination, something so utterly abhorrent that it must be destroyed. It doesn't matter that she has the basic right to exist—she is unlike them. The Volturi judge her based off the past and their experiences with it, and that is how mass media usually deal with people of mixed lineage in our country. Instead of judging people by *who* they are, they are judged by *what* they are. What Renesmee represents is a changing world. Aro states in a condescending speech to the Volturi witnesses:

> "There is no broken law. However, it does follow then that there is no danger? No. That is a separate issue. She is unique . . . utterly, impossibly unique. Such a waste it would be, to destroy something so lovely. Especially when we could learn so much. But there *is* danger, danger that cannot simply be ignored. . . . Now our status as mere myth in truth protects us from these weak creatures we hunt. This amazing child, if we could but know her potential—know with *absolute certainty* that she could always remain shrouded with the obscurity that protects us. But we know nothing of what she will become! Her own parents are plagued by fears of her future. We *cannot* know what she will grow to be. Only the known is safe. Only the known is tolerable. The unknown is . . . a vulnerability." (Meyer, 2008)

The philosopher Jean-Paul Sartre declared "hell" to be "other people" (Sartre 1944) and he couldn't have been more right. For the Volturi, Renesmee represents the very essence of their hell—someone who is not like them and can't be controlled by them. The Cullens are a dimension of hell for the Volturi because of their alternative lifestyle. Aro and Caius specifically are "looking" for any sort of excuse to rid their world of what they believe to be a serious threat. All because of behavior that boiled down to what could be classified as being racist, the Volturi cannot see the proverbial forest for the trees. They seek to keep things the way they've always been, but if they would think philosophically about the situation, they'd know that nothing has ever kept the same. Every time that Aro accepts some new vampire into the coven, it changes; especially if said new vampire has special abilities. The coven changes, thereby making it stronger, newer . . . better. And that's all well and good, as long as people look and act the way you want them to.

Yoji Cole (2008) states, "Being multi racial is an experience unique to each person who is the offspring of parents of different races. But it seems to me that more than other mixtures, people who are both Black and White are forced to choose a side—or maybe the struggle of that mixture is more public. People want to know 'What are you?' so they can put you in a box and identify your allegiance." Writer and philosopher W. E. B. Dubois (1986) described this as *double-consciousness*, seeing yourself one way, while others see you as something completely different (364–65).

Racial allegiance also appears to be a uniquely American trait. In other countries, people identify first with who they were, second with their nationality, and lastly with their race. But in America, people must know "what" you are. So, in this context, what does it mean to have personal identity? The philosopher John Locke believed in the idea of *Tabula Rasa* or "blank slate." He believed that each person has an identity that is an organization of parts in one coherent body partaking of one common life. Renesmee is that coherent body (or life). She is the embodiment of the identity of a living organism that, over time, is constituted by a continuous history of such an organized life. In the short span of time that Renesmee has lived, she has seen and experienced and created a history of her own that will go on to define who she is and what she does with her life. And really, isn't that what we all want? We want to *be*. Locke goes on further to describe what personal identity is, which is what Aro and the Volutri are so desperate to know about Renesmee. Locke (1975) states, "A person is a thinking, intelligent being that has reason, and reflection, and considers itself the same thinking thing in different times, which it does only by that consciousness which is inseparable from thinking and essential to it" (335).

I affirm that people of mixed-raced background should be free to identify with every part of their racial heritage. Multiracial people, just like Renesmee, "experience a 'squeeze' of oppression *as* people of color and *by* people of color. People of color who have internalized the vehicle of oppression in turn apply rigid rules of belonging or established 'legitimacy' membership" (Root 1992). One of the very first things the Volturi want to establish is whether or not Renesmee is a vampire. Does she or doesn't she belong? However, as Alice provided evidence, there was another multiracial identity in the *Twilight* world. Someone who made Nessie's existence non-singular, and that was Nahuel. One could say that Nahuel's multiracial identity proved to the Volturi that there could be multiracial vampires in the world without "threatening" the status quo, just as multiracial humans prove each day that we are no different from anyone else and have the right to exist without others questioning us.

We must begin the process of asking questions about the world beyond our immediate experience and culture. Popular culture is something we can put together using whatever materials happen to be available (e.g., old TV shows made into movies, cable channels endlessly replaying favorite old shows, trivia games, etc.). Media outlets have been the foundation for ideologies and structures in human history that have often been oppressive, particularly to the most vulnerable members of Western society, that is, people of different race and color (Jay 2010). They have become the all purpose "other." *Twilight* showcases that you can have these great cultural differences yet still evolve beyond yourself and begin to accept the inevitable changes that come with understanding.

In the United States, one in seven new marriages is between spouses of different races or ethnicities, according to data from 2008 and 2010 that was analyzed by the Pew Research Center. As the 2010 census counted, there are nine million Americans that identify themselves as being two or more races. And of those nine million, 51 percent were younger than eighteen. Multiracial and multiethnic Americans (usually grouped together as "mixed race") are one of the country's fastest growing demographic groups. Among American children, the multiracial population has increased almost 50 percent, to 4.2 million, since 2000, making it the fastest growing youth group in the country. The number of people of all ages who identified themselves as both white and black soared by 134 percent since 2000 to 1.8 million people. Census 2010 is the first comprehensive accounting of how the multiracial population has changed over ten years, since statistics were first collected about it in 2000.

Renesmee's character is timely and the perfect illustration of the ever-changing atmosphere toward multiracial people in this country. Rainer Spencer, director of the Afro-American Studies Program at the University of Nevada, says he believes "the mixed-race identity is not a transcendence of race, it's a new tribe." For many, that is not the point. They are asserting their freedom to identify as they choose. As the philosopher Plato once stated, "Know thyself." Renesmee chooses to be Renesmee, and that's something the Volturi either can't or won't understand. She has the innate freedom to be herself and to live simply because race or ethnicity will not automatically tell you her story. Richard Buckminster Fuller states:

> Never forget that you are one of a kind. Never forget that if there weren't any need for you in all your uniqueness to be on this earth, you wouldn't be here in the first place. And never forget, no matter how overwhelming life's challenges and problems seem to be, that one person can make a difference in the

world. In fact, it is always because of one person that all the changes that matter in the world come about. So be that one person.

Cultural differences erode over time due to globalization, changing identities, and consumption patterns, while most local and regional reactions to cultural differences generate new identities and differences. Amid this flux, the old notions of "otherness" are increasingly outdated. Meyer's books share actual teaching moments within their binding, despite the fact that stereotypes are extremely common in the media. Whether stereotypes assume the form of unrealistic portrayals of minorities or an equally unrealistic invisibility, they often fulfill this double function of oppression and reaffirmation. People like popular media, but until they make the proper adjustments as to how stereotypes are viewed, they will continue to perpetuate the misconceptions we still use. The *Twilight* saga, with its positive depictions of all races, fictional or not, is a positive step in the right direction.

Karl Marx (1977) once wrote that "religion is the sigh of the oppressed creature; the feeling of a heartless world. It is the opium of the people" (127). Much the same can be said of pop culture; it dulls the pain of reality and creates a euphoria from which we can escape. It is a drug that can be very addictive. Just like opium, the stereotyping that sometimes comes with pop culture is detrimental to society's better judgment and well-being. However, as long as there are stories like the *Twilight* saga where we can see the shortcomings and growth of the characters involved, they will always be "exactly my brand of heroin."

## REFERENCES

Anthony, Susan B. 1860. *On the Campaign for Divorce Law Reform.* Accessed June 20, 2013. https://www.womanbuddy.com/content/susan-b-anthony.

Bean, Jonathan J. 2009. *Race and Liberty in America: The Essential Reader.* Lexington: University Press of Kentucky. Accessed June 20, 2013. http://multiracial.com.

Bellah, Robert. 2006. *Morality Ethics: Discussion of Philosophy Metaphysics of "Do Unto Others" as Fundamental Morality.* Accessed June 20, 2013. http://www.spaceandmotion.com/Philosophy-Morality-Ethics.htm.

Brontë, Charlotte. 2005. *Jane Eyre.* New York: Random House.

Cole, Yoji. 2008. "Being Multiracial: It's About Synergy, Not a Choice." Diversity Inc. Accessed June 19, 2013. http://www.diversityinc.com.

Dictionary.com. 2013. *Entry: Race.* Accessed June 20, 2013. http://dictionary.reference.com/browse/race.

Dubois, W.E.B. 1986. *W.E.B. Du Bois' Writings: The Suppression of the African Slave-Trade / The Souls of Black Folk / Dusk of Dawn / Essays and Articles.* New York: Literary Classics of the United States (pages 364-65).

Egalitarian Liberal Feminism. *Stanford Encyclopedia of Philosophy: Liberal Feminism.* Accessed June 20, 2013. http://www.intellectualtakeout.org/library/research-analysis-reports/liberal-feminism.

Einstein, Albert. 1954. *The Collapse of Human Civilization – On Human Insanity, Stupidity, and its Cure – Wisdom from Truth and Reality.* Accessed June 20, 2013. http://www.spaceandmotion.com/society/insanity-stupity-collapse-society.htm.

Frost, Robert, Richard Poirier, and Mark Richardson. 1995. *Robert Frost: Collected Poems, Prose, and Plays*. New York: Library Classics.

Fuller, Richard Buckminster. *Good Reads: Quotes About Making a Difference*. Accessed June 20, 2013. http://www.goodreads.com/quotes/tag/make-a-difference.

Gunn, Giles. 1979. *The Interpretation of Otherness*. New York: Oxford University Press.

Jay, Dr. Gregory S. 2010. "Racism and the Production of Whiteness in Popular Culture." *Whiteness Studies: Deconstructing (the) Race*. Accessed June 20, 2013. https://pantherfile.uwm.edu/gjay/www/Whiteness/analyzingstereotypes.htm.

Kant, Immanuel. 1993. *Groundwork for the Metaphysics of Morals*. Indianapolis: Hackett.

———. 2009. *Groundwork for the Metaphysics of Morals*. New York: Harper Perennial Modern Thought Edition.

Lecouteux, Claude. 1992. *Witches, Werewolves, and Fairies: Shapeshifters and Astral Doubles in the Middle Ages*. Rochester, VT: Inner Traditions.

Locke, John. 1975. *An Essay Concerning Human Understanding*. Oxford: Clarendon.

Marx, Karl. 1977. *Critique of Hegel's "Philosophy of Right."* Ed. Joseph O'Malley. New York: Cambridge University Press.

Meyer, Stephenie. 2005. *Twilight*. New York: Little, Brown.

———. 2007. *Eclipse*. New York: Little, Brown.

———. 2008. *Breaking Dawn*. New York: Little, Brown.

Mill, J. S. 2002. *Utilitarianism*. Ed. George Sher. Indianapolis: Hackett.

Mill, J. S., and Jeremy Bentham. 1987. *Utilitarianism and Other Essays*. Ed. Alan Ryan. New York: Penguin.

Nietzsche, Frederick. 1989. *Beyond Good and Evil: Prelude to a Philosophy of the Future*, trans. by Walter Kaufman, Vintage Books Edition. New York: Random House.

Root, Dr. Maria P. P. 1992. *Racially Mixed People in America*. Newbury Park, CA: Sage.

Sartre, Jean-Paul, and Stuart Gilbert. 1944. *No Exit*. New York. Vintage International.

Saulny, Susan. 2011. *The "New York Times" Upfront*, vol. 143.

Velez-Ibanez, Carlos. 1996. *Border Visions: Mexican Cultures of the Southwest United States*. Tucson: University of Arizona Press.

*V*

# Beyond the *Twilight* Universe

## Chapter Thirteen

# Mainstream Monsters

*The Otherness of Humans in* Twilight, The Vampire Diaries, *and* True Blood

## Emma Somogyi and Mark David Ryan

The representation of vampires in horror movies and television programs has changed considerably over the last two decades. No longer is the vampire portrayed simply as a monster or representation of death. Now, the vampire on our screen, such as *True Blood*'s Bill Compton or *Twilight*'s Edward Cullen, passes as human, chooses to make morally sound decisions, becomes an upstanding assimilated citizen, works in the community, and aspires to be a husband to mortal women. What this chapter terms "the mainstreamer" or "mainstreaming vampire," by way of definition, is one that chooses to assimilate into society. They do not necessarily forgo the partaking of human blood but may choose to drink from volunteer humans or from packets of donated blood from a local hospital. Synthesized blood (e.g., TruBlood) or animal blood is also the food of choice for some mainstreaming vampires.

The emergence of the mainstreaming vampire marks a distinct shift in the representation of otherness in contemporary vampire screen narratives. The concept of otherness has always been central to the demarcation between monstrosity and normality (or what is deemed socially acceptable) in the horror movie. While it has been argued that representations of the monster have evolved from exotic otherness (for example, Count Dracula) to more everyday otherness in postmodern horror movies (such as the serial killer next door) (Pinedo 1997), monstrosity in the vampire movie for the most part has been represented along distinct lines of good versus evil and monstrosity versus humanity. Two notable exceptions include *Interview with the Vampire* (1994) and *Blade* (1998), among others, where such boundaries are blurred, and in terms of the former, the narrative revolves around a vampire with a conscience, while in the latter, a half-human half-vampire defends humans against a sinister vampire underworld. However, the success of recent series, such as the *Twilight* saga (2009, 2010, 2011, 2012), *The Vampire Diaries* (2009–) and *True Blood* (2008–) has popularized the idea of vampires who cling to remnants of their humanity (or memories of what it means to be human) and attempt to live as human, which builds upon similar—albeit embryonic—themes that emerged from the vampire subgenre in the 1990s. Within these narratives, representations of the other have shifted from the traditional idea of the monster, to alternative and surprising loci. As this chapter argues, humans themselves, and the concept of the human body, now represent, in many instances, both abject and other.

This chapter examines key issues around the ways in which otherness is portrayed in contemporary vampire movies and television shows and the shift of other from monsters to mortals. The discussion in this chapter focuses on three popular contemporary vampire texts, namely the *Twilight* saga, *True Blood*, and *The Vampire Diaries*, which exemplify primary trends in the representation of mainstreaming vampires. The chapter begins by considering the nature of the abject and otherness in relation to representations of classical vampires and how they have traditionally embodied the other. This provides a backdrop against which to examine the characteristics of the contemporary mainstreaming vampire "monster." An examination of the broad thematic and representational shifts from other to mainstream vampire demonstrates how mainstream monsters are increasingly assimilating into mortal lifestyles with trappings that many viewers may find appealing. The same shifts in theme and representation also reveal that humans are frequently cast as mundane and unappealing in contemporary vampire narratives.

## OTHERNESS AND THE ABJECT

Throughout cinema history, the horror movie has exploited humanity's fear of death, particularly what Stephen King has labeled a "bad death"—a grotesque and painful end (Worland 2007, 8). As this suggests, horror is an affective cinematic form, one that attempts to elicit the emotional responses of fear, disgust, terror, and horror inter alia in an attempt to frighten an audience. To achieve this, scary movies prey upon humanity's primal fears of death, fear of harm to the body, and fear for other people—especially loved ones. Horror movies allow audiences to engage with society's worst nightmares, the taboo, and bodily ruination at a safe distance, providing "a safely distanced and stylized means of making sense of and coming to terms with phenomena and potentialities of experience that under normal conditions would be found too threatening and disturbing" (Grixti 1989, 164). According to Isabel Cristina Pinedo (1997), an audience's engagement with horror derives from a desire to experience recreational terror where danger is simulated, providing a bounded experience of fear. While there are various theories that attempt to address the paradox of why audiences willingly subject themselves to their worst nightmares on screen, at the core of the horror film's narrative function—and thus the transgressive and affective nature of the genre—is the monster. As Rick Worland (2007, 17) argues, "Horror films, foremost, revolve around the monster and its threat to characters. . . . The horror story turns fear, whether personal or social, into a specific type of monster; and seeks to destroy it." The monster, a polymorphous figure that represents or embodies social, cultural, and personal fears, typically functions not only as a threat to protagonists but also as a disruption to the normative social order within the narrative.

At the core of discussion around monstrosity and horror film are the concepts of the "abject," and the "other." In terms of the former, as Julia Kristeva explains, abjection is not about uncleanliness or health; rather, the abject "disturbs identity, system (and) order." Abjection is "what does not respect borders, positions, rules. The in-between, the ambiguous, the composite. . . . He who denies morality is not abject. . . . Abjection . . . is immoral, sinister, scheming, and shady" (1982, 4). As a creature that blurs the boundaries between the humane and the monstrous, and the living and the dead, the vampire has always been the in-between and the ambiguous, an amalgam of humanity and death and, hence by Kristeva's definition, the abject.

Moreover, for Barbara Creed (1993, 10), the vampire is monstrous because of its lack of a soul. As Creed puts it, "The corpse is . . . utterly abject. It signifies one of the most basic forms of pollution—the body without a soul. As a form of waste it represents the opposite of the spiritual. . . . In relation to the horror film, it is relevant to note that several of the most popular monsters are 'bodies without souls'" (21) and, as well as Dracula (and his countless incarnations), include zombies, werewolves (when transformed), and some of the most prominent slashers from Freddy Krueger (*A Nightmare on Elm Street* 1984) to Michael Myers (*Halloween* 1978). The term *soul*, in the classical vampire tradition, has referred to a God-given animating life force with biblical and religious implications. The contemporary understanding of the term *soul*, however, can refer to a concept encompassing notions of mind and consciousness. Anna Wierzbicka (1989) explains that the modern use of soul is philosophically and religiously neutral, makes no references to "another world," and focuses more so on the psychological and moral aspects of a person's existence (44–45). With the increasing secularization of contemporary society has come the secularization of the monster. It is no longer a loss of soul, a loss of entry into a heaven that we are to fear and which the vampire represents. This secularization is reflected in texts such as *The Vampire Diaries* and *True Blood*, where the antiquated concept of the sacred soul is not a pivotal idea, with the focus more on retaining ties to human morals and ethics in order to mainstream, and in the *Twilight* saga, where both body and soul border on the abject, as obstacles between Bella and immortality.

"The other" is another key concept central to the analysis of the vampire. The idea of the other is fundamentally connected to the self and refers to the concept: that which is not the same as I/us is something other and something to be feared. The other can be explained in terms of alienation or estrangement from someone or something, by adopting an "I–It" attitude, viewing the other as impersonal and inhuman, an "it" or "object" or "thing" (Stoehr 2006, 84). Vampires have traditionally been represented on screen as the other in society, embodying the monstrous, the anxieties of the time. Robin Wood (2002, 27) suggests that, in the horror movie, the other is usually dealt with in one of two ways: it is rejected and, if possible, annihilated, or it is rendered safe and is assimilated. In contemporary vampire movies and television programs, boundaries are blurred between the other and "I/us." The following section examines the representation of early and classical vampires as other and the monster's evolution in contemporary narratives.

## VAMPIRE TRANSFORMATIONS: FROM CLASSICAL MONSTER TO CONTEMPORARY MAINSTREAMER

Vampire stories became popular in literature during the nineteenth century, with one of the earliest being *Varney the Vampire* (Prest 1845–1847), which is believed to have introduced some of the enduring monstrous traits we now expect of the vampire—fangs, leaving puncture wounds, the ability to glamour (a form of mind control), and inhuman strength. This narrative is often regarded as having influenced Bram Stoker's classic, *Dracula* (1897), which defined and cemented the supernatural and superhuman characteristics of the vampire, although at this point the vampire could still transmogrify into a lizard, wolf, or bat and could walk in the daylight. Vampires burning in sunlight was a characteristic not added until twentieth-century films (Nelson 2012, 123). The vampire on screen can be traced back to the silent era of cinema. The first representation of the vampire in film was the 1922 German Expressionist horror *Nosferatu* directed by F. W. Murnau (a film closely based on, yet not credited to, Bram Stoker's literary classic, *Dracula*). The vampire in this film, Count Orlok, is a fearful creature. He is animalistic and physically abhorrent with rat-like fangs, pointed ears, long fingernails, bald head, and emaciated physique—the epitome of the monstrous vampire of legend. Count Orlok was not charming or seductive, unlike Count Dracula who graced the screen in *Dracula* in 1931, portrayed by the dashing and seductive Bela Lugosi. David J. Skal (1990) explains that Dracula seduces his female victims, courting before he kills and, unlike other monsters, is not always recognizable as a monster, mocking concepts of society and civility, donning patent-leather shoes and "patent-leather hair" (4). As this suggests, Dracula was a seductive predator looking to feed, but there was arguably little attempt made to integrate into regular society beyond looking the part of a gentlemen of the era. Although Count Dracula often fits into his surrounds, his choices of residence (castle ownership in Transylvania and Carfax Abbey in England), contribute to his otherness and exoticism. The Hammer films of the 1950s launched Christopher Lee as the quintessential vampire figure. Themes explored in vampire horror in this decade include the political other—the red menace of communism invading the West (Weinstock 2012, 93–94). Indeed, over the last six decades, the vampire has represented not only monstrous otherness but also social otherness. The vampire is a flexible metaphor of the outsider, "a convenient catch-all figuration for social otherness" (94), whatever the contemporary social anxiety may be—political (*The Horror of Dracula* 1958), racial (*Blacula* 1978), sexual (*Interview with the Vampire* 1994; *Vampyros Lesbos* 1971), economic (*Blood for Dracula* 1974), or religious (*Salem's Lot* 1979; *Priest* 2006). The vampire character can condense the social anxieties of our time and has traditionally been presented as a threat to be overcome.

The shift in the representation of vampires can be traced to the cinematic vampire of the 1980s and 1990s. This shift aimed to directly appeal to "youth culture" (Gelder 1994). Films such as *The Lost Boys* (1987) presented audiences with a young, attractive vampire gang whose appeal lay in their physical appearance and their rebellious subculture (Gelder 1994, 103). Typical of the teen film, the protagonists display teenage anxieties around family relationships, sexuality, and law(lessness). The 1994 film adaptation of Anne Rice's *Interview with the Vampire* (1976) shifted the representation of the vampire from the rogue predator to the vampire with a conscience. Louis (played by Brad Pitt) is mocked by his creator, Lestat (Tom Cruise), for choosing to drink the blood of animals rather than take a human life. This is the first time audiences explicitly see the vampire struggle with moral choices. This film also raises, as Ken Gelder (1994, 112) observes, the concept of vampirism as an act. The interviewer in the film is told by Louis that vampire lore (crosses, garlic, etc.) is "bullshit." Gelder states, "There is no reality or meaning behind vampirism . . . but one can still 'be' a vampire because—since there is no reality behind it—acting and being collapse into each other" (112). The vampire Armand tells the newly turned Louis that vampires are not "children of Satan" and that they have "no 'discourse' with either God or the devil," explaining that "if God doesn't exist then vampires have the 'highest consciousness' of any being in the world because they have the perspective to understand the passage of time and the value of human life" (Nelson 2012, 124–25). This evolution in the way vampires were portrayed is an important one and a trend that continued in the late 1990s and early 2000s.

Over this period, Joss Whedon's work explored, and introduced, the concept of the vampire with a soul, in particular, *Buffy the Vampire Slayer* (1997–2003) and *Angel* (1999–2004). *Buffy the Vampire Slayer* (Whedon 1997,–2003) provided a principally female audience the opportunity to identify with a female warrior triumphing over her attackers and battling evil in a similar vein to a traditional masculine hero (transforming the stereotype of the female victim who needs to be saved) (Jenson and Sarkeesian 2011, 68). Buffy is still, however, allowed to fall in love with two vampires, knowing that she is equal to them in skill and cunning. So a female audience is now presented with female role models embodying strength, equality, and heroism and the girl who could have it all, including the immortal vampire husband. It is here where we first note that serialization as a narrative form "is unable to sustain the clear categorisation of the moral universe through the unambiguous depiction of good and evil. Serialised narrative produces shifting perspectives and extended middles that . . . contribute to the moral complications that surround characters" (Williamson 2005, 48).

Despite the vampire's transformations in literature and on screen, a number of defining characteristics have remained. As Erik Butler (2010) observes, the vampire:

- is neither wholly dead nor alive and does not respect the boundaries of either state of being;
- "goes about its work by expropriating and redistributing energy"—the drinking of blood is the key feature in vampire text that represents strength and life;
- draws out life and infuses victims with death "and makes the living resemble them";
- defies boundaries of space and time, actively seeking to spread terror. (11)

This fourth point, however, is changing in early twenty-first-century vampire narratives. Vampires have evolved from being creatures ruled solely by instinct and blood-lust, to complex beings with an inner life. "Once audiences cheered for the vampire's destruction. Now they often see a vulnerable side and root for him to escape the stake" (Ellen Datlow in Ramsland 1989, 33).

A constant across the centuries of vampire literature and film is the notion of vampire as predator. As Edward Cullen declares to Bella in the original *Twilight* movie, "I'm the world's best predator, aren't I? Everything about me invites you in— my voice, my face, even my smell. As if I need any of that!" However, a question that arises is: if vampires are such predatory creatures, why then do we find ourselves attracted to their stories, and why do their stories endure? Jeffrey Andrew Weinstock identifies a number of factors at the core of the appeal of vampires for audiences:

- Vampire narratives are predominantly about sex. Vampires are dangerously attractive and representations of tabooed sexuality.
- The vampire is more interesting than those who pursue it. The undead are more alive than the humans—the vampire lives for pleasure alone and is a figure of excess.
- The vampire always returns. We created this monster that gives shape to deep-seated anxieties and tabooed desires that vary with the times but never vanish.
- The cinematic vampire condenses what a culture considers other. (2010, 4–5)

Part of the enduring appeal of vampires is that they often lead extraordinarily luxurious lives, and excessive or extreme forms of capitalism are tropes that have always been prominent in contemporary vampire fiction (Gelder 1994, 22). A glance at the Cullens' light, airy mansion (a striking contrast to Dracula's dark and dilapidated castle) confirms the wealth of the Cullen family—no doubt due to centuries of compound interest and Alice's forecasting abilities. Their wealth is also evidenced by seventeen-year-old Edward Cullen's ride to school (a silver Volvo), the suite of luxury vehicles in the Cullens' garage, including a Mercedes and Porsche, and the honeymoon destination (the Cullen's privately owned island off the Brazilian coast). This theme of wealth and excess has been an enduring one. As Gelder (1994) argues:

> The vampire's nature is fundamentally conservative—it never stops doing what it does; but culturally, this creature may be highly adaptable. Thus it can be made to appeal to or generate fundamental urges located somehow "beyond" culture (desire, anxiety, fear), while simultaneously it can stand for a range of meanings and positions in culture. (141)

Contemporary vampire narratives explore reasons for vampires to mainstream and become contributing members of society. The idea that vampires had a choice to maintain their humanity becomes pivotal to the plot of the *Twilight* saga. Because of the Cullens' acceptance of Bella as a family member, and extending an invitation to her to play baseball with them, the stage is set for a showdown between the "good" vampires (the Cullens) and the monstrous vampires (Victoria, James, and Laurent), a showdown that lays the foundations for the entire saga. Carlisle's choice to mainstream, to "save" his family from their fragile human condition by turning them (or in the case of Jasper who was already turned, saving him from being a monstrous vampire) sets up the conditions for a community of vampires to live in (relative) peace among humans. "Like everything in life, I just had to decide what to do with what I was given" (Carlisle Cullen, *The Twilight Saga: New Moon*). For Carlisle, the choice to mainstream came from knowing who he was, and although he never claims it was an easy path, for him, it was an obvious one. Not all mainstreaming vampires were as willing to embrace the mainstream lifestyle. Stefan Salvatore from *The Vampire Diaries* lives on the blood of animals largely because he has trouble controlling the "ripper" frenzy he is thrown into when he consumes human blood. Accepting his humanity, he realizes that he has to abstain from human blood, in much the same way as a human addict must abstain from his or her drug of choice. The addiction support model is even reinforced:

> Stefan (to vampire Caroline): You're so good at it. Being a vampire.
> Caroline: Because of you, Stefan. I'm good at it because of you. . . . Come to me, whenever you want and I won't let you lose control. (*The Vampire Diaries* 2012, season 4, episode 3)

In *True Blood*, the choice for vampires to mainstream is made easier by the invention of an artificial drink called TruBlood. This gives the vampires a choice of whether to continue feeding from humans or, for those with some semblance of humanity and guilt remaining, to become accustomed to the taste of the substitute and live among humans. With the invention of Tru-Blood came the "outing" of vampires worldwide. The world was made aware of another species living among humans, and with this, the boundaries of other became blurred. The vampire community is now divided, with traditionally monstrous vampires, such as Victoria, James, Laurent, and the Originals (the original vampire family in *The Vampire Diaries*), now cast in opposition to the "good" vampires, who actually want to mainstream for the sake of maintaining their humanity—not to live among humans for their own nefarious purposes, such as Klaus in *The Vampire Diaries*, who is intent on building an army of werewolf/vampire hybrids. This is also quite different from vampires who live in society but segregated and hidden from humans as depicted in *Blade* (1998) and *Underworld* (2003). The other is now no longer confined to the single category of "vampire" and is depicted through the actions and intentions of any creature in the vampire horror story. For example, some of the Faerie (such as Queen Mab) in *True Blood* are as amoral as some vampires, and in the beginning of season 5, episode 1, we are shown the deceptive and true face of the Faerie when Sookie refuses to partake of the "light fruit," which is essentially a glamour spell casting the Faerie as beautiful, the land of Faerie as opulent, and distorting the Faerie inhabitants' perceptions of time.

## HUMANS AND THE BODY AS OTHER

When the other is no longer viewed as simply an object or thing, as humans, we "become more personally connected to the Other, who is also a 'self'" (Stoehr 2006, 83). It is in this shift in how we view the other that we are able to view ourselves, and humanity, and recognize the other inherent in our species. Milly Williamson (2005, 50) explains that contemporary vampire narratives "share the themes of personalising and individualising moral dilemmas"; however, the vampire is now perceived as:

- innocent (having vampirism unwillingly thrust upon it, as all of the Cullen clan did);
- simultaneously glamorous and an outsider (the Cullens are all extraordinarily beautiful yet never quite fit in at school);
- a victim of circumstances outside of its control (the Cullens have to operate within the rules of the Volturi and the human world and had no inkling that a child such as Renesemee could have even been conceived).

The contemporary vampire can thus be seen "to personify dilemmas of the self: how to have meaning in the world which demands it, how to act in circumstances we did not choose, how to be a good human" (Williamson 2005, 50).

Although a mainstreaming entity in many films and television shows (*True Blood*, *The Vampire Diaries*, the *Twilight* saga, among others), the vampire can still be representative of the other. However, it is not just the vampires that are represented as the abject and the other, but now it is also the humans (and their various minority groups), the devoutly religious, and those who are seen to sympathize with vampires who are also portrayed as other. In *True Blood*, not only is the other explored in traditional ways through the vampire creature but also through the impact the mainstreaming vampire has on human society and society's reaction to their desired integration. The audience is asked to draw parallels between the treatment of vampires and the treatment of human slaves in the American Deep South, to engage with the discourse of the variants of sexuality, and to understand and respect the societal (and feudal) structure of the vampire subculture. In the *Twilight* saga, the assimilated Cullen coven are other in the eyes of Bella's school friends, being judged not because they are vampires but because of their wealth, looks, and the seemingly strange interfamilial relationships. Bella crosses the boundaries into the realm of the other, and overcomes the estrangement of the family, by getting to know the Cullens as their true selves first and vampires second. When Edward asks Bella to come to dinner at the Cullens' house, Bella responds, "What if they don't like me?" to which

Edward replies, "So you're worried, not because you'll be in a house full of vampires, but because you think they won't approve of you" (*Twilight* 2008).

While the mainstreaming vampire works to maintain the good qualities of their former human selves and to become unnoticed through assimilation into mainstream middle-class society (Greenberg 2010, 167), humans themselves are constructed as other in many vampire texts. When Bella arrives in Forks, leaving her mother and stepfather in Arizona by choice and coming to live with her loner father, she immediately casts herself as an outsider. The local teenagers of Forks hold little appeal for Bella, they seem mundane in comparison to the intoxicating world of the supernatural, and although Bella tries conform, she but feigns interest in regular human teenage pursuits. Although she has an instant group of friends at her new school, based on her looks and newness, she has trouble fitting in due to her socially awkward manner and her quickly struck relationship with the outsider, Edward. She rejects human companionship for the friendship of the supernatural community, including the Quileute werewolves and the Cullen vampire coven. Even the local police force—primarily through Charlie Swan—is other to the werewolves working with him to track the "animals" thought to be targeting locals.

The appeal of wealth, affluence, immortality, beauty, and superpowers is proffered to the audience as a glamorous alternative to the natural, human life we are meant to lead. In the *Twilight* saga, Bella constantly argues with Edward to be changed, to live an immortal life with him forever. Edward never willingly changes her, yet when Bella is finally turned, after her mortal life is cut short during childbirth, Bella is depicted as a being who is finally able to reach her full potential—not as a human but as a vampire. All along, she has claimed that she belongs in Edward's world, as the final scene from *Eclipse* shows:

> This wasn't a choice between you and Jacob. It was between who I should be and who I am. I've always felt out of step. Like literally stumbling through my life. I've never felt normal, because I'm not normal, and I don't wanna be. I've had to face death and loss and pain in your world, but I've also never felt stronger, like more real, more myself, because it's my world too. It's where I belong.

Isabel Santaularia (2002, 118) writes that "vampires, endowed with an ethical dimension . . . become enticing alternatives to ordinary humanity, especially if we take into account that humanity, as it emerges from the narratives, is presented as a tangle of darkness, evil and sorrow." In contemporary vampire texts, human lives (and humans) are represented as traumatic, mundane, and at times expendable. Certainly, Sookie Stackhouse, whose parents were killed when she was young, lives a distressing life as a telepath with most of the town thinking she's a bit mad. Similarly, Elena Gilbert in *The Vampire Diaries* has also lost her parents and is still grieving as she encounters the vampire Stefan. And Bella, an only child, is torn between parents, an outcast and socially awkward. The vampires these three humans meet proffer a relief from insanity, tragedy, and the mundane.

Unlike Bella, the new vampires in *The Vampire Diaries*, Caroline and Elena, do not initially want to be turned. However, we follow Caroline's journey as she comes to enjoy the power and perks of her new life, in particular, the heightened sexuality that comes with being a vampire—an enduring trait throughout vampire horror from the classical to contemporary vampire. In *True Blood*, the rejection of human life is clearly exemplified by Jessica's joy at becoming a vampire and not having to adhere to the confining rules laid down by her human (and oppressively religious) family. As more characters in *True Blood*, *The Vampire Diaries*, and the *Twilight* saga are turned, and revel in their vampire lifestyle, it could be argued that there is a trend in serialized vampire texts to portray the life of a vampire as preferable to a human's life and that the powers of the immortal body are preferable to the fragility of the human state. This trend continues in the literature in Richelle Mead's *Vampire Academy* series (2007–2010), where humans are only featured as utilitarian "feeders" or "Alchemists," and the Moroi and Dhampir are the superior races, with heightened strength, agility, powers, and longevity.

As Ariadne Blayde and George A. Dunn (2010) explain, vampires tend to think of their human companions in the same way we regard our pets—as useful, amusing, and even loveable but never as equals. Ultimately, human beings are *property*—"Sookie is mine!" (*True Blood* 2010) This is particularly true of James in the *Twilight* saga, who, upon smelling the presence of Bella on the baseball diamond states, "Oh, you brought a snack." Although the Cullens have never considered Bella as an option for a snack, they have always recognized her human fragility and make jokes at her expense. After punching Jacob Black in the face for kissing her, and spraining her hand, Emmett watches on while Carlisle tends to her wound and remarks, "trying to walk and chew gum at the same time again Bella?" (the *Twilight* saga: *Eclipse* 2010). Things take a turn for the worse, however, when Bella sustains a paper cut, causing Jasper, the newest Cullen vampire, to launch himself at her in an attack. Edward pushes Bella away, causing further injury and blood loss. This sets in motion the storyline for *New Moon*, where the Cullens feel obliged to leave town so they can live their lives without fear of harming Bella. Bella is portrayed as the other, her blood is abject, she is a complication in their otherwise calm lives, and they cannot find a way to assimilate her human fragility into their superior lives and lifestyle. The *True Blood* vampires, particularly the older vampires such as Eric and Pam, also do not grant equality to human life. For example, Eric is originally not aware that Sookie is actually part Faerie. It is only once he learns this, that his regard for her changes.

In the horror genre, the human body is often represented as the thing that becomes abject throughout the film, for example *The Thing* (1982) and *the Fly* (1986). In vampire horror, the vampire traditionally could be interpreted as the abject body. However, in contemporary vampire narratives, there is a shift to abjectifying the human body. In *True Blood*, the human body is seen as food and even referred to as "blood bag" or "meat sack" (*True Blood* 2012, season 5, episode 12). In *The Twilight Saga: Breaking Dawn Part 2* (2012), Bella completes her transformation as a vampire, after suffering a painful human death, and arises as a beautiful immortal. Bella is much more comfortable in her vampire skin than her clumsy human form, which is shown as an abject corpse before her transformation into beauty and immortality. Indeed, the beauty of all members of the undead Cullen coven makes us wonder about the abjection of the corpse, as the portrayal of the contemporary vampire as "immortal" is much more appealing than the "undead" portrayal of the classical vampire. The sparkly vampire body becomes the ideal and the divine, the human body and human blood, abject. The Cullens not only reject the consumption of human blood, but also Carlisle is seen burning the blood soaked gauze he has used to treat Bella's wounds. Stefan Salvatore is portrayed as having an addiction to human blood, which, if he consumes too much, turns him into a bloodthirsty killer. Edward Cullen, in *Twilight*, explains to Bella how when a vampire consumes human blood "a kind of frenzy takes over, and it's almost impossible to stop." For the vampire with a conscience, and choosing to mainstream, control of the consumption of human blood, and thus control of addictive traits, is a theme perpetuated in the *Twilight* saga, *True Blood*, and *The Vampire Diaries*.

Over time, the abject in cinema has moved "closer in reference and identification to the audience itself . . . abject terror begins as something 'out there'" (Magistrale 2005, xv) and gradually is relocated into our everyday environments. As we have previously explored in this chapter, the classical vampire has historically been characterized as abject, a representation of the other in society, and the antithesis of the normal and socially acceptable "I." Now, humans in contemporary vampire horror are represented in their full spectrum from loving and kind to sinister, shady, and immoral. No longer are the dichotomies of alive/undead and good/evil clear cut. No longer is the cold, undead vampire body the abject. Indeed, if Bella's attraction to Edward, Elena's attraction to both Stefan and Damon, and Sookie's attraction to both Bill and Eric are anything to go by, then the vampire is not just a sexually alluring being, but the creature itself is a viable option for long-term relationships and happiness.

CONCLUSION

This chapter has discussed the ways in which the notion of the "other" is represented in contemporary vampire texts. We have examined the shift in characterization of the vampire from monster to mainstreamer and observed that humans and the human body are frequently being represented as abject and other in vampire texts. As modern societies have departed from traditional, religiously defined notions of morality, the "sacred" has been replaced with the "self" as a central category of meaning. "The discourses of individualism, which continue to mark the modern condition, arose as part of the larger bourgeois challenge to the old order; science over superstition, merit over rank, man over nature, so that the individual comes to be the repository of moral life and significance" (Brooks 1995, 16). The "individual" representing moral life and significance, as we have seen in this chapter, can be human, vampire, Faerie. In other words, the vampire is no longer by default the monstrous other; rather, the other can be associated with any individual character—supernatural, mortal, or otherwise. With the beautifying, humanizing, and secularizing of the vampire has come a change in its cultural status; on-screen the vampire has transcended its fearsome traits to become a loving husband, father, and contributing community member.

Off-screen, the vampire now exists in popular culture as romantic hero (Edward) to swooning young adults or as vigilante hero (Blade) to action-flick fans. Through social media (fan blogs, Facebook, and Twitter), audiences are able to engage with their vampire hero/romantic obsession long after the curtain has come down, extending the audience relationship with the vampire beyond simply a cinematic experience and bringing the vampire figure into quotidian life. Whereas once the schoolgirl would swoon over a human bad guy who might ride a motorcycle, dress in leather, and break the rules, now the girls swoon over the beautiful vampire pinup. The thirteen-year-old girl not only engages with the horror genre, but also she engages with the romantic fantasy of Bella and Edward. Not only is this seen as acceptable and normal, but also it is perpetuated by the pervasive (and invasive) marketing that the digital age enables. Ian Conrich (2010, 3) explains that the digital age has extended the connections of the horror community, which previously relied on print culture for fanzines and specialist magazines. This extended engagement by fans with the vampire figure, and the impacts this has on audience engagement and perception, and vampire text itself, is an emerging area of research.

The trend of vampires becoming mainstreamers and mortals being represented as "other" is one set to continue. At the time of writing, the *Vampire Academy* series and *A Discovery of Witches* are both currently in development for film production; *The Vampire Diaries* is currently filming series 5, and *True Blood* series 6 is also in production, indicating that for some years to come the mainstreaming vampire will remain on our screens. While the mainstreaming vampire has become a dominant trope in contemporary vampire narratives in film and television, we are not suggesting that the monstrous vampire is in danger of becoming redundant or archaic. The popularity of young adult fiction, such as the *Vampire Academy* series, still provides a place for the monstrous vampire (the Strigoi) but juxtaposes the truly monstrous vampire with the virtuous vampire (the Moroi, with whom we are encouraged to empathize) and halfbreed guardians (the Dhampir, with whom we are urged to sympathize). The continued popularity of the *Underworld* films, where the vampire does not aspire to humanity and assimilation and (for the most part) retains a monstrousness that harks back to the early cinematic vampire, suggests that the *Twilight* saga and the other series discussed in this chapter may be part of a protracted aesthetic cycle that allows an audience to fantasize about an immortal existence with superhero powers, where they can forgo their mundane humanity and live happily forever after.

## REFERENCES

Anderson, Lance. 2012. *The Vampire Diaries*, season 4, episode 3, "The Rager." Viewed October 25, 2012.
Blayde, Ariadne, and George A. Dunn. 2010. "Pets, Cattle, and Higher Life Forms on *True Blood*." In *"True Blood" and Philosphy: We Wanna Think Bad Things with You*, ed. William Irwin, R. Housel, and G. Dunn. Hoboken, NJ: Wiley.
Brooks, P. 1995. *The Melodramatic Imagination: Balzac, Henry James, Melodrama, and the Mode of Excess*. New York: Yale University Press.
Butler, Erik. 2010. *Metamorphoses of the Vampire in Literature and Film: Cultural Transformations in Europe, 1732–1933*. Rochester, NY: Camden House.
Condon, Bill. 2012. *The Twilight Saga: Breaking Dawn, Part 2*. Performed USA.
Conrich, Ian. 2010. *Horror Zone: The Cultural Experience of Contemporary Horror Cinema*. New York: I. B. Tauris.
Creed, Barbara. 1993. *The Monstrous-Feminine: Film, Feminism, Psychoanalysis*. London: Routledge.
Gelder, Ken. 1994. *Reading the Vampire*. London: Routledge.
Greenberg, Louis. 2010. "Sins of the Blood: Rewriting the Family in Two Postmodern Vampire Novels." *Journal of Literary Studies* 26 (1):163–78. Accessed April 24, 2012. http://dx.doi.org/10.1080/02564710903495495. doi: 10.1080/02564710903495495.
Grixti, Joseph. 1989. *Terrors of Uncertainty: The Cultural Contexts of Horror Fiction*. London: Routledge.
Jenson, Jennifer, and Anita Sarkeesian. 2011. "Buffy vs. Bella: The Re-emergence of the Archetypal Feminine in Vampire Stories." In *Fanpires: Audience Consumption of the Modern Vampire*, ed. Gareth Schott and Kirstine Moffat. Washington DC: New Academia.
Kristeva, Julia. 1982. *Powers of Horror: An Essay on Abjection*. New York: Columbia University Press.
Lehmann, Michael. 2012. *True Blood*, season 5, episode 12, "Save Yourself." Viewed August 26, 2012.
Magistrale, Tony. 2005. *Abject Terrors: Surveying the Modern and Postmodern Horror Film*. New York: Peter Lang.
Mead, Richelle. 2007. *Vampire Academy*. New York: Razorbill.
Murnau, F. W. 1922. *Nosferatu*. Performed Germany.

Nelson, Victoria. 2012. *Gothicka: Vampire Heroes, Human Gods, and the New Supernatural.* Cambridge: Harvard University Press.

Pinedo, Isabel Cristina. 1997. *Recreational Terror: Women and the Pleasures of Horror Film Viewing.* Albany: State University of New York Press.

Prest, Thomas Preskett. 1845–1847. *Varney the Vampire; or, The Feast of Blood.* Project Gutenberg.

Ramsland, Katherine. 1989. "Hunger for the Marvelous: The Vampire Craze in the Computer Age." In *Psychology Today.* New York: Sussex.

Santaularia, Isabel. 2002. "The Fallacy of Eternal Love Romance, Vampires and the Deconstruction of Love in Linda Lael Miller's *Forever and the Night* and *For all Eternity.*" In *The Aesthetics of Ageing: Critical Approaches to Literary Representations of the Ageing Process,* ed. Maria O'Neill and Carmen Zamorano Llena. Catalunya: University of Lleida.

Skal, David J. 1990. *Hollywood Gothic: The Tangled Web of Dracula from Novel to Stage to Screen.* New York: Norton.

Slade, David. 2010. *The Twilight Saga: Eclipse.* Performed USA: Summit.

Stoehr, Kevin. 2006. *Nihilism in Film and Television: A Critical Overview from "Citizen Kane" to "The Sopranos."* Jefferson, NC: McFarland.

Weinstock, Jeffrey Andrew. 2010. "Vampires, Vampires, Everywhere!" *Phi Kappa Phi Forum* 90 (3):4–5.

———. 2012. *The Vampire Film: Undead Cinema.* London: Wallflower.

Whedon, Joss. 1997–2003. *Buffy the Vampire Slayer.*

Whedon, Joss, and David Greenwalt. 1999–2004. *Angel.*

Wierzbicka, Anna. 1989. "Soul and Mind: Linguistic Evidence for Ethnopsychology and Cultural History." *American Anthropologist* 91 (1): 41.

Williamson, Milly. 2005. *The Lure of the Vampire: Gender, Fiction, and Fandom from Bram Stoker to Buffy.* London: Wallflower.

Wood, Robin. 2002. "The American Nightmare: Horror in the 70s." In *Horror, The Film Reader,* ed. Mark Jancovich, 25–32. London: Routledge.

Worland, Rick. 2007. *The Horror Film: An Introduction.* Malden, MA: Blackwell.

*Chapter Fourteen*

# Individuality and Collectivity in *The Hunger Games, Harry Potter,* and *Twilight*

## Lisa Weckerle

*Twilight, Harry Potter*, and *The Hunger Games* have much in common: huge popularity, die-hard fans, and critical acclaim. Another thing they have in common, and perhaps a partial explanation for their popularity, is their focus on individuality, community, and the tensions between the two. All three series center on teen heroes who must fit into new cultures: *Twilight*'s Bella must learn to navigate the world of vampires; Harry Potter must learn the ways of the wizarding world; Katniss must adjust to the foreign world of the Hunger Games. As adolescents, these heroes also must learn to embody the cultural norms of adulthood, while simultaneously experiencing individuation as they break away from childhood and family norms. The primary audience for these series is also that of the adolescent, poised on the precipice of individuation and sexual maturity and enmeshed in a complex network of competing communities, such as family, peers, and social networks.

Young-literature critic Allison Waller (2009) states, "The models or frameworks we use to understand adolescence—including developmentalism, identity formation, social agency, and subjectivity within cultural space—can also be found symbolically represented in the common tropes of teenage fantastical realism and its sister genres . . . metamorphoses, haunting, doppelgangers, and invisibility" (136). These tropes reverberate throughout *Twilight, Harry Potter*, and *The Hunger Games* and are inscribed with anxieties about the self that relate to adolescence, globalization, technology, and the overall human condition. The metamorphoses of werewolves and vampires in *Twilight* symbolize fears about the malleability and instability of the self. Haunting, a metaphor for anxieties about the discreteness of the self, is

213

present in the way Bella can hear Edward in her head and the way Harry Potter can sense Voldemort's thoughts. The creation of multiple Harry Potter doppelgangers in *Deathly Hallows* parallels concerns about the self's uniqueness and authenticity. Finally, the use of camouflage in *The Hunger Games* and invisibility in *Twilight* and *Harry Potter* relate to the fear of blending into the background and loss of individual significance and agency.

Desires and fears about collectivity also permeate the series. Bella, Harry, and Katniss must adapt to new communities but also struggle to retain their individual will. Similarly, current developments in networked technologies promise users a greater sense of community but foster new anxieties about loss of individualism and privacy (Fitzpatrick 2006). Just as being subsumed into a collective is undesirable, so is social and political isolation. The protagonists' isolation and desire for community mirror concerns about social isolation caused by overuse of technology (Turkle 2012). *Twilight, Harry Potter*, and *The Hunger Games* depict community as essential for forging political change but also recognize the difficulty of bridging identity differences in order to act collectively. Likewise, current social movements, such as global feminism, struggle to build solidarity among diverse individuals (Weldon 2006).

I posit that *Twilight, Harry Potter*, and *The Hunger Games* resonate with audiences because they offer "literature as equipment for living" (Burke 1967; Brummett 2006). Kenneth Burke originated the theory that literature provides insight into culture because culture gets encoded into literary artifacts. Barry Brummett extended the theory to multiple kinds of texts: "An author, poet, or political speaker puts symbols together in an essay, poem, movie, oration, or other texts as a way of trying to understand and respond to certain problems in life. Once a way of understanding is encoded in a text that text becomes a place to which others may turn for perceptions and motivations" (180). By exploring the tensions between individualism and collectivity in fantasy settings, these series serve as symbols that offer "a selection, reflection, and deflection of socio-cultural realities" (Mahan-Hays and Aden 2003, 32). In this chapter, I will trace how portrayals of individualism and collectivism in these texts help readers to process cultural anxieties about (1) increases in state authority and suppression of individual will, (2) fragmentation of community and difficulty in building solidarity, (3) narcissistic culture, and (4) balancing individuality with collectivity. As I analyze how group belonging and individuality circulate through these three series, I will draw on theories from group dynamics/political psychology, psychoanalysis, and mythic criticism.

## DEMONIZING COLLECTIVITY: SURVEILLANCE AND THE STATE REPRESSION OF INDIVIDUAL WILL

Surveillance has emerged as a major concern in modern society, especially the state's surveillance of its citizens in a post-9/11 world. Victor Fan (2012) argues, "The supernatural in the narrative can in turn be read as a symptom, or an allegory, of the sovereign authority or state power to which individuals consign the right to manage their lives" (35). A staple of speculative fiction, omniscience serves as a metaphor for surveillance. Vampires Edward and Aro are both able to read the thoughts of others, and they use this power against their enemies. Harry Potter and Voldemort are able to sense each other's actions and emotions, and they also exploit this connection. In *The Hunger Games*, the Capitol uses technology to achieve omniscience by constant monitoring and broadcasting of the Hunger Game participants. Not only do these forms of surveillance reflect contemporary anxieties about the state monitoring its citizens, but also they relate to concerns about lack of privacy and technology.

The governmental groups that operate within these fictional worlds highlight contemporary concerns about expanding state power and suppression of individual will. In *Twilight*, the Volturi are the powerful ruling vampire authority that represents the threat of dogmatic control by a pseudo-aristocracy (Mutch 2011, 86). I posit that the Volturi embody the shadow side of collectivity by portraying authoritarianism. Two of the defining characteristics of authoritarianism are demanding respect for authority and allowing punishment of deviance (Gelfand, Triandis, and Chan 1996). Authority and punishment work dialectically: the Volturi's ability to exert their authority is reinforced by their public punishments of those who break vampire law; and their punishments are largely unchallenged because of their monopolistic authority over vampire society. The problem with the Volturi is endemic to groups that exercise absolute power: they start to abuse their authority and serve their own interests rather than the common good. The Volturi ensure their continued rule through preemptive strikes against those that are powerful enough to challenge them. The Volturi also disguise these strikes as official judicial proceedings. Thus, the Volturi parallel many aspects of authoritarianism in contemporary times, including unchecked power, using violence to control their own people, and disguising their abuse of power with sham trials. Stephenie Meyer adopts a critical stance toward authoritarianism because she demonizes the Volturi and clearly "privileges listening to one's conscience over following orders from an established authority" (Toscano 2010, 27).

In *Harry Potter*, the Ministry of Magic is depicted as a group of "self-interested bureaucrats bent on increasing and protecting their power," which parodies governmental dysfunction in Great Britain and the United States

(Barton 2006, 1525). The Ministry of Magic is a hyperbolic embodiment of group think. I. L. Janis (1973) defines "group think" as a dysfunction in which groups suppress independent critical thinking in favor of concurrence seeking, often leading to deteriorations in "mental efficiency, reality testing and moral judgments as a result of group pressures" (22). Janis describes group think as fostering "over-optimism, lack of vigilance, and sloganistic thinking about the weakness and immorality of out-groups" (1971, 22–23). The Ministry of Magic demonstrates a myopic focus on concurrence; it is constantly trying to reach consensus on trivial matters and thereby overlooking the approaching apocalypse. When confronted with news that Voldemort has returned, the Ministry displays over-optimism and lack of vigilance by denying his return. By demonizing Dumbledore and Harry for reporting Voldemort's return, the Ministry situates them as a dangerously hysterical out-group. Like the Volturi, the Ministry conducts sham trials, which bring charges capriciously and convict on hearsay rather than evidence. The Ministry of Magic also spreads group think to the populace by controlling the messages of all official media channels, employing slogans such as "The Boy Who Lies" to discredit Harry (Rowling 2007).

District 13 subordinates the rights of individuals to the well-being of the state through the practice of Machiavellianism, which is generally defined as valuing pure instrumentality over morality (Wiener 1973). Machiavellian leadership subordinates the volition of individuals in a group to the achievement of group goals. Machiavellianism allows for the individual conscience to be manipulated because "leaders and followers assume that the cause they serve is of such surpassing importance that deception or cruelty in its behalf is in fact a moral virtue." (Scharfstein 2005, "Machiavellian Rule"). As leader of the rebellion, President Coin demonstrates both deceptiveness and cruelty when she secretly orders the bombing of Capitol children and District 13's medical team in order to frame the Capitol leader. She tricked her own people into believing the enemy was responsible for the bombing and harnessed the resulting moral outrage to win the war. President Coin's Capitol bombings show that she is Machiavellian; she deceives her own people and sacrifices innocent lives for propaganda purposes.

## SEARCHING FOR SOLIDARITY AND NEGOTIATING DIFFERENCE

Along with modern society's fears of suppression of individual will by the state, we also struggle with how to form meaningful communities in an age of fragmentation and instability. Globalization and the rise of multinational companies require heterogeneous groups to navigate cultural and geographical difference in order to function effectively. Coalition building between different factions of oppressed groups is also essential to enacting social change. Coalition building is challenging, especially when the groups that need to unite have unique identities and conflicting interests. Laurel S. Weldon (2006) argues that solidarity among diverse members is facilitated by developing norms of inclusivity that allow for both consensus building and internal dissent.

These series all feature groups that successfully unite diverse groups, thereby assuaging their audience's anxieties about how to form communities among disparate peoples. The differences that are being bridged correspond to the nature of the oppressions that are perpetrated by the villains. For example, the diversity of beings united against *Twilight*'s Volturi include vampires and their sworn enemies, the werewolf pack. Thus, *Twilight* emphasizes the ability of long-standing rivals to cooperate with each other if they are united in common hatred (for the Volturi). In the final battle of *Harry Potter*, the army fighting against Voldemort's pure-blood Death Eaters includes muggles, wizards, minotaurs, giants, and house elves. Thus, *Harry Potter* highlights the need for different races to come together to stop Voldemort's program of ethnic cleansing. In *The Hunger Games*, the people who join to fight against the Capitol include people from the affluent Capitol and from all thirteen of the starving Districts. Thus, *The Hunger Games* underscores the need for different socioeconomic classes to work together to stop the exploitation of workers by the minority ruling classes.

*Twilight* reassures fans that internal conflicts can be negotiated in order to build solidarity. In *Breaking Dawn*, the vampires and the werewolves are sworn enemies, but they join forces to stand up to the Volturi. The coalition is able to temporarily put aside differences that would prevent any long-standing friendships in order to accomplish its goal. In the end, the coalition achieves its goals because its members are able to retain their individuality and act collectively. Indeed, *Twilight* makes an argument for the strength of diversity in groups by ending with an image of hybridity. Deborah Mutch (2011) states, "The completed *Twilight* ends with a niche hybrid community of cordial relations between vampires and weres and a multicultural future as the half-white American human, half-vampire Renesmee 'imprints' with the Native American were, Jacob, for a life-long relationship" (86).

The *Twilight* coalition is also ephemeral: it forms, serves its purpose, and then quickly dissolves. The idea of collectives that spring up and then dissipate parallels the nature of community in the modern world. For example, today's job seekers are likely to work for multiple employers over the course of their lifetime (Friedman 2005, 284). In terms of technology, the lighting-fast speed of communication and centrality of social networks enables the sudden erupting of flash mobs, viral videos, and Internet friendships. The sudden formation and dissolution of the coalition also mimics the dynamics of teen (and for that matter, adult) friendships. While some friendships may last a lifetime, most erupt spontaneously and disappear after they have served their developmental purpose. Through the portrayal of the formation, success, and dissolution of the coalition, *Twilight*'s finale reassures readers that social bonds need not be long standing in order to have deep meaning and significant purpose.

*Harry Potter* and *The Hunger Games* depict similar coalitions. In *Harry Potter*, rivalry between the houses is encouraged in the earlier volumes, but inner division is depicted as a weakening force later in the series. The sorting hat warns: "For our Hogwarts is in danger / From external, deadly foes / And we must unite inside her or we'll crumble from within" (Rowling 2003, 206–7). *Harry Potter* portrays loyalty and teamwork as the solutions to factionalism and infighting (Carey 2003). Like the alliance against the Volturi, resistance groups form in response to danger from Voldemort, but then disband when Voldemort dies. In *The Hunger Games*, the rebellion movement is composed of disparate people from the affluent Capital and thirteen different Districts. Ironically, it is Katniss's singularity as the Mockingjay that unifies these forces. She demonstrates the ability to reach across divisions and form alliances not based on strategy but on mutual respect.

In all three series, the presence of a common enemy strengthens the tenuous bonds between group members. Whether it is stopping the Volturi from executing a child, stopping Voldemort from taking over the world, or stopping the Capitol from exploiting the Districts, these coalitions model how diverse groups of people can take collective action when united by a common cause.

## FEARS OF THE UNBOUNDED SELF: NARCISSISM AND THE STUNTED SELF

While the balance between self and other is a long-standing theme, the prevalence of modern reality television and social networking serve to foreground our anxieties about narcissism. Reality shows reflect both a growth of cultural narcissism and a decline in self-control (Slosar 2009). Since 2000, Americans have tested as more narcissistic on psychological tests, and some researchers posit a connection to the predominance of social networks (Grossman 2010). Narcissism is characterized by a constellation of attributes including self-importance and grandiosity, fantasies about unlimited success and power, displays of entitlement and exceptionalism, and inability to express empathy (Rhodewalt 2007). Failure to recognize the limits of the self then leads to the inability to form social bonds (Rhodewalt 2007). Characteristics of narcissists include lack of remorse, lack of empathy, and cunning manipulation (Hare 2003), all of which are associated with the villains of the series. I argue that the villains of the series resonate with audiences because they serve as hyperbolic projections of society's concerns about narcissistic culture.

Because vampires are driven by hunger, they are linked to the id-dominated stage of an infant's development (Day 2006). Freud describes the oral stage in which the infant is driven by the id and pleasure principle, unaware of any boundaries between self and other (Felluga 2013a). As the infant develops, the pleasure principle becomes moderated by the reality principle, and the id becomes balanced by the superego. Blood thirsty vampires symbolize the stunted self whose id-driven hungers are never moderated by the development of the superego. The vampire's sucking of blood evokes the infant's sucking on its mother's breast as well as the merging of self with victim (Copjec 14, as quoted in Day 2006, 182).

Vampires also symbolize Jacques Lacan's concept of the undifferentiated stage in which the infant cannot distinguish between self and others (Lacan 1977; Felluga 2013b). Like the infant, the vampire is undifferentiated, meaning it does not yet recognize difference between self and other but thinks that the entire world is a part of the self. Because vampires do not recognize the difference between self and other, they lack the ability to form healthy social bonds. Thus, *Twilight*'s vampires are usually solitary creatures that are unable to live peacefully with each other because of their inherent territorialism and competitiveness.

Vampires also represent a fear of assimilation; they are figures whose unbounded selves absorb or destroy others. Vampires assimilate their victims physically through feeding on them or culturally through turning them into vampires (Hallab 2009). Aro, one of the Volturi, exemplifies the vampire as "the ultimate self before whom all things, even death, must make way" (Hallab 2009, 65). He is able to read every thought someone has ever had by touching him or her, and he uses this skill to discover his enemy's weaknesses. His omniscience symbolizes the unbridled self; he violates the boundaries of others without their consent to serve his own purposes. He also uses the guise of group membership and duty to mask his personal agenda of collecting vampires with extraordinary gifts. Since his collected vampires are also under his power and command, available as weapons if he so desires, he is in a sense assimilating them.

Voldemort demonstrates dysfunctions of self, including projection, undifferentiation, and lack of boundaries. As an orphan born to Muggle parents, he projects his self-hatred outward. His goal of eradicating wizard society of Muggle blood is actually an attempt at cleansing himself of his Muggle ancestry. Instead of resolving his internal conflict about his heritage, Voldemort projects this conflict onto the world around him, seeing the world as a microcosm of his self. The entire world seems to be present only as an extension of the Voldemort's self and for the purpose of fulfilling the desires of the self. Like the vampires, Voldemort demonstrates stagnation in the undifferentiation stage. His quest to make himself immortal further demonstrates Voldemort's inability to accept the boundaries of his self. Because Voldemort is stuck in the undifferentiated stage of development, he is unable to form connections. Even his loyal followers receive no loyalty from him; Voldemort disposes of his servants when they displease him or outgrow their usefulness (Duriez 2007).

An excessive concern with the self permeates the culture of the Capitol. The Capitol citizens display an excess of appetite, similar to that of the vampire. They practice overeating, followed by self-induced vomiting, followed by yet more overeating. Like the vampire, the Capitol citizen is stuck in the id-stage in which the world exists for their own pleasure and consumption. Through the voyeuristic enjoyment of the Games, the Capitol audience objectifies and consumes the District members. Capitol citizens also display narcissistic entitlement, the belief that they should get more resources than others because of their superiority (Campbell and Foster 2007). Furthermore, the Capitol's obsession with fashion and plastic surgery resonates with narcissistic aspects of our own cultures, including superficiality, materialism, and commodification of the body.

## RECOVERING INDIVIDUAL AGENCY AND SIGNIFICANCE: THE HERO'S BALANCING ACT

In an age when individuals are often thought of as powerless cogs in the machines of democracy, capitalism, and other systems, these narratives offer reassurance about the potential for individual agency. All of the heroes are portrayed as being unique and valuable to society. Bella is an especially powerful vampire endowed with unique gifts; Harry Potter is the only one who was able to survive or kill Voldemort; Katniss as the Mockingjay is the only one who can unite the Districts. Rather than positioning the individual as subordinated by systems, these stories remind audiences that extraordinary individuals are needed to stand up to seemingly insurmountable systems.

The success of these heroes is due in part to their ability to balance the tensions between collective and individualistic characteristics. Geert Hofstede defined individualistic cultures as having loose social ties in which people are usually responsible for taking care of themselves and their immediate family and collectivist cultures as having strong, cohesive in-groups that expect loyalty and provide protection (2001). Each national culture demonstrates aspects of both individuality and collectivism, though cultures such as China's tend to display more collectivist markers, and cultures like the United States' tend to display more individualistic markers. Researchers found that Harry Potter appealed equally to both the collectivistic and individualistic cultures: "Potter is (likely) both sociable enough to appeal to readers from collectivistic cultures and at the same time at least sufficiently independent and assertive to appeal to readers from individualistic cultures as well" (Schmid and Klimmt 2011, 263). Like Harry, Bella and Katniss combine independence with interdependence, thus suggesting a possible explanation for their cross-cultural appeal.

Bella's heroism is defined by combining individuality and collectivity harmoniously. Her shielding power is most useful when she is able to protect the entire coalition and allow others to exercise their individual gifts in concert with hers. Harry is a more solitary hero, relying on friends and mentors along the journey to face Voldemort's army and surrogates but ultimately facing Voldemort alone (Cronn-Mills and Samens 2010). Katniss is perhaps the most independent hero of all, a hero who is able to see through the unifying rhetoric of her own side—the rebellion group—and execute its leader in order to prevent the rebellion from perpetuating the same evils that the Capitol engaged in.

As the heroes progress on their journeys, they must make decisions about when to act independently and when to draw on the strength of the group. Bella demonstrates individuality by choosing Edward, choosing to keep her baby, and choosing to become a vampire (Toscano 2010). Yet, Bella also demonstrates collectivity through her joining of the Cullen family and vampire community. The hero must also be able to distinguish between positive and negative manifestations of individuality and collectivity and respond accordingly. For example, when Katniss decides to go against the resistance and assassinate her former ally, President Coin, to save the future of Panem, she resists a corrupted collective. However, when Harry runs off to rescue Sirius without waiting for help, his actions are construed as reckless and arrogant.

All three heroes follow a pattern that reflects Campbell's description of the hero's journey: "A hero ventures forth from the world of common day into a region of supernatural wonder: fabulous forces are there encountered and a decisive victory is won: the hero comes back with the power to bestow boons on his fellow man" (2008, 23). The hero's journey can be conceptualized as a roadmap for how to negotiate one's dual role as an individual and a member of a society. As the hero proceeds on the journey, he or she is often assisted by mentors, friends, and guides. However, as the hero comes closer to the end of the journey, the helpers may withdraw so that the hero must prove him or herself as an individual. After the hero's triumph, the hero shares whatever special gifts were won with the community and is then reintegrated into the group.

Bella's experience of herself as alienated from her family, her peer group, and even her species positions her as an individual without a community. Bella's separation extends beyond not fitting in with her family or community to not fitting in with humanity: "Sometimes I wondered if I was seeing the same thing through my eyes that the rest of the world was seeing through theirs" (Meyer 2005, 10–11). It is only by falling in love with Edward, joining the Cullen family, and becoming a vampire herself that she is able to overcome her alienation. *Twilight* emphasizes the importance of family belonging by imbuing Edward with paternalistic characteristics and portrays "adult identity as being formed within the context of the family" (Silver 2010, 127). Thus, Bella's integration focuses on romantic relationships and family.

Bella is called to adventure when she simultaneously realizes that Edward is a vampire, that he thirsts for her blood, and that she loves him unconditionally and irrevocably (Meyer 2005). By accepting the call, she moves from the human world into the supernatural realm. Bella is assisted by helpers as she completes her journey: Edward socializes her to vampire ways, and Zafrina teaches her how to use her mind as a shield. Bella's final showdown with the Volturi synthesizes her individual talent with collective cooperation: Bella's shielding is only effective because it works in concert with the actions of her allies. The boon that Bella brings to her community is the ability to resist the Volturi and greater integration between the vampire, werewolf, and human communities.

Janne Stigen Drangsholt (2011) draws parallels between *Twilight* and the narrative topos of katabasis, a mythological journey in which the hero descends into an underworld in search of an Other. She describes Bella as the hero who searches for the Other, who may be conceived of as Edward or alternatively as her vampire self. Once immersed in the underworld, Bella must "undergo a series of tests and challenges, culminating in the dissolution of her sense of selfhood and ending with a return to the world, where she brings back truth (*aletheia*), love or power" (Drangsholt 2011, 97). Thus, she claims that Bella gives up herself over the course of the novel to commune with the Other. Silver (2010) conceptualizes Bella's balance between self and others quite differently: "Meyer's implication in *Breaking Dawn* is that self is found in community, particularly in marriage and parenthood (whether biological or adoptive), but also in family and groups such as the werewolf pack. . . . Bella finds her sense of identity not through individual achievement but through a relationship" (132–33). Whether Bella sacrifices the self to be a part of community or finds her true self through integration with a community, she is constantly negotiating her role as individual and community member.

Harry Potter also begins his journey as isolated, an orphan who is ostracized by his adopted family. Harry's call to adventure is his invitation to join Hogwarts, and he makes the decision to answer the call in the isolation of his room. Through immersion into the wizarding world, Harry forms deep friendships, becomes a member of Gryffindor House, and becomes bonded to Hogwarts. Harry forms family bonds through his interaction with the Weasleys and eventually officially joins the family by marrying Ginny Weasley. Harry's integration also focuses on group belonging to a family. Although Harry and Bella both marry into their surrogate families, Bella's integration is more centered on romantic bonds than Harry's. Harry's integration is centered on belonging to Hogwarts, which represents integration into tradition, ritual, and place. He is assisted by various mentors, but as he matures, they fall away so that Harry can accept greater responsibility. Harry triumphs over Voldemort because he is willing to sacrifice himself for the good of his community. Harry brings back the boon of Voldemort's defeat and the corresponding beginning of an age of peace in the wizarding world.

Katniss's journey does not fit the hero's journey as neatly as Bella's and Harry's, but it weaves together the themes of alienation and integration. Katniss starts as a solitary person whose main bonds are to her sister and her hunting partner Gale. Katniss's call to adventure is a combination of individual action and social ritual. She demonstrates willingness to sacrifice self and strength of bond to family by volunteering to take her sister's place in the Games. In a sense, she intercedes in Prim's call to adventure and substitutes herself, thereby depicting her as the most active of the heroes in the acceptance of the call. During the Games and the rebellion, Katniss forms alliances with other others but also disregards orders and acts independently at strategic times. Most notably, she assassinates the leader of the rebellion that she helped succeed because she realizes the leader has been corrupted. The boon that she brings to her community is the end of the Hunger Games and the overthrow of the Capitol; however, the price of winning is that her sister is killed, her friendship with Gale is ruined, and she is exiled from the community. She ends her journey starting a new family with Peeta but as an outcast with no role in the new government. Although many of her friends and allies are killed in the revolution, Katniss ends the series by remembering all of those she has lost, drawing strength from their kindnesses. Thus, Katniss's heroic journey does not end with a traditional reintegration into the community, but she is nevertheless connected to others, even if they are not physically present.

## CONCLUSION

*Twilight, Harry Potter,* and *The Hunger Games* offer readers and viewers valuable "equipment for living" by providing representations of individual and collective identities, actions, and tensions. First, the corruption and incompetence of fictional government institutions resonate with audience's questioning of the abilities and motives of their own governments. The power of the state to usurp individual will for the good of the community is a focal point for both fictional and real world governance. Second, the texts' exploration of how to form solidarity among different races and classes references our own anxieties about how to form communities in an age of increasing intercultural contact, rapid change, and identity politics. Third, the villains of the texts demonstrate society's concerns about narcissism, lack of self-control, and lack of empathy. While the villain's personification of the dysfunctional self allows audiences a fictional "steam valve" for their own anxiety about the narcissistic culture, the destruction or limitation of the villains also suggests to audiences that the unbridled self will eventually be tamed. Finally, the heroes of the series reassure readers and viewers that individual agency is both possible and necessary to society. Each series depicts a singular hero who embodies the positive manifestation of individuality and independent action but also integrates collective action and community belonging. Bella, Harry, and Katniss model how individuals can weave together independence and interdependence and in so doing benefit both themselves and their communities.

In conclusion, *Twilight*, *Harry Potter*, and *The Hunger Games* are pleasurable to readers and viewers because they offer "literature as equipment for living." They provide both an imaginative space upon which to project cultural anxiety about individualism and collectivism and reassuring models for how these fundamental human needs can be negotiated.

## REFERENCES

Barton, Benjamin H. 2006. "Harry Potter and the Half-crazed Bureaucracy." *Michigan Law Review* 104 (6): 1523–38.

Brummett, Barry. 2006. *Rhetoric in Popular Culture*. London: Sage.

Burke, Kenneth. 1967. *The Philosophy of Literary Form*. Berkeley: University of California Press.

Campbell, Joseph. 2008. *The Hero with a Thousand Faces*. Novato, CA: New World Library.

Campbell, W. Keith, and Joshua D. Foster. 2007. "Narcissistic Entitlement." In *Encyclopedia of Social Psychology*, vol. 2, ed. Roy F. Baumeister and Kathleen D. Vohs, 606–7. Los Angeles: Sage.

Carey, Brycchan. 2003. "Hermione and the House Elves: The Literary and Historical Contexts of J. K. Rowling's Anti-Slavery Campaign." In *Reading Harry Potter*, ed. Giselle Liza Anatol, 103–16. Contributions to the Study of Popular Culture 78. Westport, CT: Praeger.

Cronn-Mills, Kristin, and Jessica Samens. 2010. "Sorting Heroic Choices: Green and Red in the *Harry Potter* Septology." In *Millenial Mythmaking*, ed. John Perlich and David Whitt, 5–31. Jefferson, NC: McFarland.

Day, Peter. 2006. *Vampires: Myths and Metaphors of Enduring Evil*. Amsterdam: Rodopi.

Drangsholt, Janne Stigen. 2011. "Managing the Self: A Study of *Katabasis* in *Twilight*." In *Interdisciplinary Approaches to "Twilight,"* ed. Mariah Larsson and Ann Steiner, 97–110. Lund, Sweden: Nordic Academic.

Duriez, Colin. 2007. *The Field Guide to "Harry Potter."* Downer's Grove, IL: Intervarsity.

Fan, Victor. 2012. "The Poetics of Addiction: Stardom, 'Feminized' Spectatorship, and Interregional Business Relations in the *Twilight* Series." *Camera Obscura* 27 (79): 31–67.

Felluga, Dino. 2013a. "Modules on Freud." *Introductory Guide to Critical Theory*. Purdue University. Accessed February 21, 2013. http://www.purdue.edu/guidetotheory/psychoanalysis/freud 5.html.

———. 2013b. "Modules on Lacan." *Introductory Guide to Critical Theory.* Purdue University. Accessed February 21, 2013. http://www.purdue.edu/guidetotheory/psychoanalysis/ freud 5.html.

Fitzpatrick, Kathleen. 2006. *The Anxiety of Obsolescence: The American Novel in the Age of Television.* Nashville, TN: Vanderbilt University Press.

Friedman, Thomas L. 2005. *The World Is Flat.* New York: Farrar, Strauss and Giroux.

Gelfand, Michele J., Harry C. Triandis, and Darius K.-S. Chan. 1996. "Individualism versus Collectivism or versus Authoritarianism?" *European Journal of Social Psychology* 26 (3): 397–410.

Grossman, Lev. 2010. "Person of the Year 2010 Mark Zuckerberg." *Time Magazine,* December 5. Accessed February 21, 2013. http://www.time.com/time/specials/packages/article/ 0,28804,2036683_2037183_2037185-8,00.html.

Hallab, Mary Y. 2009. *Vampire God: The Allure of the Undead in Western Culture.* Albany, NY: SUNY Press.

Hare, R. D. 2003. *Manual for the Revised Psychopathy Checklist.* 2nd ed. Toronto: Multi-Health Systems.

Hofstede, Geert. 2001. *Culture's Consequences: Comparing Values, Behaviors, Institutions and Organizations across Nations.* 2nd ed. Thousand Oaks CA: Sage.

Janis, I. L. 1971. "Groupthink." *Psychology Today* 5 (6): 43–46, 74–76.

———. 1973. "Groupthink and Group Dynamics: A Social Psychological Analysis of Defective Policy Decisions." *Policy Studies Journal* 2 (1): 19–25.

Lacan, Jacques. 1977. *Écrits: A Selection.* Trans. Alan Sheridan. New York: Norton.

Mahan-Hays, S. E., and R. C. Aden. 2003. "Kenneth Burke's 'Attitude' at the Crossroads of Rhetorical and Cultural Studies: A Proposal and Case Study Illustration." *Western Journal of Communication* 67 (1): 32–55.

Meyer, Stephenie. 2005. *Twilight.* New York: Little, Brown.

Mutch, Deborah. 2011. "Coming out of the Coffin: The Vampire and Transnationalism in the *Twilight* and Sookie Stackhouse Series." *Critical Survey* 23 (2): 75–90.

Rhodewalt, Frederick. 2007. "Narcissism." In *Encyclopedia of Social Psychology,* vol. 2, ed. Roy F. Baumeister and Kathleen D. Vohs, 604–6. Los Angeles: Sage.

Rowling, J. K. 2003. *Harry Potter and the Order of the Phoenix.* New York: Scholastic.

———. 2007. *Harry Potter and the Deathly Hallows.* New York: Scholastic.

Scharfstein, Ben-Ami. 2005. "Machiavellism." *New Dictionary of the History of Ideas.* Encyclopedia.com. Accessed March 07, 2013. http://www.encyclopedia.com/doc/1G2-3424300446.html.

Schmid, Hannah, and Christoph Klimmt. 2011. "A Magically Nice Guy: Parasocial Relationships with Harry Potter across Different Cultures." *International Communication Gazette* 73 (3): 252–69.

Silver, Anna. 2010. "*Twilight* Is Not Good for Maidens: Gender, Sexuality, and the Family in Stephenie Meyer's *Twilight* Series." *Studies in the Novel* 42 (1/2): 121–38.

Slosar, J. R. 2009. *The Culture of Excess: How America Lost Self-Control and Why We Need to Redefine Success.* Santa Barbara, CA: Praeger.

Toscano, Margaret M. 2010. "Mormon Morality and Immortality in Stephenie Meyer's *Twilight* Series." In *Bitten by "Twilight": Youth Culture, Media, and the Vampire Franchise,* ed. Melissa A. Click, Jennifer Stevens Aubrey, and Elizabeth Behm-Morawitz. New York: Peter Lang.

Turkle, Sherry. 2012. *Alone Together: Why We Expect More of Technology and Less of Each Other.* New York: Basic Books.

Waller, Allison. 2009. *Constructing Adolescence in Fantastic Realism.* London: Routledge.

Weldon, S. Laurel. 2006. "Inclusion, Solidarity, and Social Movements." *Perspectives on Politics* 4 (1): 55–74.

Wiener, Phillip P., ed. 1973. *Dictionary of the History of Ideas: Studies of Selected Pivotal Ideas.* New York: Scribner.

*Chapter Fifteen*

# From *Twilight* to *Fifty Shades of Grey*

*Fan Fiction, Commercial Culture, and Grassroots Creativity*

Sonia Baelo-Allué

What do *Twilight* and *Fifty Shades of Grey* have in common? What can these two series of novels possibly share? *Twilight* is a mostly chaste fantasy romance between a 104-year-old vampire and a teenage girl, whereas *Fifty Shades of Grey* is an erotic series dealing with a college graduate and a young business magnate who is into BDSM (bondage, discipline, sadism, and masochism). Apparently, they have a lot in common since both series have struck a chord in our society, becoming full-fledged cultural phenomena. Bearing in mind that *Fifty Shades of Grey* was in origin fan fiction of *Twilight*, this chapter deals with what happened between 2005, when *Twilight* was first published, and 2012, when *Fifty Shades of Grey* became the biggest hit, topping bestseller lists for months. There are both cultural and ideological implications emerging from the transformation that the *Twilight* series has undergone. From a set of novels and films written by a Mormon American author and addressing a young adult audience, *Twilight* has turned into *Fifty Shades of Grey*, an erotic saga labeled by the media "mommy porn," written by a British fan of *Twilight* and addressing an adult female audience. The story of this journey is worth exploring in full since it also shows a common tension in contemporary culture, that between corporate-driven and consumer-driven processes, between commercial culture and grassroots creativity.

# FROM FAN FICTION TO MAINSTREAM SUCCESS: A CULTURAL JOURNEY

Both *Twilight* and *Fifty Shades* are by now international franchises that respond to the rise of global fan and popular culture. By the end of October 2010, *Twilight*'s translation rights had been sold in nearly fifty countries and the saga had sold 116 million copies worldwide ("Little, Brown to Publish Official *Twilight* Guide" 2010). To date, the *Fifty Shades* trilogy has sold more than thirty-five million copies in the U.S. and sixty-five million copies worldwide (Deahl 2012). For twenty consecutive weeks, *Fifty Shades of Grey* was number one on *USA Today*'s Best-Selling Books list, and in the UK, it has sold more than five million copies, making it the best-selling book in Britain since records began and even outselling all seven *Harry Potter* books on Amazon.uk (Jones 2012). The foreign rights for the trilogy have been sold in forty-four territories and translated into more than forty languages (Metcalf 2012). In Spain, my home country, the books were published by Editorial Grijalbo in June and July 2012, and topped the Spanish bestseller list for months. As Claudia Bucciferro details in the introduction to this book, the *Twilight* series has been adapted to the screen and turned into five very successful films. In the same way, Universal Pictures and Focus Features are preparing the big-screen adaptation of the first book in the *Fifty Shades* trilogy (Meza 2012). As we can see, the global success of both series in terms of sales and media buzz is remarkably similar and inextricably linked.

In 2008, E. L. James, whose real name is Erika Leonard, was a British television executive and mother of two children, who, after watching the first *Twilight* film, read the books and liked them so much that in January 2009 decided to write her own fiction based on the original characters:

> Just after Christmas, I sat down and read the books [*Twilight*], and I escaped for five days. I just loved them. . . . And on the 15th of January I sat down to write an *original* book for the first time ever. I finished it in April, and then I started another one. I kind of came to a halt with it 96,000 words later, in August, and then I discovered fan fiction. I thought, "This is interesting." I just wrote one in three weeks. And while I was doing that I had the idea for what would eventually become "Fifty Shades," and I started writing that there and then. (In Johnson 2012, my emphasis)

She called her stories *Master of the Universe* (MOTU) and, under the pen name Snowqueens Icedragon, decided to share them with the fan community on http://www.fanfiction.net (the largest archive of fan fiction), in http://www.twilighted.net (a *Twilight* fan-fiction site), and later on the author's webpage http://www.50Shades.com. It is important to note that in the quotation above E. L. James claims she has written "an original book" but *Master of the Universe* was fan fiction that took off from the beginning, which helped the author build her original fan base, the Bunker Babes. In fact, she hit a note and earned a massive following, receiving more than 50,000 comments on her stories. *Master of the Universe* used the same character names and traits as in *Twilight*, though developing a different storyline. Edward turns into a twenty-seven-year-old billionaire with a dark past and a liking for sadomasochism and Bella into a twenty-one-year-old inexperienced college graduate who, being a virgin, is more into classical romantic British literature than into hardcore sexual relationships. Edward wants Bella to play the submissive to his dominant sexual nature, but she's not entirely convinced. Although we will see that the large dynamics are similar, the initial conflict that triggers *Master of the Universe* seems to differ from *Twilight*'s original conflict: the impossible relationship between a vampire in love with a human girl whose blood he is desperate to drink.

In any case, what has made *Fifty Shades of Grey* a cultural phenomenon is not just that it started as fan fiction based on *Twilight* and freely available on the Internet but that it successfully broke into the mainstream. Firstly, The Writer's Coffee Shop, which is a small, independent Australian publisher, decided to publish the series in the e-book format and print-on-demand but renamed the characters to avoid copyright infringement (Edward and Bella became Christian and Anastasia). Word of mouth publicity or, rather, word of mouse, mainly e-mails, chat rooms, social media networks, newsgroups, and blogs, played an important role into its initial success. According to Joel Rickett, an editor at Penguin, readers have more power than ever because they have online communities that can berate overhyped books promoted by publishing houses and promote unexpected titles by word of mouth ("Of Brooms and Bondage" 2012). As a result, the books sold 250,000 copies, and they even hit the *New York Times* e-book bestseller list (Metcalf 2012). Vintage, a Random House division, acquired the series and republished it on a large scale: new e-books were released in March 2012 and paperbacks in April 2012, which have turned into the worldwide success. As we can see, even though the series had an established audience in the fan-fiction community, it still needed the traditional publishing system to reach a worldwide audience. As Rachel Deahl puts it: "As it turns out, E. L. James needed Vintage as much as Vintage needed E. L. James. The Writer's Coffee Shop could not handle the distribution demands of a series as successful as James's" (2012).

## FAN FICTION AND CANON: A LOVE–HATE RELATIONSHIP

*Twilight* was an original work, whereas *Master of the Universe* was its "alternate universe" (AU) fan fiction, a deliberate departure from canon. AU may involve altering one aspect of the canon or answering "what if" questions or more radical changes in place and time. E. L. James takes the main characters from *Twilight*, keeps some of their character traits, and puts them in a very different situation without the vampire plot line. This is what fan fiction does since it is a type of writing that

> makes use of an accepted canon of characters, settings and plots generated by another writer or writers. This source material may come from books, films or TV, and in the latter two cases it will not derive purely from writers but also from directors, producers and even actors, all of whom have a hand in the creation of characters. (Pugh 2005, 26)

Therefore, fans of a book, film, or TV series turn into creators who write stories about existing characters and situations and post them online (either in dedicated websites or in general ones like http://www.fanfiction.net). In these webpages, other fans read the stories and provide feedback by introducing comments. Thus, we are not talking about individuals but online fan communities or fandoms. In fact, one of the characteristics that makes fan fiction different from traditional publishing is the degree of interaction between authors and readers, who are usually also authors of other fan fiction. The scope of this interactive review culture has been transformed by the advent of Web 2.0. As Sheenagh Pugh points out, in the 1960s, there were fan clubs, conventions, fanzines, and letterzines, but communication between fans was difficult and slow (2005, 117). With the advent of the Internet, posting fan fiction is easy, free, and there is no need for any technical knowledge. The source material is also more easily available and the feedback instantly provided through email, mailing lists, and forums.

As Pugh underlines, fan fiction has been transformed from an individual activity to a global, online workshop with a very large audience (2005, 128). FanFiction.net hosts several million works and is the largest fan fiction site. There are more than 200,000 stories based on *Twilight* and more than 600,000 based on *Harry Potter*. The initial readership of *Master of the Universe*/*Fifty Shades of Grey* did not come from the traditional channels but from the fan fiction community, which, according to *Publishers Weekly*, makes "a bold statement about what happens when the audience can lay claim to the discovery process" (Deahl 2012) and is one of the reasons why E. L. James was named *Publishers Weekly*'s Person of the Year in 2012, an annual award that had never gone to an author before and is usually given to publishing leaders that have shaped and transformed the publishing industry.

Fan fiction has to do with a continuation of the original canon, in this case *Twilight* (books and films), but also with a departure from the cannon. As Henry Jenkins explains, there should be a balance between fascination and frustration. On the one hand, because fans are fascinated with the canon, they write fan fiction, and on the other hand, because they are frustrated with some aspects of the canon, they rewrite and remake it (2006, 258). Jenkins has borrowed Michel de Certeau's concept of active reading as "poaching" and has applied the term to fan fiction where fans are in a position of cultural marginality and lack power to influence entertainment industry's decisions but they can still "poach" from texts. Poaching is "an impertinent raid on the literary preserve that takes away only those things that are useful or pleasurable to the reader" (1992, 24). As Pugh has also put it, fan fiction stems from the need to have "more of" and/or "more from" the original cannon (2005, 19). The former ("more of") would entail continuation; once the stories stop being published or the main character dies, fans will continue the story because they like it so much they don't want it to end. "More from" involves readers feeling there is something wanting or missing in the original canon that can be filled in with new stories. For example, many female fans of science fiction and police shows in the 1970s liked the action but missed more character development and stronger female figures so they wrote their own stories to fill in this gap (Pugh 2005, 21).

It is remarkable that fan fiction writers and consumers are largely female. According to John Fiske, this type of popular creativity "is typical of subordinated groups who have no, or limited, access to the means of producing cultural resources, and whose creativity therefore necessarily lies in the arts of making do with what they have" (1989, 151). Henry Jenkins has also pointed out that the mass media "constructs more vivid and compelling male protagonists than female secondary characters" (1992, 200). Fiske and Jenkins wrote these words in 1989 and 1992, and since then, the situation for female writers and characters has improved, especially in the young-adult market where women have lately dominated with the success of three book-to-movie franchises: Suzanne Collins's *The Hunger Games*, J. K. Rowling's *Harry Potter*, and Stephenie Meyer's *Twilight*. However, there is always room for improvement, and fan fiction writers are active consumers who try to change what they don't like. *Twilight* was written by a woman, has a female protagonist and a largely female readership. The target readership is mainly teen and tween girls, but it has also been very successful with female adult readers also known as "Twilight Moms" or "Twi-Moms." They even have their own fan sites and Facebook and Twitter pages with more than 45,000 followers. According to *New York Magazine, Twilight* "reinvents sex for women who might have placed it at the bottom of a to-do list" and creates bonds for adult women (Em and Lo 2009). In her fan fiction, E. L. James attracted part of this female adult audience that found in her stories what they missed in the original novels, a more adult relationship in which sexuality is fully explored. Because of *Fifty Shades of Grey*'s mainstream success among Twi-Moms and female adult readers, the press has labeled this erotic trilogy "mommy porn."

Romance and pornography have always gone hand in hand in fan fiction. There are in fact three main categories: "Slash" (same-sex pairings), "Het" (heterosexual pairings), and "Gen" (general fiction). Most fan fiction stories are posted with a pairing label that is marked by a slash between the names of the characters involved in a relationship. In fact, pairing and rating (from G-rated stories to NC-17 stories) are usual search terms in the archives of fan fiction. According to Catherine Driscoll, sex acts are usually depicted in fan fiction in two ways: plot sex and porn sex. Plot sex is the dominant mode, and in it, sex marks story development, intimacy escalates in the standard shape of romance narrative, and sexual intercourse closes the narrative. Porn sex provides minimum narrative context for the scene as seen in the PWP (Plot? What Plot?) genre. However, as Driscoll underlines, a single story often includes both plot and porn sex and porn and romance (2006, 85–86, 91). Driscoll also concedes that characterization is more necessary in fan fiction than in most porn, and it is supplemented by the canon from which it evolves. In fan fiction, porn and romance define one another: "pornography is structured in relation to the conventions of romance, and romance fiction is sustained by porn's ecstatic relationship to exposure" (95). *Fifty Shades of Grey* is the result of the interactions of both romance and pornography in fan fiction. It provides both porn sex and plot sex along its three volumes. The sexual encounters intensify the romantic features that *Twilight* provides since these encounters are also structured around the romance genre of this original canon. In fact, when Ana is pondering whether to sign the contract that will turn her into Grey's submissive, she turns to her romance heroines for guidance:

> I flush and stare down at my hands. That's what I'm hindered by in this game of seduction. He's the only one who knows and understands the rules. I'm just too naïve and inexperienced. My only sphere of reference is Kate, and she doesn't take any shit from men. My other references are all fictional: Elizabeth Bennet would be outraged, Jane Eyre too frightened, and Tess would succumb, just as I have. (James 2012a, 224–25)

In the world of pornography Ana looks for guidance in romance classics like *Pride and Prejudice*, *Jane Eyre*, and *Tess of the d'Urbervilles*, underlining the connection that we often find in fan fiction between the two genres and also repeating the pattern of *Twilight*, the original canon, where there are also references to *Pride and Prejudice*, *Romeo and Juliet*, and *Wuthering Heights*.

## *TWILIGHT* AND *FIFTY SHADES OF GREY*: SIMILARITIES AND DIFFERENCES

For fan fiction to work, some similarities with the canon have to be kept. The comparison between *Twilight* and *Fifty Shades of Grey* shows some remarkable similarities and of course some striking differences given the fact that they are directed at different audiences: the young-adult female public in the case of *Twilight* and the female adult market in the case of *Fifty Shades of Grey*. Both stories take place around Seattle and both use a first-person narrative voice that prizes female subjectivity. They follow a similar story-line, typical of the romance: there's a meet-cute, a relationship, an early marriage, early motherhood, and a happy ending in which the couple is consolidated. In both series of books, the couple has to face a long list of power imbalances: their differences in age, experience, wealth, and social power and some enemies that try to separate the couple: Victoria and the Volturi in *Twilight*, Mrs. Robinson and Jack Hyde in *Fifty Shades of Grey*.

The main characters in both works share common traits. Edward in *Twilight* and Grey in *Fifty Shades* are both refined, mature, wealthy, powerful, attractive, and have a dark secret that they try to keep to themselves. Initially, they are monsters (Edward is a vampire, Grey is a sadist) and a threat to Bella/Ana. However, one of the most interesting lines in the story is the way these "predators" try to protect Bella/Ana by controlling their impulses (Edward's wish to drink Bella's blood and Grey's wish to hurt her in the playroom or "red room of pain" as Ana calls it). They also have to learn to control their domineering nature and their jealousy.

Bella in *Twilight* and Ana in *Fifty Shades of Grey* also have a lot in common: they both play the archetype of the waif. They are clumsy, innocent, sexually inexperienced, insecure, and uninterested in money, consumer culture, and fashion items, though thanks to Edward and Grey they have full access to these consumer pleasures. They both have a male best friend who belongs to a minority and who is in love with them: Bella has Jacob, who is Native American, and Ana has José, who is Hispanic. Jacob and José seem to challenge Bella/Ana's love interest through the introduction of a love triangle, which is much less developed in *Fifty Shades of Grey*. Bella and Ana also have a talent for putting themselves in danger with several sexual near-assaults on them (Bella is threatened by strangers in Port Angeles and Ana by her boss in her new job). In all cases, they are saved by their heroes, who, in spite of their monstrous nature, often play the knight in shining armor in the typical damsel-in-distress situation. As a summary, both series of books are shaped by the conventions of the romance: the waif gains the heart of the monster or the bad-boy who is reformed in the process. Apparently, this is still a well-known fantasy for many women of all ages.

There are some obvious differences too that can be explained by the change in the target audience. As we have mentioned, fan fiction writers are not passive consumers that simply repeat stories that they love. They also change them to fit their likings. When E. L. James started to write her fan fiction *Master of the Universe*, she was changing her role from reader to writer and transforming the original content of *Twilight* into something else. *Twilight* is a vampire paranormal romance, whereas *Fifty Shades* is an erotic romance set in realist grounds. As a result, Edward and Grey hide very different secrets. Edward is a "vegetarian" vampire that has a thirst for human blood but that bends his impulses by only drinking animal blood. Grey, on the other hand, is a sadist that cannot truly love and cannot stand to be touched but who has a traumatic past of abuse that accounts for his behavior. Like a nineteenth-century gentleman, Edward has a strong, old-fashioned sense of morality and wants to protect Bella's soul by waiting for marriage to have sex. On the other hand, Grey only enjoys sadomasochist sex and sees Ana's virginity as something that needs to be "solved" with some vanilla sex rather than something that needs to be protected. Going against the cultural standard, *Twilight* builds on the erotics of abstinence, while *Fifty Shades of Grey* builds on the erotics of full sexual exploration. The only restraint in *Fifty Shades* is Ana's unwillingness to become Christian's submissive and his initial inability to love.

In this sense, the type of secrets they hide (vampirism and sadism) also point to the different genres used. Unlike *Twilight*, in *Fifty Shades of Grey* all traces of fantasy have disappeared, and there is no escapist supernatural solution to overcome the power imbalances of the couple. These imbalances are solved in *Twilight* by Bella becoming a vampire and in *Fifty Shades of Grey* by Ana turning into a stronger woman who is able to face her enemies, cure her traumatized husband, have a successful career, be the mother of two children, and have a spicy sex life (combining vanilla sex with visits to the playroom for consensual submissive sex).

This also leads to another of the important differences in the series: the goal of the main female characters. In *Twilight*, Bella has no interest in continuing her studies after high school or developing a career. Her only wish is to become a vampire and live forever with Edward. Thus, she puts marriage, motherhood, and vampirism at the expense of everything else. In contrast, Ana has just finished college and wants a career in publishing. Throughout the saga, she advances up the company ladder from commissioning editor assistant to commissioning editor to Grey Publishing owner. She knows what she wants and refuses Grey's initial attempts to make her give up work. This is a source of conflict because Grey sees Ana's career as a rival, but in the end, she gets it all: love, marriage, motherhood, a successful career, and a spicy sex life. Bella turns into a wife-mother-vampire-girl and Ana into a wife-mother-submissive-career-girl.

In her seminal book *Archetypal Pattern in Women's Fiction*, Annis Pratt deals with the traditional, more conservative novel of development in which the supreme goal of the heroine is to groom the young hero for marriage; from the world of freedom, the heroine enters the social world of enclosure. Bella's mother married young and divorced Bella's father to escape the small, enclosed world of Forks. She has followed her new younger husband, who is a baseball player, and left Bella with her father in the same enclosed world she escaped from. Bella wants to avoid early marriage at all costs so as not to repeat her mother's mistake, but Renee's actions are not an example either since she has to pay for her freedom by playing a very secondary role in her daughter's life. Bella is left without an example to follow since she doesn't want to feel trapped by an early marriage and early motherhood but she doesn't want to cut all ties with her family, either.

In her human form, Bella is also limited by being clumsy, powerless, weak, and even unable to exert her sexual freedom for fear that Edward will kill her. Her objective is not marriage in a traditional sense, but her willingness to give everything up for Edward takes the "happily ever after" to a much higher level of commitment. In the novel of development, the archetypal heroine desires "freedom to come and go, allegiance to nature, meaningful work, exercise of the intellect, and use of her own erotic capabilities [which] inevitably clashes with patriarchal norms" (Pratt 1981, 29). This conflict is solved in the final book of the series with Bella's transformation into a powerful vampire and with the destruction of her old human world.

Much has been discussed as to the ideological change that is introduced in *Breaking Dawn*. Turning into a vampire is Bella's chance to transform into Edward's equal and to explore her desire for sexual fulfillment. Kristine Moruzi argues that Bella is a postfeminist heroine that "takes charge of her destiny in order to achieve her dreams" (2012, 48). In the safe confines of their relationship, she becomes a vampire and has sexual intercourse with Edward. Even in *Breaking Dawn*, Bella explores her postfeminist agency as spouse and mother, offering "a transformative possibility to wives and mothers as well" (Moruzi 2012, 62). In contrast to Moruzi's view that the fantastic elements of *Twilight* serve to invigorate the romance genre, Anne Morey argues that the resources of fantasy show the difficulty in showing an empowered young woman in the context of the present and in the context of the romance (2012, 16). I share Morey's point of view since by the end of the series *Twilight* turns into a coming-of-age novel that rather than progress toward maturity introduces the fantasy world of wish fulfillment and regresses from full participation in adult life.

*Fifty Shades of Grey* follows a similar pattern. Grey and Anastasia need to explore and negotiate their own sexual limits, there is even a contract that Ana never signs but that is discussed in detail in the first volume. After establishing a relationship, there comes the point of painful separation. Unlike in *New Moon*, where Edward leaves Bella because he fears she is in danger when she is close to him and his family, in *Fifty Shades*, Ana decides to leave Grey because she fears she may get hurt if she continues their sadomasochist sexual encounters. This change in the fan fiction version of *Twilight* may point to the need for a woman to take control of her life in our contemporary world rather than consider suicide as a response to being abandoned. *Eclipse* explores the relationship between Edward and Bella and the way it is threatened by Victoria and the Volturi on the one hand and Jacob and the life he represents on the other. By contrast, *Fifty Shades Darker* centers on the return of Christian's past in the form of Mrs. Robinson (the mother/lover figure that initiated him in BDSM ) and Leila, an ex-submissive that wants to take revenge. However, the volume is really about Ana helping a psychologically vulnerable Christian overcome his inner demons, work through his trauma, and get him to admit: "I'm a sadist, Ana. I like to whip little brown-haired girls like you because you all look like the crack whore— my birth mother" (James 2012b, 329). This conflict that Christian and Ana need to solve is much more mature than the threats that Victoria or Jacob pose in *Eclipse*. This is the story of how Christian will open up and accept that he also deserves to love and be loved. The suspense is not to be found just in external threats but in inner ones.

In *Breaking Dawn* and *Fifty Shades Freed*, the final volumes of both sagas, the couples get married and deal with power inequalities in very different ways. Neither Bella nor Ana is comfortable with the world of wealth that Edward and Christian provide. However, Bella accepts it as part of her future life as vampire where money will not be an issue and it will not be necessary for her to worry about how to make an income. Ana has a more realistic attitude and feels guilty about the situation and the woman that Christian wants her to become: "I am rich . . . stinking rich. I have done nothing to earn this money. . . just married a rich man" (James 2012c, 30). Rather than passively accepting the situation, she refuses to give up her job:

> I'm just trying to establish a career, and I don't want to trade on your name. I have to do *something*, Christian. I can't stay imprisoned at Escala or the new house with nothing to do. I'll go crazy. I'll suffocate. I've always worked, and I enjoy this. This is my dream job; it's all I've ever wanted. But doing this doesn't mean I love you less. You are the world to me. (James 2012c, 146)

Their pregnancy comes unexpectedly to both couples, and neither Edward nor Christian accepts the new situation, Edward because he fears the half-vampire baby will kill the human Bella, Christian because he fears parenthood will be the end of their active sexual life. Once more, the differences concern the worlds they inhabit: the supernatural versus the day-to-day strains of contemporary partnership, parenthood, and family life. Both Bella and Ana have been empowered by the end of the saga and achieve an equal relationship, but whereas Bella simply turns into a vampire, Ana succeeds in making Christian accept that she is not his abusive mother and that neither of them needs to be punished for his mother's actions: "I'm not her. I'm much stronger than she was. I have you, and you're so much stronger now, and I know you love me. I love you, too" (James 2012c, 256). Both Edward/Bella and Christian/Ana are equally strong by the end, but *Fifty Shades* is placed in a recognizable reality, however fantastic given Grey's incredible wealth, where all traits of the supernatural disappear. This is not to say that Ana is the ultimate feminist and that she represents what all women want. In fact, in the first volume, she unwillingly engages in a dominant/submissive relationship, and this is something that has been especially underlined in the media. However, this does not imply either that women want to be submissive or want to be beaten; the novel is a mainstream success because all the sexual experimentation is safely wrapped in a monogamous relationship typical of the romance and fully used in *Twilight*. In the books, Christian Grey's most repeated sentence is "We aim to please," and he does please Ana by giving her innumerable orgasms but also by being tender and washing her hair.

## PARTICIPATORY CULTURE, MEDIA CONVERGENCE, AND THE POSSIBILITIES OF GRASSROOTS CREATIVITY

The story of *Twilight* and *Fifty Shades of Grey* is only one example of today's participatory culture that transforms content from static to dynamic and the message from informative to interactive. Participatory culture is a logical result of media convergence or convergence culture, which, according to Henry Jenkins, represents a paradigm shift. Content is not medium-specific anymore but flows across interdependent media channels changing the creation of content, its distribution and its consumption, since the roles of the publisher, author, and reader are sometimes blurred (2006, 254). The Internet has made the access to media production and distribution easier and cheaper and has facilitated the interaction of readers and producers and the formation of communities of readers, who, in turn, can easily transform content and turn into publishers and broadcasters.

This success is also the result of the emergence of four ecosystems that combine a device and a bookstore: the Nook, the Kindle, Apple's iBookstore, and Google Books (Jopson and Edgecliffe-Johnson 2012, 9). In the last few years, electronic readers and tablets like Kindle Fire, Nook Tablet, and the iPad have become increasingly popular, and they have provided readers with the possibility of rapid access to books in a private way and without revealing the contents of what they are reading. This is something important for readers of erotica since covers tend to be very explicit. In fact, erotica and romance novels were among the first genres to adapt to the digital format, and at present, 40 percent of the sales of these books come from this format (Rosman 2012, D.1). E. L. James is the first author selling more than one million copies via Kindle, and this success is the result of both the growing popularity of digital fiction, the emergence of affordable electronic readers, and the role of social media, literature blogs, and the fan-fiction community.

As a conclusion, I would like to take Henry Jenkins's description of convergence culture as both "a top-down corporate-driven process and a bottom-up consumer-driven process. Corporate convergence coexists with grassroots convergence" (2006, 18). Fan fiction represents grassroots creativity as new technologies permit people to recirculate, expand, and modify media content, even changing the nature of the marketplace. As Jenkins puts it: "The power of participation comes not from destroying commercial culture but from writing over it, modding it, amending it, expanding it, adding greater diversity of perspective, and then recirculating it, feeding it back into the mainstream media" (2006, 268). The story of *Twilight* and *Fifty Shades* certainly shows the power of participation and how readers can change commercial culture (*Twilight*), but it also shows the power of corporations and the mainstream to take the new product (*Master of the Universe*) and market it again as *Fifty Shades of Grey* to profit from the free work of fans. An optimist would say that fans have pressured major publishing houses to open up a mainstream market for erotica that can be discretely enjoyed by women in their electronic readers. Also, fan fiction is now more easily entering the mainstream with other *Twilight* fan fiction like *Gabriel's Inferno* being published by Penguin. A pessimist would say that major publishing houses are only trying to profit from the new trend. For example, Clandestine Classics has released a series of erotically charged versions of nineteenth-century literature, like *Jane Eyre, Wuthering Heights*, and *Pride and Prejudice*. These are classics that featured prominently in both the *Twilight* and *Fifty Shades* series. The idea that any text can turn into canon for new fiction can also be seen in the success of books like *Pride and Prejudice and Zombies, Android Karenina*, and *Sense and Sensibility and Sea Monsters*, among other titles.

In any case, participatory culture is producing a cultural feedback loop, and *Fifty Shades of Grey* is already begetting more fan fiction that takes a saga that was in origin fan fiction as a new canon. There are more than one thousand stories based on *Fifty Shades* already available at http://www.fanfiction.net, some dealing with gaps in the story, others continuing Christian and Ana's life as parents, and still others developing crossovers with characters from erotic romances, like Sylvia Day's *Bared to You*. Right now, it is difficult to decide if this recycling of culture is something positive. When *Publishers Weekly* named E. L. James "Person of the Year," part of the media responded with utter horror: "Civilization Ends" could be read in the

*New York Daily News* (Young 2012), and "What was *Publishers Weekly* thinking?" in *Los Angeles Times* (Kellogg 2012). However, sociologists and media-studies scholars have argued in the last decade that the new digital, participatory culture is blurring hierarchical structures, democratizing society and culture in the process (Rheingold 2002; Surowiecki 2004; Shirky 2008). Fan fiction and the feedback provided by many readers transformed *Twilight* and made it more enjoyable for a different audience and within the bounds of a different genre. This grassroots creativity was absorbed by corporate power and turned into a new consumer product, which has already become canon for new fan fiction. Whether this ongoing struggle for possession of texts is the end of our civilization or a new, bright future is unclear; what is for sure is that participatory culture and fan fiction have opened *Twilight* to a more adult audience, showing in the process both the power and the limitations of grassroots creativity.

## NOTE

The research carried out for the writing of this article is part of a project financed by the Spanish Ministry of Economy and Competitiveness (MINECO) (code FFI2012-32719). The author is also thankful for the support of the government of Aragón and the European Social Fund (ESF) (code H05) and the University of Zaragoza (JIUZ-2012-HUM-01).

## REFERENCES

Deahl, Rachel. 2012. "E. L. James: PW's Publishing Person of the Year." *Publishers Weekly*, November 30. Accessed December 28, 2012. http://www.publishersweekly.com/pw/by-topic/industry-news/people/article/54956-e-l-james-pw-s-publishing-person-of-the-year.html.

Driscoll, Catherine. 2006. "One True Pairing: The Romance of Pornography and the Pornography of Romance." In *Fan Fiction and Fan Communities in the Age of the Internet: New Essays*, ed. Karen Hellekson and Kristina Busse, 79–96. Jefferson, NC: McFarland.

Em and Lo. 2009. "*Twilight*, Take Me Away! Teenage Vampires and Mothers Who Love Them." *New York Magazine*, November 23. Accessed December 28, 2012. http://nymag.com/movies/features/62027/.

Fiske, John. 1989. *Understanding Popular Culture*. London: Routledge.

James, E. L. 2012a. *Fifty Shades of Grey*. London: Arrow Books.

———. 2012b. *Fifty Shades Darker*. London: Arrow Books.

———. 2012c. *Fifty Shades Freed*. London: Arrow Books.

Jenkins, Henry. 1992. *Textual Poachers: Television Fans and Participatory Culture*. London: Routledge.

———. 2006. *Convergence Culture*. New York: New York University Press.

Johnson, Steve. 2012. "Who Is E. L. James? *Fifty Shades* Author and Her Fans Bond over Improbable Success Story" *Chicago Tribune*, May 3. Accessed December 28, 2012. http://articles.chicagotribune.com/2012-05-03/entertainment/ct-ent-0502-50-shades-of-grey-20120501_1_fan-fiction-book-signing-event-fans-bond.

Jones, Toni. 2012. "*Fifty Shades of Grey* Outsells *Harry Potter*. The 'Mummy Porn' Novel Breaks Another Record and Outsells All Seven J. K. Rowling Books on Amazon." *Daily Mail*, August 2. Accessed December 28, 2012. http://www.dailymail.co.uk/femail/article-2182618/Fifty-Shades-Grey-outsells-SEVEN-Harry-Potter-books-Amazon.html.

Jopson, Barney, and Andrew Edgecliffe-Johnson. 2012. "Publishing: The Bookworm Turns." *Financial Times*, May 4: 9.

Kellogg, Carolyn. 2012. "Blinded by Dollar Signs? *PW* Names E. L. James Person of the Year." *Los Angeles Times*. November 30. Accessed December 28, 2012. http://www.latimes.com/features/books/jacketcopy/la-et-jc-pw-names-el-james-person-of-the-year-20121130,0,6233202.story.

"Little, Brown to Publish Official *Twilight* Guide." 2010. *Publishers Weekly*, October 6. Accessed December 28, 2012. http://www.publishersweekly.com/pw/by-topic/childrens/childrens-book-news/article/44733-little-brown-to-publish-official-twilight-guide.html.

Metcalf, Fran. 2012. "'Mummy Porn' *Fifty Shades of Grey* by E. L. James becomes Australia's Bestselling Book." *The Courier Mail*, August 22. Accessed December 28, 2012. http://www.couriermail.com.au/news/mummy-porn-fifty-shades-of-grey-by-el-james-becomes-australias-bestselling-book/story-fnek2nxs-1226455801169.

Meza, Ed. 2012. "Bertelsmann Soars on *Fifty Shades* Success: Random House Trilogy Boosts Bottom Line." *Chicago Tribune*, August 31. Accessed December 28, 2012. http://articles.chicagotribune.com/2012-08-31/entertainment/sns-201208310926reedbusivarietynvr1118058532-20120831_1_net-profit-trilogy-e-book-sales.

Morey, Anne. 2012. "'Famine for Food, Expectation for Content': *Jane Eyre* as Intertext for *The Twilight Saga*." In *Genre, Reception, and Adaptation in the "Twilight" Series*, ed. Anne Morey, 15–27. Farnham, UK: Ashgate.

Moruzi, Kristine. 2012. "Postfeminist Fantasies: Sexuality and Femininity in Stephenie Meyer's *Twilight* Series." In *Genre, Reception, and Adaptation in the "Twilight" Series*, ed. Anne Morey, 47–64. Farnham, UK: Ashgate.

"Of Brooms and Bondage: How to Publish a Bestseller." 2012. *Economist*, May 5.

Pratt, Annis. 1981. *Archetypal Pattern in Women's Fiction*. Bloomington: Indiana University Press.

Pugh, Sheenagh. 2005. *The Democratic Genre: Fan Fiction in a Literary Context*. Glasgow: Bell and Bain.

Rheingold, Howard. 2002. *Smart Mobs: The Next Social Revolution*. Cambridge: Basic Books.

Rosman, Katherine. 2012. "Books Women Read When No One Can See the Cover." *Wall Street Journal*, March 14: D.1.

Shirky, Clay. 2008. *Here Comes Everybody: The Power of Organizing without Organizations*. New York: Penguin Books.

Surowiecki, James. 2004. *The Wisdom of Crowds*. New York: Anchor Books.

Young, Christopher. 2012. "Civilization's Ends: E. L. James Named *Publishers Weekly*'s 'Person of the Year.'" *New York Daily News*, November 30. Accessed December 28, 2012. http://www.nydailynews.com/blogs/pageviews/2012/11/civilization-ends-eljames-named-publishers-weeklys-person-of-the-year.

# Closing Thoughts

## Claudia Bucciferro

Throughout this book, we have explored some of the most prominent aspects of the *Twilight* saga, taking into consideration how the novels and the movies fit within larger cultural and social contexts. It has been our intention to also go beyond the specifics of the *Twilight* texts, addressing the interrelationships they establish with their audiences and with other texts, especially considering trends involving literature and media.

*Twilight* provides an excellent instance for studying how works of fiction that emerge from a specific environment go on to transcend national boundaries and become global popular culture referents. As such, *Twilight* has been translated and interpreted in multiple (and sometimes contradictory) ways; it has been appropriated and "glocalized" to fit particular environments; it has been loved and embraced by different kinds of people and has been imitated in a number of ways. At the same time, it has been mocked, ridiculed, and parodied in many venues. The *Twilight* saga is a controversial franchise, one that rouses strong feelings among people—whether they like it or not—and that is what makes it particularly interesting. In the years that it took for the series to be completed, few people could remain oblivious to its presence. The sheer power of this realization is part of the *Twilight* puzzle— how come it got so big? What is in it that attracts audiences worldwide? Why do some people hate it so much?

Multiple factors have contributed to make the *Twilight* series a huge success. The books benefitted from well-coordinated author appearances, the formation of fan clubs, and the strategic use of online resources for marketing efforts. The movies capitalized on the casting of attractive actors, the addition of computer-generated special effects, the recruiting of popular bands to compose soundtracks, and the release of highly coordinated publicity campaigns that spanned across multiple platforms. But there is more to

*Twilight* than this or else it would not have been possible for a debut novel by an unknown author to become so popular. The not-too-perfect characters inspired the fans from the very beginning, and people identified with their struggles and journeys. The storyline merged timeless topics with contemporary concerns relevant for today's young adults, providing a virtual space for people to sort through various issues. Although the movies are somewhat different from the books, they stay true to the characters' essence and the major challenges they face. Both formats are, in this case, complementary.

*Twilight* presents well-known yet mysterious creatures, emphasizes their existential struggles, puts a teenage girl at the center of the story, and stresses the transformative power of love—it is a formula apt for crossing borders. Although the 2012 release of the final film, *Breaking Dawn Part 2*, marked the official end of the *Twilight* saga, there are rumors of additional books and perhaps even something more. Edward and Bella's story may be over, but Renesmee and Jacob's love is just beginning, and the series' finale made a point of leaving things open, even hinting at a new love triangle. From an industry point of view, it will be hard to resist the temptation of expanding the franchise a little further. Stephenie Meyer's partial manuscript of *Midnight Sun*, for example, is still unfinished. Meanwhile, *Twilight* followers continue to hold their ground.

Even if the franchise is effectively over, its influence lingers still—and it is likely to be felt for years to come. *Twilight* reignited the public's interest in classic pieces by Jane Austen and Charlotte Brontë, which led to new readings and new films. It helped mainstream the paranormal romance as a genre, which has experienced spectacular growth in the last few years. By introducing fangless, handsome vampires that sparkle in the sun, play the piano, and quote classic literary works, *Twilight* broke the mold of the vampire as a scary monster. And by portraying werewolves that are as charming as they are handsome and are also imbued with a strong sense of duty and morality, it blurred the boundaries between the human and the nonhuman *Other*. Therefore, it opened the door to a plethora of attractive supernatural creatures, which now populate the fantasy stories that fill the shelves of booksellers everywhere. The saga even influenced the development of a new classification within the book industry: "new adult" (NA), which includes works that could otherwise be considered young adult but that appeal to older audiences because they deal with mature themes.

The present volume is about *Twilight*—but is not *only* about *Twilight*. The saga has things in common with other series such as *Harry Potter* and *Fifty Shades of Grey*—disparate as they may seem—and there are even conceptual threads that go further back, linking it to other fictional stories. So, this book is also about the appeal of fantasy and romance, the features that make a story rise above the rest and become "a cultural phenomenon," the role that media (old and new) play in the development of a popular franchise, and what this all means for people. In the research that informs this book, we have paid special attention to cultural contexts and audiences, and we have tried to understand the role that fictional works such as *Twilight* play in our contemporary world. On this may rely much of this volume's contribution, because it is true that book series and movie franchises come and go, but the appeal of romance and fantasy, as they say, may last *forever*.

# Index

abuse, 19, 98–99, 104, 159, 216, 234, 236
adults, 4–7, 9, 20, 27, 47, 54–59, 69–70,
    73–76, 79, 82, 100, 112–114, 117, 123,
    130, 133–135, 158, 165, 213, 217, 221,
    227, 231–238, 242
agency, 3, 19, 159, 213, 220–223, 235
American Indian, 37, 44, 148. *See also*
    Native American
anti-fans, 11, 56, 93–105
archetypes, 17, 22–25, 72–73, 76, 233, 235
audience, 4–7, 17–22, 27, 29–30, 49,
    54–59, 79–84, 115, 129, 158, 159, 163,
    169, 178–179, 198, 202–204, 220, 241
Austen, Jane, 119n1, 242. *See also Pride
    and Prejudice*

Blake, William, 111, 112–113, 117
boundaries, 9, 11, 17–20, 25, 28–30, 89,
    94–98, 114, 181, 197–202, 204–205,
    219, 241, 242
Brontë, Charlotte, 110, 125, 129, 183, 242
*Buffy the Vampire Slayer*, 49, 127, 130,
    132, 135, 161, 202
Burke, Kenneth, 3, 30, 40, 214
Byron, Lord, 110, 119n1–119n3; Byronic
    hero, 23, 110–111, 112, 119n3

Campbell, Joseph, 22, 24–25, 221
capitalism, 171–172, 174, 177–178, 203,
    220. *See also* materialism
characterization, 155, 157, 209, 232

chastity, 18–19, 102, 155–158, 162, 166.
    *See also* virginity
children, 35, 41, 74, 109–119, 134, 157,
    161, 184, 188–189, 205–206, 218
choice, 7, 18–19, 25, 29, 39, 53, 67, 72–73,
    103, 123–124, 127, 150, 155, 187,
    197–201, 203–204, 206
class, 140, 143, 148, 169–171, 217
collectivity, 23, 51, 213–224
community, 56, 70–72, 81, 88, 116, 185,
    203–204, 206, 209, 213–217, 221–224,
    229, 230, 237
consumers, 81, 171, 173–174, 178–179,
    231, 234; consumerism, 53, 174–175
convergence, 237–238
crisis, 34, 65–76
criticism, 40, 56–57, 95, 100, 104, 162,
    175, 214
cross-cultural, 10, 17–19, 22, 25, 26, 29,
    220
cultural studies, 4, 17, 52. *See also* media
    studies

death, 27, 29, 35–41, 67, 71, 100, 112–113,
    118, 134, 147, 197–202, 206–208,
    217–219
discrimination, 2, 173, 185
Dracula, 49, 94, 100–101, 103, 105, 116,
    155, 157, 159, 161, 197, 199, 200, 203.
    *See also* Bram Stoker

emasculation, 100–101, 104–105
empowerment, 9, 51–53, 124–134,
    159–166, 235–236
entertainment industry, 4, 6–8, 9, 17, 28,
    48, 230
erotic, 19, 23, 24, 132, 166, 227, 231,
    234–235, 237–238
escapism, 29–31, 51, 55, 59, 68–69, 76, 84,
    118, 127, 141–142, 149, 169, 192, 228,
    234
ethnicity, 86, 90, 143, 145, 183, 191, 217
ethnography, 50, 67, 76, 79, 80

fandom, 4, 47–49, 56, 73–76, 80–82, 87,
    88–89, 93–105
fan fiction, 9, 29, 80, 116, 227–238
fantasy, 5, 6, 18, 20, 25, 27–29, 30–31, 69,
    75–76, 79, 98, 139–142, 149–150, 163,
    170, 209, 214, 227, 233–235, 242
fear, 25, 38–41, 55, 82, 93, 103, 127, 129,
    134, 148–149, 159, 189, 198–203,
    207–209, 213–214, 218–219, 235–236
femininity, 5, 53, 123–124, 135, 161
feminism, 48, 52–53, 60, 123, 127, 214,
    235
*Fifty Shades of Grey*, 4, 9, 10, 11,
    227–238, 242
folklore, 19, 23, 24, 25, 155
franchise, 4–9, 28, 48–49, 54, 93–98,
    101–105, 156, 241–242
friendship, 49, 67, 75–76, 80, 83, 84–90,
    147, 206, 217–222

gaze, 6, 95, 125, 141, 159–160, 166
gender, 21, 29, 47–53, 94–105, 139–149,
    169
global, 2–5, 8, 29, 30, 35–37, 155, 192,
    213–216, 228–230, 241
gratification, 155, 164, 166

Hall, Stuart, 4, 17, 18
*Harry Potter*, 29, 159, 213–224, 242
hegemonic, 93, 97, 101, 140, 143–149
heterosexual, 100, 103, 114, 141, 145, 232
history, 21–22, 25–26, 33–44, 149,
    190–191, 198
horror, 23, 93–105, 116, 159, 173,
    197–204, 207–209

humanity, 39, 98, 102, 157–158, 184–185,
    188, 197–199, 203–209, 221
*Hunger Games, The*, 8, 10, 213–224, 231
hypersexuality, 94, 100–105, 133, 135, 156

identity, 30, 65, 86, 96, 103, 126, 141, 161,
    173, 181–191, 199, 213–214, 221–223
ideology, 42–44, 50–52, 76, 96, 105, 134,
    142, 191, 227, 235
individuality, 19, 52, 213–223
*Interview with the Vampire*, 23, 116, 157,
    197, 200–201

James, E. L., 9, 228–231, 234, 237–238
Jung, Carl, 20–21, 22–23, 25, 72

Kristeva, Julia, 199

literature, 18, 19–20, 22, 24–25, 33, 48–50,
    72, 112, 124, 155–161, 169, 200–202,
    207, 214, 224, 238, 241

marketing, 3, 7–8, 17, 26, 171–174, 209,
    241
masculinity, 22, 94, 97, 100–103, 139–150.
    *See also* emasculation
materialism, 169, 170–175, 177–179, 191,
    220
media studies, 3, 4, 18, 47–48, 238
men, 3, 7, 9, 24, 36, 48, 70–72, 95, 101,
    125, 130–134, 139–149, 156–163, 187,
    232
metaphor, 9, 17–19, 26–30, 72, 73,
    100–101, 162, 200, 213–215
Meyer, Stephenie, 5–6, 21, 33, 65–66, 75,
    76, 79, 102, 109, 115, 124, 125, 141,
    147, 155, 182, 187, 215
modernity, 18, 26, 30, 49, 76, 85, 86, 101,
    123–129, 135, 186, 197–199, 209,
    215–218; postmodernity, 86, 197
monster, 19, 20–21, 25, 30, 94, 130, 147,
    158–160, 182, 197–203, 209, 233, 238,
    242
mortality, 17, 25, 33–34, 39–42, 57, 67–68,
    73–76, 97, 110, 113, 115, 139,
    156–157, 164–165, 173, 187, 197–202,
    206–209, 219
motherhood, 9, 24, 132–135, 233–235

myth, 17–18, 20–25, 29–30, 33–42, 130, 187–189, 214, 222

Native American, 7, 40, 119, 146–147, 182, 217, 233

otherness, 157, 159, 181, 192, 197–200; the Other, 20, 30, 100, 105, 182, 197–200, 204–209, 222; othering, 96, 98–100, 105, 181–182

parenthood, 165, 222, 236. *See also* motherhood
parents, 19, 67, 69, 98, 118, 158, 166, 189–190, 206, 219, 238
participatory culture, 48, 237–238
patriarchal, 51–52, 94, 101–105, 114, 124, 128, 134–135, 235
pop culture, 4, 19, 29, 174, 181–183, 192
porn, 50, 103, 132, 227, 231–232
power, 2, 18–19, 24–29, 36–38, 42–44, 51–53, 73, 97, 103–105, 110, 117, 124–134, 139–150, 155–166, 176, 184, 207–209, 215, 218–223, 229–238. *See also* empowerment
prejudice, 181–185, 187, 189
*Pride and Prejudice*, 110, 232, 238
privilege, 97, 100, 169

race, 4, 84, 140, 143–144, 148–150, 169, 175, 181–187, 188–192, 207, 217, 223. *See also* whiteness
Radway, Janice, 22, 47, 48–55, 56–51, 59–60, 144
relationships, 19–23, 25–27, 30, 55–59, 68–73, 79–86, 87–90, 95–99, 102, 114, 123, 145, 201, 205, 208, 221
representation, 18, 22–23, 30, 34, 47–53, 94–101, 105, 140, 169–173, 177, 197–203, 208, 223
research, 1, 2, 3, 8–11, 21–22, 26, 47–49, 54, 59–60, 80, 87–90, 191, 209, 218–220, 242
Rice, Anne, 23, 49, 116, 157, 201. *See also* *Interview with the Vampire*
romance, 5, 9, 10, 19, 21–23, 29, 33–35, 44, 47–60, 69, 93–98, 101–105, 109–119, 123–126, 126–132, 155–158, 227–238, 242

Romantic literature, 20, 110–119, 119n1–119n4
Rowling, J. K., 215, 218

sadism, 159, 227, 228, 233–235
Scott, Sir Walter, 34–35
sex, 19, 21, 29, 55, 59, 95, 100, 103, 133–134, 145–149, 155–166, 203, 228–234
sexuality, 6, 18, 28–29, 69, 94–98, 103, 123, 132–134, 145–146, 155–166, 213, 228, 232–236. *See also* hypersexuality
sexualization, 19, 157, 165
social networking, 82–83, 85, 218
status, 90, 97, 105, 140–141, 143–144, 146–147, 149–150, 169–171, 174, 209
stereotypes, 21, 40, 96, 144–148, 181–192
Stoker, Bram, 116, 155, 157, 200
Summit Entertainment, 6, 8, 48, 60n1

teenagers, 6, 17, 54–59, 103, 126, 156–163, 201, 206, 213, 227
tradition, 6, 17–18, 21, 26, 30, 33–35, 100–103, 109–111, 116–118, 123–124, 127, 135, 144–145, 162–163, 197–202, 204–209, 222–223, 229–235
transformation, 9, 23, 26–27, 39, 44, 141, 148, 160, 172–174, 179, 187, 200–202, 208, 227, 235
trauma, 117–118, 206, 234–235
*True Blood*, 10, 197–199, 204–209
*Twilight* moms, 49, 65–70, 73–74, 231

*Vampire Diaries, The*, 11, 126, 127, 135, 197–209
vampire genre, 50, 95, 116–118, 199–201
vampirism, 39, 100, 103, 111, 126, 134, 147, 156, 201, 205, 234; vampiric, 114, 123, 126, 132, 157, 158, 159–160
*Vampyre, The*, 23, 119n3
Victorian, 110, 123–135
violence, 19, 31, 40, 98, 100–105, 132–133, 143, 215
virginity, 96, 102, 132–133, 162–163, 164–165, 219, 228

werewolves, 21, 24–29, 34, 37–41, 55, 66, 76, 135, 179, 181–184, 187, 199, 204–206, 213–217, 222, 242 whiteness, 2, 7, 53, 113, 141–150, 169, 190–191, 217

women, 6, 17, 22, 24, 27, 47, 49–59, 65–76, 79–90, 95, 101, 105, 123–129, 133–135, 139–149, 156–166, 197, 231–238

Wordsworth, William, 111–113, 117

worldwide, 3–9, 17, 29, 48, 76, 79, 155, 165–166, 169, 204, 228–229, 241

young adult, 6, 79, 93, 98, 213–214, 217

# About the Editor and Contributors

## ABOUT THE EDITOR

**Claudia Bucciferro** is assistant professor in the Department of Communication Studies at Gonzaga University, where she teaches courses in international/intercultural communication, communication theory, and language and social interaction. She has a PhD in communication from the University of Colorado at Boulder and a master's degree in linguistics from the University of Concepción, Chile. Her research focuses on the relationship between media representations and social processes within the context of globalization, including issues regarding international cultural trends and civic activism. Her first book was titled *FOR-GET: Identity, Media, and Democracy in Chile* (University Press of America, 2012). Her work has also appeared in the *Handbook of Gender, Sex, and Media*, the *Journal of Mass Communication*, the *Journal of Global Mass Communication*, and the *Journal of American Culture*. Occasionally, Dr. Bucciferro works as a consultant for projects involving market research. She lives with her husband and children in Spokane, Washington.

## ABOUT THE CONTRIBUTORS

**Sonia Baelo-Allué** is associate professor in the Department of English and German Philology at the University of Zaragoza, Spain, where she primarily teaches U.S. literature. She has published articles on the genre of blank fiction, the concept of intermediality, and the representation of violence in literature. Her current research centers on trauma studies, 9/11 fiction, and popular culture. She recently published the book *Bret Easton Ellis's Controversial Fiction: Writing between High and Low Culture* (Continuum, 2011) and coedited with Dolores Herrero *The Splintered Glass: Facets of Trauma in the Post-Colony and Beyond* (Rodopi, 2011) and *Between the Urge to Know and the Need to Deny: Trauma and Ethics in Contemporary British and American Literature* (C. Winter, 2011).

**Michelle Bernard** is an adjunct instructor of philosophy at the New England School of Communications at Husson University in Bangor, Maine. She attended the University of Maine and graduated with a bachelor's degree in philosophy and theatre, and later completed her master's degrees in liberal studies with a concentration in philosophy and theatre (racial studies and pop culture). She is now working on advanced degrees that include a focus on Native American studies, history, and English. Michelle has been married for twenty-two years to her husband, Peter, and has two children. She has lived in Scotland and Japan.

**Brynn Buskirk** holds a master's degree from Lehigh University in American studies and a bachelor's degree from Moravian College in English and sociology. She recently completed her thesis entitled, "Why Is Everyone Hatin' on Bella? Choice Feminism and Free Agency in *The Twilight Saga*." Buskirk served on a vampire and gender studies panel at the 2012 Popular Culture Association/American Culture Association National Conference in Boston. She has also presented on "Vampires and Philosophy" and "The Paranormal in Pop Culture." Her areas of study include popular culture, occult literature and film, gender in horror film, and anything related to Dracula. When not studying the undead, she works as a marketing director. Buskirk resides with her husband and son in Northampton, Pennsylvania.

**Barbara Chambers** is a visiting assistant professor in the area of management at the Rawls College of Business at Texas Tech University. She teaches courses in managerial communication, organizational management, and business professionalism. Barbara has more than twenty years of experience in marketing, advertising, and public relations with a specialization in brand development, strategic planning, and research. Her research interests include strategic planning, consumer behavior, brand relationships, organizational behavior, and small business brand management. Barbara also serves as a consultant on projects related to strategic planning, marketing research, management, and product/service development. She received her PhD from the College of Mass Communications at Texas Tech University, where her dissertation was titled "Measuring the Brandfan: Exploring a Model for Predicting the Fandom of Brands."

**Laura K. Dorsey-Elson** is associate professor of communication studies at Morgan State University in Baltimore, Maryland. She specializes in leadership development, strategic organizational communication, diversity/global communication, and conflict management. Her formal research interests include the intersection of leadership, culture, and conflict in various organizational contexts. While Laura's initial interest in the *Twilight* saga was personal, it grew into an academic pursuit as the impact of the series on global popular culture increased and became ripe for study. In addition to being an academic, Laura is a communication consultant and coach in the area of leadership development and shares her life with her husband, Omowale, and two children.

**Victoria Godwin** holds a PhD from Indiana University. She is an assistant professor of languages and communications at Prairie View A&M University. Her research interests incorporate fan studies, media studies, gender studies, and cultural studies. Recent publications include "'Never Grow Old, Never Die': Vampires, Narcissism and Simulacra" in *Interactions: Studies in Communication and Culture* and "Love and Lack: Media, Witches, and Normative Gender Roles" in *Media Depictions of Brides, Wives, and Mothers* (Lexington Books).

**Michelle Groover** is a lecturer in the Communication Arts Department at Georgia Southern University in Statesboro, where she teaches public-relations courses. She is currently completing her PhD in communication from Regent University. Her research interests include social media, popular culture, and public relations. She has presented several *Twilight*-themed papers at professional gatherings, including the national Popular/American Culture Association conference, the Popular/American Culture Association in the South conference, and the Southern States Communication Association conference.

**Gaïane Hanser** has a PhD in British literature from the Université Sorbonne Nouvelle–Paris 3, in France. She is an adjunct professor of English at Education Nationale and Paris 3, where she teaches courses in English, debate, theater, and textual analysis. Her doctoral dissertation is titled "Naugrette: Intrication Textuelle et Déchiffrement du Sens Dans l'œuvre de C. Brontë." Her publications include the articles "Women's Voices in Charlotte Brontë's Novels" and "La Bit Lit et ses stratégies de contournement des cadres patriarcaux pour dire la féminité."

**Paul A. Lucas** is an assistant professor at the University of Pittsburgh at Johnstown in Pennsylvania. Paul primarily teaches courses in advertising, marketing, and rhetoric and holds a PhD in rhetoric from Duquesne University, with a concentration in integrated marketing communication. Paul has presented papers on mass media and marketing at conferences such as the

Popular Culture Association, the Eastern Communication Association, and the Pennsylvania Communication Association.

**Michelle Maloney-Mangold** is a PhD candidate in English at the University of Connecticut. Her research focuses on twentieth-century American literature and culture, particularly on issues of class and race. She is currently working on her dissertation, "Under the Table, Off the Grid: Fictional Representations of the American Underclass in the Age of Neoliberalism, 1970 to the Present," which identifies fictional representations of underclass methods of resistance, community building, and survival in a period of divestment by the state (and the private sector) in the poorest and most invisible communities of the United States.

**Lisa Nevárez** is associate professor of English at Siena College, in upstate New York. She holds a doctorate in comparative literature from Vanderbilt University. Her research and teaching interests include British romanticism and Latino/a literature, in addition to vampires, horror fiction, and the Gothic. Her recent work has included essays on Matthew "Monk" Lewis's *Journal of a West India Proprietor* and on Lady Maria Nugent's *India Journal*. She is the editor of the collection *Out of the Coffin and Into the Classroom: Essays on Teaching the Vampire*, soon to be published by McFarland.

**Robert Moses Peaslee** is assistant professor in the College of Media and Communication at Texas Tech University, where he teaches coursework related to popular culture, fandom, visual communication, and qualitative research methodologies. His research focuses on relationships between media texts, audiences' practices, and space, and his work appears in a number of journals, including *Transformative Works and Cultures*, the *International Journal of Communication*, *Mass Communication and Society*, *Visual Communication Quarterly*, and *Tourist Studies*, among others. He is also the coeditor, with Robert G. Weiner, of *Web-Spinning Heroics: Critical Essays on the History and Meaning of Spider-Man* (McFarland, 2012). He lives in Lubbock, Texas, with his wife, Kate, and children.

**Mark David Ryan** is a lecturer in film and television for the Creative Industries Faculty, Queensland University of Technology. He is a national expert on Australian horror films and genre cinema and a media commentator on anything horror, cult film, or cinema related. He has written extensively on popular-genre cinema, industry dynamics of cultural production, and cultural policy. His research interests include Australian film and horror movies, gothic film and literature, the horror genre, popular movie genres (action, science-fiction, thriller, crime, etc.), entertainment industries, next-generation filmmaking, and cultural policy. His publications can be viewed online at: http://eprints.qut.edu.au/view/person/Ryan,_Mark.html.

**Emma Somogyi** is a PhD student in the Creative Industries Faculty at Queensland University of Technology, Brisbane, Australia. Her research interests include the classical and contemporary vampire, the shift in representations of the vampire, ideas of the "other" in contemporary vampire text, and audience reception to the vampire horror genre. Emma's academic background includes a master of arts in applied linguistics, a graduate diploma of education, and a bachelor of arts with a double major in English language and literature and majors in French and medieval studies.

**Lisa Weckerle** is an associate professor of communication studies at Kutztown University in Pennsylvania. She has an MA from the University of North Carolina–Chapel Hill and a PhD from the University of Texas at Austin. She teaches and studies in the areas of performance of literature and mediated communication, especially in how they relate to culture and gender. Her previous publications include an article on film adaptation in the *Edith Wharton Review* and a short story in *Berkley Fiction Review*.

**Nicole Willms** is a visiting instructor of sociology at Gonzaga University, with a PhD from the University of Southern California. Her research and teaching focuses on the representation, performance, and negotiation of gender, race, and class in American sports. Nicole's publications include a coauthored work about media representations of female athletes titled "This Revolution Is Not Being Televised" and a study of the relationships between elite female athletes and their fathers in *Fathering through Sport and Leisure*. She is currently working on projects examining the construction of Japanese American identity through basketball, the negotiation of gendered spaces on school playgrounds, and discourses surrounding women's basketball.